Rediscovering the Eucharist

ECUMENICAL CONVERSATIONS

Rediscovering the Eucharist

ECUMENICAL CONVERSATIONS

Edited by Roch A. Kereszty, O. Cist.

Paulist Press
New York/Mahwah, N.J.

Cover design by Valerie Petro
Book design by Celine M. Allen

Library of Congress Cataloging-in-Publication Data

Rediscovering the Eucharist : ecumenical conversations / edited by Roch A. Kereszty.
        p. cm.
Includes bibliographical references and index.
    ISBN 0-8091-4144-2
    1. Lord's Supper—Congresses. 2. Lord's Supper and Christian
union—Congresses. I. Kereszty, Roch A.
    BV825.3 .R43 2003
    234'.163—dc21

                                                                    2002156405

Published by Paulist Press
997 Macarthur Boulevard
Mahwah, New Jersey 07430

www.paulistpress.com

Printed and bound in the United States of America

In memory of William R. Farmer
who lived and worked
for the unity of all Christians
in the one Eucharist

CONTENTS

INTRODUCTION

The articles presented in this volume are the fruit of an ecumenical conference on the Eucharist sponsored by and held at the University of Dallas on November 9–11, 2000. The active participants and
observers represented a variety of backgrounds in the Jewish, Protestant, Greek Orthodox, and Roman Catholic traditions. Though the
idea of the conference originated with Fr. Roch Kereszty, O. Cist.,
and Dr. William Farmer, the entire Theology Department of the
University soon embraced the project as a fitting response to John
Paul II's call to reflect on the Eucharist in the Jubilee Year of 2000. In
1999 the president of the University of Dallas, Monsignor Milam
Joseph, approved and endorsed the conference and a planning committee was formed to organize and implement it. The committee
consisted of Roch Kereszty, William Farmer, John Norris, and Mark
Goodwin from the University of Dallas, Brian Daley from Notre
Dame University, and Durwood Foster from the Pacific School of
Theology, Berkeley.

At the preliminary stages, the committee deliberated on how to
focus the conference on a topic that would be manageable and yet
rich enough for scholarly exploration. Building on two previous conferences, both initiated by William Farmer,[1] we eventually chose the
topic of the Eucharist as sacrifice for several reasons. While it has
been an essential aspect of the Roman Catholic understanding of the
Eucharist throughout the centuries, recently the meaning and importance of eucharistic sacrifice has come under increasing scrutiny in
Catholic circles: Why and how is the Eucharist a sacrifice rather than
a memorial meal? While the Council of Trent gave a broad magisterial definition on this topic for Roman Catholic teaching, it did not

articulate the meaning of Christ's sacrifice clearly enough nor did it fully elucidate the relation of the eucharistic sacrifice to the one-time sacrifice of Jesus on the cross. How can the Mass be a real sacrifice without detracting from the perfection of the one historical sacrifice of Christ? This last issue has remained a source of conflict and misunderstanding between different Christian groups for centuries up to this very day. Thus, in choosing the theme of the Eucharist as sacrifice, the committee hoped to eliminate some historical misunderstandings and contribute to an eventual ecumenical consensus.

Finally, we saw that the theme of the Eucharist as sacrifice is broad and rich enough to encompass scholarly exploration across several disciplines, such as biblical exegesis, historical theology, and systematic theology. The choice of this topic would enable an approach that would not be limited by the scope and methods of any single discipline, but rather would be more integrated and broadly based than has been typical of past research on the topic. The conference papers were thus defined according to the three interrelated areas of biblical, historical, and systematic theology, and participants were encouraged to speak across the respective disciplines, integrating insights from all three areas in their discussions.

After settling on the sacrificial character of the Eucharist as the focus for the conference, the committee turned its attention to defining specific paper topics. To this end, we convened a pre-conference on the Eucharist in May of 1999 at the University of Dallas. Participants in this pre-conference included Rev. Denis Farkasfalvy, O. Cist.; Charles Talbert of Baylor University; Rev. Brian Daley, S.J., of Notre Dame University; Jeff Bingham of Dallas Theological Seminary; Durwood Foster of the Pacific School of Theology; John Norris of the University of Dallas; and others from a variety of liturgical, pastoral, and academic backgrounds. The pre-conference served its purpose well in highlighting areas to be researched in preparation for the main conference of 2000. Following the pre-conference, the committee settled on an arrangement of two major papers in each of the three areas of biblical studies, historical theology, and systematic theology. These six major papers were to be accompanied by two responses.

This volume, then, represents the six major papers along with some of the responses given at the conference on November 9–11,

2000.[2] In the area of biblical studies, the first paper is by Rabbi David E. Stern of Temple Emmanuel in Dallas, Texas, and is entitled "Remembering and Redemption." Rabbi Stern's paper looks at the issue of "remembrance" (*zakhor*) in the context of Jewish Passover celebration and also examines the Israelite *todah* sacrifice as a potential parallel to the Eucharist. Toni Craven of Texas Christian University and Richard Taylor of Dallas Theological Seminary gave the responses. The second biblical essay comes from Rev. Denis Farkasfalvy, O. Cist., abbot of the Cistercian community in Irving, Texas. His paper is entitled "The Eucharistic Provenance of New Testament Texts." Building on previous scholarship, he explains that "the literary heritage of the apostolic church represented by the books of the New Testament is so closely and organically related to the Eucharist that one can truly say that the whole of New Testament scripture has a eucharistic provenance." The respondents were the Rev. Francis Martin of the John Paul II Institute, Washington D.C., and Charles Talbert, Distinguished Professor of Religion at Baylor University.

In the area of historical theology, Robin Darling Young of the Catholic University of America and D. Jeffrey Bingham of Dallas Theological Seminary presented the two major papers. Robin Darling Young's paper explores the role of the Eucharist in the theology of Clement of Alexandria. She intends to show how pervasively albeit elusively the Eucharist imbued and oriented Clement's theology as a whole. Her two respondents were Brian Daley, S.J., of Notre Dame University and Everett Ferguson of Abilene Christian University. D. Jeffrey Bingham's paper, entitled "Eucharist and Incarnation," examines in the second century and in Luther the central position of the Eucharist in salvation history uniting creation, the pre-incarnate Logos, incarnation, redemption, and eschatology. Susan J. White of Brite Divinity School and David N. Power, O.M.I., of Catholic University provided the responses.

In the area of systematic theology, the two major papers were those of D. Bentley Hart of Duke University on "Thine Own of Thine Own: Eucharistic Sacrifice in Orthodox Tradition" and Avery Dulles, S.J., of Fordham University on "The Eucharist as Sacrifice." D. Bentley Hart's paper focuses on Byzantine eucharistic theology, attempting to draw together its various strands "in a single, internally consistent theological reflection." David Balás, O. Cist., of the University of Dallas and William J. Abraham of Southern Methodist University offered responses to Hart's paper. Avery Dulles's essay, "The Eucharist as Sacrifice," provides a lucid synthesis from a carefully balanced Catholic perspective and was responded to by Peter Casarella of the Catholic University of America and Durwood Foster of the Pacific School of Theology. In order to enrich the systematic presentation, we inserted here an essay by Peter Casarella on the "Presence of a Gift," which deals with the eucharistic sacrifice from a new, existential perspective.

Two papers conclude the volume. The first, by Avery Dulles, "The Eucharist and the Mystery of the Trinity," was presented as the keynote address in a public lecture on the opening day of the conference. It shows how the eucharistic liturgy "provides unparalleled opportunities for salvific encounter with the three divine persons."

As usually happens, the presenters and respondents accumulated data and insights on a much wider scale than the original theme of the Eucharist as sacrifice. This overabundance of material prompted the eventual choice for the title of this volume, "Rediscovering the Eucharist: Ecumenical Conversations," as well as the inclusion of the essay "The Eucharist of the Church and the One Self-Offering of Christ" by Roch Kereszty, O. Cist., from the University of Dallas. In its original form, Kereszty's paper served as the position paper for the preparatory phase of the conference. Revised after the conference, it is meant to re-focus the discussion on the theme of the Eucharist as sacrifice. Drawing on the insights of the preceding essays, responses, and discussions, Kereszty's concluding study attempts to outline a biblical, historical, and systematic synthesis as well as spell out the ecumenical implications of the original theme.

Obviously, a conference of this scope would not have been possible without the dedicated work of many individuals. The committee is indebted to Msgr. Milam Joseph, president of the University of Dallas, who was supportive of the conference from its inception and who contributed in many ways to its success. We also thank the two bishops of the Diocese of Dallas, Bishops Charles Grahmann and Joseph Galante, for their encouragement and advice. The planning committee is also grateful for the contributions of Fr. David Balás, O. Cist., and John Norris, the respective chairmen of the Department of Theology in the period from 1998 to 2000. They were instrumental in organizing and implementing the conference. Thanks also go to Fr. Roch Kereszty, O. Cist., for his invaluable efforts in all phases of the conference. Stacey Raab, of the Office of the International Bible Commentary, provided indispensable technical assistance in organizing the conference and in preparing the essays of this volume for publication.

This book, however, is dedicated to the one man without whom this conference would not have been realized, Dr. William R. Farmer, professor emeritus of Perkins School of Theology at Southern Methodist University and research scholar at the University of Dallas since 1991. The conference stands as a tribute to his ecumenical vision, his love for the Eucharist, and his superb organizational skills. William Farmer's lifelong passion for the unity of the church, a passion born of a heartfelt sorrow over divisions in the body of Christ, created a congenial and friendly atmosphere that assured a willingness to learn from each other far beyond the usual attitude at gatherings of this kind. At the conference, his presence behind the scenes ensured its smooth running and provided those intangible personal touches that made the conference both an intellectual and personal experience. Dr. Farmer was to serve as editor in chief of this volume of essays until his untimely death on December 31, 2000.

Mark Goodwin, Roch Kereszty, and John Norris
Editorial Committee

NOTES

1. The first, held at Cambridge University, focused on the Pauline eucharistic texts and yielded a volume of papers, *One Loaf, One Cup: Ecumenical Studies of 1 Cor 11 and Other Eucharistic Texts*, ed. B. F. Meyer (Macon, Ga: Mercer University Press, 1993); the second conference at Baylor University focused on the Suffering Servant texts which underlie the institution accounts of the Eucharist and produced a volume entitled *Jesus and the Suffering Servant: Isaiah 53 and Christian Origins*, ed. W. H. Bellinger and W. R. Farmer (Harrisburg: Trinity Press International, 1998).

2. Only those responses that were corrected after the conference are included.

David E. Stern

Remembering and Redemption

Zakhor: Memory as Imperative

The command to remember is central to the Jewish tradition.[1]
The Hebrew verb *zakhar* appears in various forms 169 times in the
Hebrew Bible, usually with Israel or God as the subject, "for memory
is incumbent upon both."[2] Yosef Hayim Yerushalmi teaches that the
biblical imperative of memory underscores the distinctiveness of
ancient Israelite religion: it was ancient Israel that first assigned a
decisive significance to history and thereby created a new view of the
world, a view carried on into Christianity and Islam. In contrast to
other primitive cultures, ancient Israel did not focus on the time of
origins and archetypes; no longer was the historical moment sub-
verted to mythical cycles of return. Instead, Judaism moves the crucial encounter between humanity and God to the plane of history.
Expelled from Eden, we live in history, and God is revealed in history.
Rituals and festivals evoke not primeval time, but a historical past.
The drama of redemption takes place in time and over time. "Far
from attempting a flight from history, biblical religion allows itself to
be saturated by it and is inconceivable apart from it."[3]

But while a paper on remembrance in Jewish tradition needs to
recognize this world-changing emphasis on historical memory, we also
need to complicate it, because remembering in the Jewish tradition
seems to mean much more than an act of historical recall. Scholars
refer to the Hebrew Bible's word plays on names (e.g., Moses means
drawn from the water) with the euphemism "folk etymologies": i.e.,

1

the word plays may be both popular and instructive, but they are not etymologically accurate. So here I would like to insert a folk etymology of my own.

Humpty Dumpty Remembered

Consider as a constructive pun that re-member might mean to put things back together—the opposite of dismembering. In a literal sense, re-membering is what all the king's horses and all the king's men try to do (in vain) for poor old Humpty Dumpty. But this kind of remembering is not just the task of the royal paramedics of Mother Goose. It is in fact at the center of the religious enterprise: to recover disparate pieces of experience and weave them together into a meaning-making whole. The conception is more than playful, because it suggests that remembering need not be restricted to the retrieval of past events. Rather, remembering in this sense implies a process of taking note of an event, an idea, a promise—in time or beyond it—and then somehow integrating it into the believer's understanding of the world.

Professor Lawrence Hoffman argues for precisely this understanding of memory in the Jewish tradition.[4] Using rabbinic and medieval texts, and especially Seder *Rav Amram*, the ninth-century prototype for the Jewish order of prayer, Hoffman asserts that the root *zakhar*, normally translated as "remember," is better rendered as "to point out," and can therefore function beyond time and history. Hoffman identifies a parallel (and our discussion of the Eucharist is foreshadowed) in the Christian concept of remembrance described as *anamnesis*, about which a dictionary on sacramental worship comments:

> This Greek word is practically untranslatable in English. "Memorial," "commemoration," "remembrance" all suggest a recollection of the past, whereas *anamnesis* means making present an object or person from the past. Sometimes the term "reactualization" has been used to indicate the force of *anamnesis*.[5]

In Hebrew, the terms *zekher* and *zikaron* are equivalent to *anamnesis*. In the Kiddush, the prayer of sanctification that inaugurates the

Sabbath and the festivals, we recite the phrases *zekher litsiat mitsrayim* (in remembrance of the Exodus from Egypt) and *zikaron le-ma-aseit vereishit* (in remembrance of the work of creation). The Sabbath and festivals are structured not simply for us to recall past events, but for us to re-experience them: on the Sabbath, we rest as God rested; on Passover, we taste affliction in the bitter herbs. As Hoffman writes, "The rabbis saw *zekher* as anamnesis: making the past present."[6] In other words, *zekher* is a pointer through time, connecting the present to the past. The Sabbath is a remembrance because it is a pointer to creation; our festivals are remembrances because they are pointers to the Exodus.[7]

Hoffman's concept of *zekher* as "pointer" helps us understand what might be meant when the Jewish tradition speaks of an omniscient God as remembering, or of our asking God to remember. In fact, in prayer we often ask God to "remember" things that have nothing to do with the passage of time. We pray, for example, "Remember Your mercy, O Lord, and Your compassion for they are eternal."[8] Reminding God, therefore, is not asking God to cognitively recall a past event; the reminder is a pointer which seeks to direct God's attention, especially in the service of our salvation. So when a Jew prays that God "remember the good deeds of the ancestors," it is not simply a request that God leaf through the ancient family photo album. Instead, it is a plea that God take note of the righteous acts of the biblical patriarchs so that those righteous acts might evoke God's grace upon us, though we be lacking in good works ourselves.[9]

The Passover Seder as Ritual of Remembrance

Keeping this construct of remembrance in mind—remembrance observances as pointers, in time and beyond time; *zekher/zikaron* as the act of making the past present; and God's remembering as a redemptive act of paying mind—we move to the Jewish observance of Passover. We will see that the Passover ritual develops into the Jewish ritual par excellence—and therefore our best example of memory as redemptive re-experience.

The Bible describes the preparation and eating of the Passover sacrifice in Exodus 12 and 13. Interestingly, the instructions for

future observance of the Passover come in the midst of the Exodus
narrative itself, so that even before the redemptive story is complete,
we receive the instructions for how to sustain and re-enact it. In particular, Exodus 12 prescribes the slaughtering of lambs locally within
the community, the daubing of the doorposts with blood, the requirement that the animal be roasted over the fire and eaten the same
night. The observance is called a *zikaron*, and it is combined with a
seven-day feast of unleavened bread. There is, however, almost no ritual per se attached to the preparation and eating. Only the rudiments
of a script are suggested in Exodus 12:26–27 and 13:8, where we are
instructed to explain the observance as: (1) a sacrifice to the Lord
because God passed over the houses of the Israelites in Egypt, and (2)
"because of what the Lord did for me when I went free from Egypt."

Joseph Tabory and others argue that the precise history of the
Passover seder starts at the end of the Second Temple period, in part
because while the biblical text attests to the prescribed eating of the
sacrifice, we do not have evidence of any ceremony or ritual connected with that eating of the paschal lamb prior to descriptions of
the Second Temple period.[10] Any attempt to trace the seder's history
therefore begins with the Mishnah, which was itself redacted only at
the beginning of the third century C.E., close to 150 years after the
destruction of the Second Temple.

The first description of the seder occurs in the last chapter of
Mishnah Tractate Pesachim, where we receive an outline for a three-
part observance: (1) recitation of the story of the Exodus from Egypt,
(2) a celebratory meal with special foods, and (3) songs of praise to
God. Hoffman, using a concept from contemporary ritual studies,
offers the idea of the seder as "sacred theater," proceeding as follows:
(1) introductory prayers set the stage, in this case the table and its
special foods; (2) the drama then opens with a rhetorical question or
questions about the food, designed to stimulate a response; (3) a free-
flowing account of the Exodus ensues; and (4) the evening ends with
praise of God through the psalms of praise known collectively as the
Hallel.[11]

Tabory, Hoffman, and others assert the well-established claim
that the seder is related to the Greco-Roman symposium meal.[12]
Using Plutarch's definition of a symposium as a banquet followed by

"a communion of serious and mirthful entertainment, discourse and actions," the scholarly consensus affirms Hoffman's statement: "The seder is a rabbinic symposium, its topic of discourse being the Exodus." The shift is significant: rather than a sacrificial meal in which the consumption of the sacrifice is the focal point of the gathering, at some time following the destruction of the temple in 70 C.E. the seder becomes what Tabory calls a "second-stage symposium," in which

> the discussions and conversations became the main elements of the evening, and many of these discussions are related to the foods consumed during the evening. Eventually, the foods were treated as symbols and were eaten in symbolic quantities. As symbols, they evoked further exegesis... this, in turn, served further to emphasize the conversational aspect of the seder.[13]

Viewing the seder as related to the symposium underscores that mealtime rites and table spirituality were an essential dimension of rabbinic Judaism, embodied within the rabbinic fellowship groups known as *chavurot*. Many now believe that the domestic table was the primary locus for Jewish prayer until the synagogue took center stage as a place of prayer in the third century.[14] The transfer from sacrificial rite to table ritual may have been especially smooth for the Passover observance, since its biblical origins include local slaughter of the sacrifice and sharing of the sacrificial meal by all.

Sometime in the second century, perhaps in response to competing Christian conceptualizations of the Passover symbols,[15] the liturgical unit of rhetorical questions, Exodus account, and Hallel praise was moved prior to the meal, with psalms included after the meal as well. As a result, with nothing to prompt them, the questions became a fixed set of stock queries known as The Four Questions, and the response became fixed as well, largely as a midrashic expansion of Deuteronomy 26, along with a mandatory explanation of the symbolism implicit in certain seder foods.[16]

The seder ritual continued to develop, and by the eighth century we see our next set of marked changes. Most important, the ritual had moved from oral theater to the written text we call the *Haggadah*.

The medieval period brought its own additions, largely messianic in tone. These include the prominent folk role given to the prophet Elijah, herald of the messianic age, as a summoned guest at every seder; and the singing of the folk song *Chad Gadya* (An Only Kid), in which God finally conquers the Angel of Death. This messianic thrust echoed longstanding rabbinic tradition that Passover eve was the time scheduled for ultimate redemption. The "night of watching" was indeed for all time; Rabbi Joshua stated: "On that night they were redeemed [in the past] and on that night they will be redeemed in the future."[17] The Passover "pointing," therefore, is both to the redemption past and the redemption yet to come.

Sacrifice and Story

Throughout the centuries of its development (which continues with a plethora of contemporary Haggadot), the effect of the Passover seder's ritual theater is profound; it is remembrance in the deepest sense. By ingesting symbolic foods, we literally internalize the narrative of redemption. The participants not only recall and rehearse the Exodus story—we are commanded to relive it, to see the story as our own. The Haggadah teaches: "In every generation, we are required to see ourselves as if we ourselves went forth from Egypt." Who is termed "wicked" by the Haggadah? The one who insists on declaring the story to be someone else's and not his own—he willfully locates himself outside the realm of redemptive possibilities. In post-destruction Passover observance, the story is the thing, and the telling itself is a step toward redemption. The sacrifice is described, and an echo of it is preserved in the eating of unleavened bread as a substitute for the paschal lamb, but it is the Exodus from Egypt, rather than the offering in Jerusalem, that serves as focal point and fulcrum to an evening of messianic hope.[18]

There is a paradox here. First and foremost, we are commanded to make the story our own. At the same time, the explicit emphasis on story as taking place in historical rather than mythic time, and the prominent place given to exegesis—i.e., the explicit and elaborate improvisations on the familiar narrative—constitute a conscious reminder that the experience of Exodus for us is in fact mediated.

Haggadah means telling, and the Haggadah as script constantly confronts the reader with the textualization of the Exodus narrative. Examples abound. Biblical citations from outside the Book of Exodus create a complicating weave. In the narrative section called the Maggid, the Haggadah presents us with numerous introductory passages that seem to both delay and broaden the fundamental story; it subverts assumptions and expands possibility in permitting an opinion that the Israelites' degradation consisted not in slavery, but in our worship of idols. The rabbis engage in serious literary play regarding the number of plagues based on an exegesis of the phrases "finger of God" (Exod 8:19) to describe God's power in Egypt, and "mighty hand" to describe God's power at the sea. Since there were ten plagues in Egypt effected by God's finger, and a hand has five fingers, then God must have brought fifty more plagues at the sea! Most striking is the fact that the passage that forms the basis for the rabbinic exegesis of the Exodus narrative does not even come from the Book of Exodus. The rabbis instead use Deuteronomy 26:5ff., which is itself not the Exodus narrative, but a script for how the Exodus narrative should be retold and remembered. Through explicit strategies that insistently mediate (and even fracture) the core narrative, the Haggadah rejects emulative re-enactment in favor of self-conscious exegesis.

What is fascinating is that in Jewish (read rabbinic) terms, the acknowledgment of story, of exegetical relationship rather than mythic re-enactment, is no less potent an act of remembrance. In fact, the mediated memory may be more powerful, because in its very mediation it recognizes not only the Exodus but the temple's destruction as well, for the mediated telling comes only as substitute for the temple sacrifice that is no longer possible. The ultimate goal of the seder, it seems to me, for all of its drama of identification, is not to make the Exodus contemporaneous to the participant. The identification with the story is only a vehicle. The goal is to re-member the reality of redemption: to reassemble our own world-view in accord with the Haggadah's progression from degradation to dignity, to reintegrate into our lives the reality of a God who hears the cry of the oppressed. The thrill of re-experiencing the redemptive moment only brings us halfway; the ultimate messianic goal of the seder is not to transport ourselves into the redemptive moment, but to insist that the redemptive moment can be realized in our world.[19]

The process of transformation in the Passover observance—from a sacrificial to an exegetical focus—might serve as an approximate analogy for Jewish response to the destruction of the temple. By definition, for Jews, the destruction of the temple in Jerusalem constituted the demise of the sacrificial system. While there is ample evidence that alternatives to the sacrificial system had been springing up both in Babylonia and even in the land of Israel for centuries, the sacrificial cult remained the essence of first-century Judaism up until the destruction. Because tradition dictated that sacrifices could be offered only at the temple (see Deut 16:2, where the originally local Passover sacrifice is "relocated" accordingly), the destruction of the temple signaled the demise of the priestly cult—and, most important, of its expiatory function. The question that Judaism (and early Christianity) had to answer was how to sustain the function of the sacrificial system—the drawing near to God through diverse offering of thanks, purification, well-being, and especially expiation—when the system itself was defunct. Judaism's response was clear: the sacrificial cult is replaced by a rabbinic Judaism that emphasizes prayer, study, and acts of loving kindness,[20] but the memory of sacrifices is preserved in various liturgical and textual reminders.

The rabbis of the Mishnah devote an inordinate amount of space to details of the practice of sacrifice even (perhaps especially) in the absence of the temple cult, and the study of those texts by subsequent generations is seen as tantamount to participating in the sacrificial system itself. In the most profound transformation, spoken prayer, defined as the "service of the heart," replaces sacrifice as the means to reach out to God, but the prayer services are given names that recall the sacrifices in the now-demolished temple. Prayers for restoration of the cult are inserted into the liturgy. On Yom Kippur, a whole section of the service is dedicated to a detailed description of the priestly ritual on the Day of Atonement. So, even as the liturgy uses images of sacrifice to fulfill the ends of sacrifice especially in the absence of sacrifice, the message is clear: once the temple is gone, one can only commemorate the ancient practices—one cannot replicate them. The messianic hope called for an eventual restoration of the cult, but, in the meantime, it is our job to tell the story and to conduct the rituals that point both to the redemption past and the redemption yet to come.

There is, of course, a Christian story to be told as well, a Christian reading of Passover's redemptive message. Israel J. Yuval sets out a thesis of parallel development:

> Following the destruction of the Temple in 70 C.E., two competing interpretations were formed for Passover, one Jewish and one Christian. To replace the ritual of the defunct paschal sacrifice, each religion adopted the strategy of mandating the telling of a story. Jews adhered to the original meaning of the festival as deriving from the initial redemption from Egypt that served as a sign of a second deliverance still to come. Christians narrated the tale of a second redemption already in place: the crucifixion and resurrection of Jesus. Both stories offered a liturgical alternative to the old sacrificial rite, addressing simultaneously the difficult question of how to celebrate a festival of redemption in an age of foreign domination and oppression. Both began with degradation (*g'nut*)—either Egyptian servitude or the crucifixion—and concluded with praise (*shevach*), holding out hope for the future.[21]

In reading the redemptive symbols, Christianity identified the *pesach* with Jesus, the lamb of God (*agnus dei*). *Matzah* was the body of the Savior (*corpus Christi*), a remembrance of the bread of the Last Supper, and *maror* became symbolic of the suffering of the Savior (*passio domini*), or of the punishment awaiting the People of Israel for what they had done to their Messiah.[22] Most important, in contrast to the Jewish observance of Passover, in the eucharistic enactment of Passover, the notion of sacrifice remains central. Exactly how to understand the Eucharist in relationship to sacrifice has long been a debate within Christianity. But setting aside the question of whether an actual sacrifice takes place during the eucharistic ritual, it is clear that, since the beginnings of Christianity, the death and resurrection of Jesus have been understood as a sacrifice (Heb 9:11–12). Moreover, the question of whether the Eucharist is an actual sacrifice directly involves the definition of remembrance ("Do this in remembrance of me") not as historical recall, but as present re-experience of the past.[23] The Last Supper narratives in the gospels are replete with sacrificial language, and in fact with sacrificial symbols that were rooted in normative Jewish practice.[24] As a result, scholars have sought to understand exactly what type of sacrifice is being echoed and transformed here. This notion of both continuity and discontinuity is vital; whatever biblical sacrifice may be the referent, it is clear that the circumstances of the Last Supper, most notably Jesus' "implied divine dignity,"[25] by definition transform (and for Christians, transcend) any normative precedent in the Old Testament. Nonetheless, the search for roots remains vital. Recent attention has been directed toward the theory that the early Eucharist may have been derived from the *todah* sacrifice, not the least reason being their common meaning of thanksgiving or gratitude. Since that question lands me back in the Hebrew Bible, where I am on somewhat more secure ground, here are some observations.

Todah and Eucharist

Chapters 1 to 3 of the Book of Leviticus describe three basic categories of sacrifice that were offered regularly by individual Israelites and their families, by kings and leaders, and by the entire community:[26] the burnt offering (*'olah*), the grain offering (*minchah*), and the offering of well-being (*zevach ha-shelamim*). Chapters 4 to 5 then detail two sacrifices of expiation, one usually translated "sin offering" (*chatat*), and the other usually translated "guilt offering" (*asham*).[27] The *todah* sacrifice is described in Leviticus 7:11–18, where it appears as a subset of the *zevach shelamim*, identified as *zevach todah*, or "thanksgiving offering." As described in Leviticus 3, the *zevach* offering was a sacred meal in which sections of the sacrifice were shared by the priests and donors of the offering. Only certain fatty parts of the animal were burned on the altar as God's share. There is also some evidence that at an early stage the *zevach* may not have required the use of an altar. The paschal *zevach*, for example, as indicated in Exodus 12 to 13, was to be roasted whole over an open fire, near one's home. Levine points out that because the eating of the *zevach* was not restricted (which actually rendered it "an offering of lesser sanctity"), its purpose seems to be clear: "to afford the worshipers the experience of joining together with the priests in a sacred meal at which God himself was perceived to be the honored guest."[28]

The *todah* offering was distinguished from the general *zevach she-lamim* because it called for the addition of a grain offering of unleav-ened cakes, as well as leavened cakes (Lev 7:12–14), and because the flesh had to be eaten on the day it was offered.

In terms of its purpose, the *todah* offering was made as an expres-sion of gratitude, often for deliverance from danger or misfortune. It was not obligatory, nor was it rooted in sinfulness or guilt. According to the rabbis, it would continue to be offered in the messianic era, when the rest of the sacrificial system was no longer operative.[29]

Most interesting for our purposes are the parallels that exist between the *todah* and the *pesach* and *miluim* (ordination) offerings. Like the *pesach* offering, the *todah* could be offered locally, had to be eaten the night it was offered, was to be shared with the community, and was accompanied by unleavened bread. (The combination of grain and animal sacrifices was a well-known pattern.) The latter two characteristics are echoed in the Mishnaic treatment of the *zevach todah*. In Tractate *Zevachim*, the offering is placed in the category of "Lesser Holy Things," precisely because of its accessibility to the community—it could be slaughtered anywhere in the temple court, it could be eaten anywhere, and it could be cooked in any way (M. Zevachim 5:6). The majority of the Mishnah's references to the thanksgiving offering are concentrated in Tractate *Menachot*, which focuses on grain offerings. Interesting again for our Passover paral-lels, two of these *mishnayot* discuss the relationship between the lamb and the bread in the thanksgiving offering (M. Men. 2:3, 7:3).

Potential parallels to the Eucharist are clear; characteristics of the *todah* offering can easily be identified in the Last Supper. I can not reach any secure conclusions here, especially since I am reading the New Testament only in its English translation, but I offer some ques-tions to consider: (1) How should Jesus' expression of gratitude as described in the Last Supper narrative be classified? Is it part of a *todah* offering, or simply the normal blessing that one would say before or after a meal?[30] (2) The parallels to the Passover offering both clarify and obscure the question. Because the *todah* offering and the Passover offering contain such similar characteristics, it is hard to tell which one (if either) is primary in the Last Supper narratives. Then again, as Fr. Kereszty suggests, linking the Last Supper to the *todah* sacrifice would allow for its commemoration in the Eucharist at all times, rather than only at the time of Passover.[31] (3) The more difficult issue is raised by Kereszty's assertion "Thanksgiving sacrifice (*Eucharistia*) and expiatory sacrifice are inseparable."[32] While that may be a valid theological conclusion, it does not seem to be supported by evidence in the Hebrew Bible, where the *zevach shelamim* does not seem to have anything to do with atonement: "Though the fat and certain other organs of the sacrifice were burnt on the altar as a 'pleasing odor' and the blood was sprinkled on the altar, nowhere do we hear of these acts as atoning for any sin."[33]

Night and Day

A passage from Mishnah Berakhot, included in the Haggadah:

R. Eleazar ben Azariah said: Behold, I am about seventy years old, and I have never been worthy to find a reason why the Exodus from Egypt should be mentioned at night-time, until Ben Zoma expounded it thus: It is stated—"That thou may remember the day when thou came forth out of the land of Egypt all the days of thy life" (Deut 16:3). Had the text said "the days of thy life" it would have meant only the days; but "all the days of thy life" includes the nights as well. The sages, however, say: "The days of thy life" refers to this world; "all the days of thy life" is to include the days of the Messiah. (*M. Berakhot* 5:1)

What does it mean to remember? To weave together the disparate pieces: day and night, past and present, one redemptive possibility and another. To weave together, but always to distinguish—to note, as God did from the first, the dignity of sacred separation. It means to stay up late thinking about the stories that make us who we are. It means telling tales of redemption even when the night is dark or the dawn yet gray. It means not only to take note of the past, but to own it as the day when *you* came forth. It is to stand between redemptions. It means to live in time and beyond time, because it is our task—Jews and Christians—to hold the vision of wholeness so near that we succeed, finally—in remembering the future.

NOTES

1. I am indebted to my teachers Dr. Michael Signer and Dr. Lawrence Hoffman for their guidance at the outset of this project, and for their numerous insights cited in this paper.

2. Yosef Hayim Yerushalmi, *Zakhor: Jewish History and Jewish Memory* (Seattle: University of Washington Press), 5.

3. Ibid., 8–9.

4. Lawrence A. Hoffman, "Does God Remember? A Liturgical Theology of Memory." Unpublished material, to appear in *History and Memory in Christianity and Judaism*, ed. Michael Signer (Notre Dame: University of Notre Dame Press).

4. Peter E. Fink, S.J., *The New Dictionary of Sacramental Worship* (Collegeville, Minn: Liturgical Press, 1990), 45. Cited in Lawrence A. Hoffman, "Jewish and Christian Liturgy," in *Christianity in Jewish Terms*, ed. Tikva Frymer-Kensky, David Novak, Peter Ochs, David Fox Sandmel, and Michael Signer (Boulder: Westview Press, 2000), 183.

6. Hoffman, "Jewish and Christian Liturgy," 183.

7. Hoffman, "Does God Remember?" 66.

8. From the *Tachanun* prayer, Seder Rav Amram A65. Cited in Hoffman, "Does God Remember?" 52.

9. Hoffman, "Does God Remember?" 48.

10. Joseph Tabory, "Towards a History of the Paschal Meal," in *Passover and Easter: Origin and History to Modern Times*, ed. Paul F. Bradshaw and Lawrence A. Hoffman (Notre Dame: University of Notre Dame Press, 1999), 62.

11. Lawrence A. Hoffman, "The Passover Meal in Jewish Tradition," in *Passover and Easter*, 13.

12. Ibid., 9. The concept was advanced by S. [Sigmund] Stein in his article "The Influence of Symposia Literature on the Literary Form of the Pesach Haggadah," *Journal of Jewish Studies* 69 (1957). Stein's thesis was challenged by Baruch M. Bokser in his book *The Origins of the Seder* (Berkeley: University of California Press, 1984).

13. Tabory, 74.

14. Hoffman, "The Passover Meal in Jewish Tradition," 11–12.

15. For a lucid and detailed treatment of the mutual influence of Jewish and Christian interpretations of the Passover ritual, see Israel J. Yuval, "Easter and Passover as Early Jewish-Christian Dialogue" in *Passover and Easter*, 98–124.

16. Hoffman, "The Passover Meal in Jewish Tradition," 14. The explanation of the symbolism is attributed to Rabban Gamliel: "Whoever did not say these three

things on Passover did not fulfill his obligation: 1. *Pesach* (paschal lamb)—because the Omnipresent skipped over the houses of our ancestors in Egypt. 2. *Maror* (bitter herbs)—because the Egyptians embittered the lives of our ancestors in Egypt. 3. *Matzah* (unleavened bread)—because they were redeemed." Cited in Tabory, 69.

17. Hoffman, "The Passover Meal in Jewish Tradition," 20. Rabbi Joshua's statement appears in *Mekilta de-Rabbi Ishmael*, Jacob Z. Lauterbach, ed. (Philadelphia: The Jewish Publication Society of America, 1933), p. 115.

18. Yuval, 114, suggests that by the second generation after the destruction, the Christian interpretation of Exodus 12, in which the paschal lamb is identified with Jesus, had emerged, and that, in response, the Haggadah distanced itself from sacrifice and instead emphasized the duty to tell the story of the Exodus.

19. I have only the most rudimentary knowledge of the Christian debate over the concept of the "real presence" of God in the Eucharist; I do not know whether this paradox of mediation *adding* to the meaning of remembrance might shed light on that discussion.

20. The midrashic collection *Avot de Rabbi Nathan* relates this account of Rabbi Yochanan ben Zakkai, who is traditionally credited with redacting the Mishnah: "Once Rabban Yochanan b. Zakkai was going forth from Jerusalem, followed by R. Joshua, when he saw the Sanctuary in ruins. Said R. Joshua: 'Woe unto us that this place, where the iniquities of Israel were expiated, lies in ruins!' Said [R. Yochanan] to him: 'My son, be not grieved! We have a means of atonement that is its equal, namely the practice of benevolence, as it is said: 'For I desire loving kindness, and not sacrifice'" (Hos 6:6). *Avot de Rabbi Nathan*, Version I, iv, 11a. in Ephraim E. Urbach, *The Sages: Their Customs and Beliefs* (Cambridge: Harvard University Press, 1987), 667.

21. Yuval, 98.

22. Ibid., 106, nn 34–37.

23. Robert Louis Wilken, "Christian Worship: An Affair of Things as Well as Words," in *Christianity in Jewish Terms*, 200.

24. Hoffman, "Jewish and Christian Liturgy," 179, points out that when Jesus refers to the bread as his body and the wine as the new covenant in his blood, he is invoking familiar Jewish symbolic associations: "Bread was already a Jewish symbol of salvation that paralleled and then took the place of the paschal lamb as the primary symbol of God's deliverance of Israel in Egypt." Wine was "widely assumed to be symbolic of blood." Blood is also seen as part of the process of expiation in Levitical sacrifices of substitution.

25. Roch Kereszty, O. Cist., "The Eucharist of the Church and the One Self-Offering of Christ," p. 240 of this volume; cf. Miroslav Wolf, "The Lamb of God and the Sin of the World," in *Christianity in Jewish Terms*, 316: "In the story of Christ's death, the two primary agents... are not strictly separate and the action must be

understood as the deed of God...Atonement, in the most fundamental sense, is an *event in the life of God* for the sake of the world."

26. Baruch A. Levine, *The JPS Torah Commentary: Leviticus* (Philadelphia: The Jewish Publication Society, 1989), 3.

27. The translation of technical terms of sacrifice in the Book of Leviticus poses unique challenges. I use the phrase "usually translated" above because there are great divergences in translation, each translation representing not just a philological conclusion, but a philosophical conviction about sacrifice. For example, Jacob Milgrom translates *chatat* as "purification offering," and contends that in fact the offering was designed not to expiate the sin of the offerer, but to purify the temple precincts of the pollution created by the offerer's transgression. *Asham* has been translated as "reparations offering," and Levine, 42, translates *zevach ha-shelamim* as "the sacred gift of greeting." See Gary A. Anderson, "Sacrifice and Sacrificial Offerings—Old Testament," in *The Anchor Bible Dictionary*, ed. David Noel Freedman (New York: Doubleday, 1992), 879.

28. Levine, 14.

29. Ibid., 43.

30. Hoffman points out that the Jewish notion of blessing (Hebrew *berakhah*) emphasizes praise rather than thanks, and that the linguistic distinction may reflect a theological difference: "The verb *levarekh* is frequently found in apposition to verbs that mean 'to praise,' not 'to offer thanks'...The Christian Eucharist is a supreme act of gratitude. The Jewish blessing is a supreme act of praise." Hoffman, "Jewish and Christian Liturgy," 186–187.

31. Kereszty, 245–246.

32. Ibid., 255.

33. Anderson, 878–879. Cf. Hans-Josef Klauck, "Sacrifice and Sacrificial Offerings—New Testament," in *The Anchor Bible Dictionary*, 888. Klauck argues against attempts to classify the Lord's Supper as a *todah* meal.

A RESPONSE TO DAVID E. STERN ON

Remembering and Redemption

BY RICHARD TAYLOR

Introduction

In the Hebrew Scriptures we find many examples of the *Magnalia Dei*, or mighty acts of God undertaken in behalf of his people. Some of these acts, like the Passover and the Exodus, are major events that point to defining moments in the survival of the ancient Israelite nation. Others are less comprehensive and more personal in nature, involving occasions of deliverance from death or extrication from tragic circumstances that threatened the life of an individual Israelite. In both cases, certain obligations attended those who had benefited from Yahweh's salvific actions. First, there was an obligation that rested on the worshiper of Yahweh to remember and not forget the mighty deeds of the Lord. In cases of great national deliverance, this remembrance was to continue for successive generations. Sometimes such remembrance would be aided by a tangible and visible memorial that was intended to cause the next generation to ask, "What do these stones mean?" (Josh 4:6–7). Second, there was an obligation on the part of the worshiper to acknowledge Yahweh's presence in the deliverance of his people by offering an appropriate sacrifice as an expression of gratitude and thanks. Such a public sacrifice would also provide others an opportunity to participate in the deliverance that the Lord had brought about for the benefit of those who stood in a covenant relationship with him. It is around these twin foci of remembrance and thanks that I would like to construct my response to Rabbi Stern's helpful paper on the role of remembrance in the worship of ancient Israel. It will be obvious from my remarks that I am very appreciative of the contribution that Rabbi Stern has made to our consideration of these important motifs.

Remembrance

That remembrance plays an important role in the Eucharist requires no elaboration. The very words of institution, "Do this in remembrance of me" (Luke 22:19), point to the important role that memory plays in the proper observance of what came to be called the Lord's table (1 Cor 10:21). It is in fact not too much to say that memory is a primary emphasis throughout the entirety of scripture.[1] But what exactly is meant by remembrance? The English word by itself does not capture very well the particular nuances that could have been assumed and taken for granted with Jesus' original audience. Rather, the word must be understood against the backdrop of the Hebrew Scriptures that informed the world-view of Jesus' earliest disciples. In what follows I would like to highlight three features of remembrance in the Hebrew Bible that Rabbi Stern, building on the work of Michael Signer and Lawrence Hoffman, has brought to our attention. Though each of them by itself gives only a partial picture of biblical remembrance, together these characteristics of ancient Israelite remembrance provide a nicely orbed summary that can inform our understanding of remembrance within a New Testament eucharistic context.

First, remembrance invariably involves recollection of a historical past. As Rabbi Stern has reminded us, a distinctive feature of Israel's religion was an emphasis on its historical moorings. By contrast, to a much greater degree than was the case with ancient Israel, the religious beliefs of neighboring cultures were taken up with mythic cycles involving the activities of the gods in primeval history. Whether we think of ancient Akkadian literature with its creation legends, or Ugaritic literature with its Baal myths, or various Canaanite mythologies, ancient Israelite literature stands out for its restraint in this regard. It is not that we cannot see within the Hebrew Bible evidences of struggle with such world-views. On the contrary, we can.

The creation account in the Book of Genesis, for example, should probably be read as something of a polemic against such alien understandings of creation. But as Rabbi Stern has emphasized, "Judaism moves the crucial encounter between humanity and God to the plane of history."[2] Redemptive history is inseparably linked to real time and space; God has chosen to reveal himself within the categories of time and space with which we are most familiar. While remembrance certainly means more than mere recall of events drawn from the past, it does not mean less than this. Memory in the Hebrew Bible begins with a calling to mind of God's salvific acts on behalf of his people at particular moments of prior history in the life of the community.

Second, I find Rabbi Stern's emphasis on the "pointing" nature of remembrance very helpful. To remember, in the biblical sense, is not only to recall an event from past history; it is to point out its meaning and to benefit from its significance for the present moment. Rabbi Stern appeals to two examples in order to clarify this observation. First, while the Sabbath points back to the creative week of Genesis 1 to 2, it also points to the present human need for rest in imitation of the pattern of divine activity. Second, while the Passover points back to the Exodus event and the experiences subsequent to the Israelite flight from Egypt, it also invites present participation in the affliction experienced by those who first made that journey. To remember is therefore more than mere recollection; it is reflection on the present significance of the event that one calls to mind for this purpose. Otherwise, as Rabbi Stern points out, it is hard to see what meaning could be attached to the fact that an omniscient God is asked in scripture to remember.[3] In divine remembering it is not that distant or forgotten facts are simply being called to mind, but rather that a contemporary application of the significance of those facts is being made. This is an important feature of what it means in the biblical sense to remember.

Third, remembrance invites participation in the salvific benefits to which the ceremonial symbols call attention. As Rabbi Stern notes, in the Passover ritual one does not merely observe the feast of celebration as a spectator; he actually participates in it by partaking of the food items that are provided. In this way he demonstrates his personal involvement in what those elements are intended to express. This internalization of the meaning of redemptive history enables the participants "to see the story as our own."[4] In that sense, Rabbi Stern observes, "the ultimate messianic goal of the seder is not to transport ourselves into the redemptive moment, but to insist that the redemptive moment can be realized in our world."[5] Remembrance is thus not only recollection of distant facts of history; it is personal appropriation of redemptive benefits and personal participation in the effects of redemptive history.

The construct that Rabbi Stern has provided with regard to remembrance in Jewish thought thus provides a helpful backdrop for understanding how remembrance would have been understood by the earliest participants in the Eucharist. Their thought-world was one based on thorough familiarity with the Hebrew Scriptures. This familiarity would have automatically informed how they thought about such things. Post-biblical Jewish thought no doubt retained and perpetrated these same notions of remembrance, especially through the evolving development of the Passover seder, which, as Rabbi Stern notes, is "our best example of memory as redemptive re-experience."[6] And even though we must be cautious about reading back into the first century notions that may be actually attested only in the later post-biblical literature, there is no doubt a great deal of continuity between these late and early Jewish traditions.

Rabbi Stern's paper has, I think, important implications for how we approach the study of those New Testament documents that deal not only with the Lord's Supper but with other topics as well. His paper has served to remind me of the degree to which Christian vocabulary is indebted to lexical antecedents found in the Hebrew Bible. Many words that appear in the Greek New Testament are in fact pregnant with Hebrew meanings that would not necessarily have been a normal part of those Greek words when used within a purely Hellenistic setting.[7] In cases where the semantic range of Hebrew and Greek words differed there was often an implied transfer of Hebrew meaning to the related Greek vocabulary. As a result, these Greek words must be studied in light of their Hebrew counterparts if we are to grasp their full significance. Remembrance is one such word, as I think Rabbi Stern has effectively shown. Consequently, it seems clear to me that the eucharistic word *anamnesis* ("remembrance") finds fullest explanation not in its usage in secular Greek literature of the day, but in the Old Testament categories of corresponding Hebrew words such as *zekher* and *zikkaron*.

Thanks

> R. Phinehas, R. Levi, and R. Johanan said in the name of R.
> Menahem the Galilean: "In the time-to-come, all offerings
> will cease, except the thank-offering: this will never cease. All
> prayers will cease except the prayer of thanksgiving: this will
> never cease..."[8]

A second area that Rabbi Stern touches on in his paper is the
matter of the *todah* offering as a possible source for the eucharistic
practice of the early church. In keeping with the wishes of our conference committee, I would like to offer a few thoughts concerning *todah*
in relation to the Eucharist. I will then return to Rabbi Stern's observations regarding the *todah* offering.

In the categories of the Hebrew Bible, the public expression of
thanks to the Almighty for deliverance from danger is linked to one
of the Levitical sacrifices provided for this purpose, namely the *zevach/*
todah, or thank offering. In reality, the *todah* is but one of several
offerings known in biblical parlance as "peace offerings" (*selamim*).
The other *selamim*, such as the *neder* ("votive offering") and the *ne-*
daba ("freewill offering"), had somewhat similar purposes but a different *Sitz im Leben* in the worship of ancient Israel. It is therefore the
todah that is most relevant for our present purposes.

Todah in the Hebrew Bible

The thirty-two instances of *todah* in the Hebrew Bible divide into
three categories: (1) sometimes the word is used in a general way for
thankful praise directed toward God;[9] (2) sometimes it refers specifically to a choir of singers who render praise within a liturgical
setting;[10] and (3) often the word is used to refer to a particular type of
Levitical sacrifice known as the "thank offering."[11] It is this latter
usage that is of special interest for discussion of the origins of the
Eucharist.

From the various biblical allusions to the *todah* we can derive a
composite picture of how this Old Testament sacrifice functioned in
the life of the Israelite community.[12] When one had gone through a

dangerous or perhaps life-threatening situation and had been rescued
by Yahweh from those circumstances,[13] it was customary for the worshiper later to gather with family and friends in the presence of a
priest at the sanctuary or temple in order to celebrate God's provision
of renewed life. It was there that an animal would be sacrificed as a
thank offering and then cooked in preparation for a meal. Wine, various breads, and other food items would also be made available to the
participants who had come in order to share that meal (Lev 7:12–15).
Once the meal was ready, the priest together with the worshiper and
his family and friends would engage in fellowship while partaking of
the meal. During the course of the events the celebrant would describe
the situation out of which the Lord had delivered him, publicly
acknowledging God's good hand of protection upon his life, while
those who were present joined in the expression of thanks being given
to Yahweh. The mood was typically different from that of other sacrifices in that it was a happy occasion. The purpose of the *todah* was not
for sorrowful confession of sin, but rather for joyful celebration of
God's provision of deliverance from which the worshiper had benefited. Certain common expressions of praise characterize the *todah* as
described in the Hebrew Bible, such as "Yahweh is good" (1 Chr
16:34; 2 Chr 5:13; Pss 106:1; 107:1; 118:1, 29; 136:1; Jer 33:11; 2 Chr
7:3; Ezra 3:11), or "his loyal-love is everlasting" (1 Chr 16:34; 2 Chr
5:13; Pss 106:1; 107:1; 118:1–4, 29; 136 [26 times]; Jer 33:11; 2 Chr
7:3, Ezra 3:11), or "his faithfulness continues to all generations" (Ps
57:3, 9; 108:5), or "Yahweh is gracious and compassionate" (Ps 111:4),
or "Yahweh is righteous" (Ps 7:17; 33:3–5, 18, 22). The reason for the
occasion was to extol the *Magnalia Dei*, or mighty deeds of God, performed on behalf of his people (Ps 111:2; cf. Pss 9:1; 26:7; 89:5; 105:1;
Isa 25:1). The assumed basis of the *todah* celebration was the covenan-
tal relationship that the worshiper enjoyed with Yahweh (cf. Ps 111:5,
9), a relationship based upon divine initiative and established upon
prior divine promises. Sometimes, but not always, in the *todah* we find
an explicit reference to the covenant (e.g., Ps 111:5, 9; 1 Chr
16:15–18; cf. Pss 89:1–49; 105:8; 106:1, 45). But whether there is overt
reference to the covenant or not, it is always understood to be the
basis for the celebration.

From this brief synthesis we can easily see that there are certain
correspondences between the Old Testament *todah* and the Eucharist

as described in early Christian literature. Perhaps no one has articulated these parallels more clearly than the Protestant scholar Hartmut
Gese of the University of Tübingen, who sees in the *todah* the historical antecedents of the Eucharist.

Gese on the Eucharist

Gese first proposed his theory of the Old Testament *todah* offering as a backdrop for understanding the origins of the Eucharist in an
essay dealing with the use of Psalm 22 in the New Testament.[14] He
later developed that thesis more fully and responded to anticipated
objections to the thesis in an essay that explored the origins of the
Eucharist in the pre-Christian Jewish tradition.[15] In what follows I
would like to summarize Gese's conclusions about the Eucharist and
offer a brief evaluation of his proposal.

A starting point for Gese is that the origins of the Eucharist are to
be sought in a Jewish milieu and not in the cultic celebrations of the
Hellenistic mystery religions.[16] Any possible Hellenistic influence on
eucharistic origins is minor and entirely secondary, according to Gese.
Given the paucity of extant information about the inner-workings of
the Hellenistic meals, and given the almost immediate progression
from Jesus' Last Supper to the eucharistic practice of the early
church, it seems certain that eucharistic origins are to be found not in
Hellenistic religious practices but instead within the Old Testament
understandings of first-century Jewish Christians.

For Gese, the Eucharist is essentially the *todah*, or thank offering,
of the resurrected Lord who has been vindicated and delivered from
death. In the Eucharist, understood in light of this Old Testament
sacrifice, the early Christian worshipers participated in a sacral meal
that celebrated the deliverance out of death experienced by the risen
Christ. In this way the Eucharist was for them both a proclaiming of
the Lord's death to those who observed the offering (1 Cor 11:26)
and an expression of praise and thanks to God for the deliverance that
he had brought about on their behalf through Christ.

In addition to the obvious continuities between the Eucharist and
the Old Testament *todah*, there are also certain discontinuities. In the
new *todah* the sacrifice and the offerer are identified. Jesus offered

not a sacrifice separate and distinct from himself; rather, he himself was the sacrifice. Like the old *todah*, the new offering was separate from the temple, although that did not take anything away from its holy nature. Furthermore, the bread of the sacrifice comes to connote the blood sacrifice involved in the offering up of the body of Jesus. The bread is thus not only a symbol of nourishment, but it has come to denote the very sacrifice of Jesus. Although in the old *todah* the meal was elaborate and intended to satisfy basic hunger, in the new *todah* the meal was a sacramental observance separated from the ordinary meal. Gese summarizes the role of *todah* in the Eucharist as follows:

> The *todah*-Eucharist is the worship in which the community experiences the saving event of Jesus' death and resurrection in its profoundest depths. In this *todah* we find the fulfillment of the meaningful development of the human experience of death and redemption, the development of the sacred meal, of the fellowship with the Savior and of the human basis of life, the development of sacrifice. The Eucharist is the end and goal of the biblical development of worship. It brings together manifold elements, and bears testimony to the unique, final saving event of Christ.[17]

Over the past several decades there has been a growing interest among both Protestant and Roman Catholic scholars in viewing the *todah* offering as a basis for understanding early eucharistic practice. Indeed, there is much to commend this proposal.[18] However, there are also certain difficulties that must be faced in connecting the Eucharist to the *todah* offering. Rabbi Stern rightly brings to our attention several problems in this regard.

First, he asks whether Jesus' expression of gratitude at the Last Supper is a part of a *todah* offering or simply a normal blessing at the Passover meal. But I wonder if this need be an either/or question. Is it possible that in offering the expected meal blessing Jesus anticipated the approaching redemptive events of his death and resurrection and offered thanks in a way that transcended the disciples' limited understanding at the time? If so, Jesus' expression of thanks at the meal may have anticipated the *todah* offering.

Second, Rabbi Stern calls attention to the overlapping characteristics of Passover and *todah* in the Last Supper narratives, which make clear identification with one of these rituals to the exclusion of the other difficult. This is a very helpful observation. But is it possible that the Passover meal described in the Synoptics was later re-signified in terms of the *todah* by the earliest Christians, partly to permit frequent celebration of the Eucharist rather than an annual observance in keeping with Passover ritual? If so, the *todah* offering of the Eucharist need not be equated with the Last Supper.

Third, Rabbi Stern raises the issue of the non-expiatory purpose of the Old Testament *todah*, which complicates viewing it as an appropriate vehicle for interpreting the atoning sacrifice of Jesus. This, I think, is a vital issue that requires further study. The *todah* offering of the Old Testament was a joyful acknowledgment of deliverance; it was not a sacrifice offered for atonement of sin. At a minimum, I think we would have to grant that the *todah* offering cannot explain all elements of eucharistic practice in the early church.

Conclusion

Rabbi Stern's paper has focused on two important dimensions of eucharistic origins: the role of remembrance in Jewish ritual, and the possibility that the *todah* offering may provide a basis for understanding the eucharistic practice of the earliest disciples of Jesus. With regard to remembrance he has helped us to see more clearly not only the strategic role that memory and remembrance played in redemptive history in ancient Jewish thought, but also the place of the specific elements of present significance and personal appropriation that were a part of what it meant in Jewish tradition to remember. As a result, we are in a better position to understand how the earliest Christians would have perceived what it meant to remember Jesus in the New Covenant economy.

With regard to viewing the Eucharist as a modified *todah* offering, Rabbi Stern seems less certain. Indeed, it seems to me that the evidence is not entirely decisive. But to the degree that the Eucharist celebrates both the deliverance from death of the Righteous Sufferer and the salvific benefits that have been brought about as a result of his suffering, the parallels make this an attractive possibility. It seems very feasible that when the early disciples of Jesus looked for an appropriate Old Testament format for celebrating on a frequent basis the merits of his death and their identification with him, they would have turned to the familiar *todah* sacrifice.

NOTES

1. So Edward P. Blair, "An Appeal to Remembrance: The Memory Motif in Deuteronomy," *Interpretation* 15 (1961): 41.

2. David E. Stern, "Remembering and Redemption," p. 1 of this volume.

3. Ibid., 3.

4. Ibid., 6.

5. Ibid., 7.

6. Ibid., 3.

7. Along this line I find helpful the following discussion: David Hill, *Greek Words and Hebrew Meanings: Studies in the Semantics of Soteriological Terms*, Society for New Testament Studies Monograph Series, ed. Matthew Black, vol. 5 (Cambridge: Cambridge University Press, 1967). See also Peter Walters, *The Text of the Septuagint: Its Corruptions and Their Emendation*, ed. D. W. Gooding (Cambridge: Cambridge University Press, 1973), 141–154.

8. William G. Braude, trans., *The Midrash on Psalms*, vol. 2, Yale Judaica Series, ed. Leon Nemoy, vol. 13 (New Haven: Yale University Press, 1959), 148.

9. Josh 7:19; Isa 51:3; Jer 30:19; Jonah 2:10; Pss 26:7; 69:31; 95:2; 100:4; 147:7; Ezra 10:11; Neh 12:27.

10. Neh 12:31, 38, 40.

11. Lev 7:12 bis, 13, 15; 22:29; Jer 17:26; 33:11; Amos 4:5; Pss 50:14, 23; 56:13; 100:1; 107:22; 116:17; 2 Chr 29:31 bis; 33:16.

12. On the use of *todah* in the Hebrew Bible, see especially the following essays: Daniel Bach, "Rite et parole dans l'Ancien Testament: Nouveaux éléments apportés par l'étude de *Todah*," *Vetus Testamentum* 28 (1978): 10–19; Walter Beyerlin, "Die *todah* der Heilsvergegenwärtigung in den Klageliedern des Einzelnen," *Zeitschrift für die alttestamentliche Wissenschaft* 79 (1967): 208–224; A. E. Goodman, "*chesed* and *torah* in the Linguistic Tradition of the Psalter," in *Words and Meanings: Essays Presented to David Win-*

ton Thomas on His Retirement from the Regius Professorship of Hebrew in the University of Cambridge, 1968, ed. Peter R. Ackroyd and Barnabas Lindars (Cambridge: Cambridge University Press, 1968), 105–115.

13. In laments of the Hebrew Bible a variety of life-threatening situations are specifically referred to on occasion: sickness (Pss 30:4–12; 32:5); drowning at sea (107:23–32; Jonah 2:1–10); agricultural reversals (Joel 1 to 2); threats from enemies (Ps 56:12–13); etc.

14. Hartmut Gese, "Psalm 22 und das Neue Testament: Der älteste Bericht vom Tode Jesu und die Entstehung des Herrenmahles," *Zeitschrift für Theologie und Kirche* NF 65 (1968): 1–22 [= *Vom Sinai zum Zion: Alttestamentliche Beiträge zur biblischen Theologie*, Beiträge zur evangelischen Theologie, vol. 64 (Munich: Chr. Kaiser, 1974), 180–201]. See also Hartmut Gese, "Psalm 22 and the New Testament," *Theology Digest* 18 (1970): 237–243.

15. Hartmut Gese, "The Origins of the Lord's Supper," in *Essays on Biblical Theology*, trans. Keith Crim (Minneapolis: Augsburg, 1981), 117–140. This article originally appeared in Gese's *Zur biblischen Theologie: Alttestamentliche Vorträge* (Munich: Chr. Kaiser, 1977).

16. Gese, "Origins of the Lord's Supper," 119.

17. Ibid., 138.

18. See, for example, the favorable review of Gese's proposal found in the following essay: Dennis R. Lindsay, "*Tôdah* and Eucharist: The Celebration of the Lord's Supper as a 'Thank Offering' in the Early Church," *Restoration Quarterly* 39 (1997): 83–100. According to Lindsay, "The Church today could benefit greatly from a renewed understanding and practice of the Lord's Supper as the thank offering of the risen Lord. In the thank offering there is no dichotomy between sacrifice and *anamnesis*, between word of proclamation and word of praise, between daily bread and spiritual bread, between physical presence of Christ and spiritual presence of Christ" (p. 99).

Denis Farkasfalvy

The Eucharistic Provenance
of New Testament Texts

Following contemporary biblical theology, one might decide to approach the theme of the Eucharist in the New Testament the following way:

First: Analyzing the four accounts of the institution in Matthew, Mark, Luke, and First Corinthians.

Second: Examining the eucharistic theology of John's discourse on the Bread of Life.

Third: Identifying the eucharistic features of the resurrection narratives (two episodes in Luke and one in John).

Fourth: Describing the eucharistic practice of the early church on the basis of Acts (mostly 2:42–47 and 20:7–12).

Fifth: Examining the eucharistic language found in Paul's Christology and ecclesiology.

Sixth: Pointing out the eucharistic references in the heavenly liturgy described in the Book of Revelation.

This method could bring about a rich harvest and lead to valuable insights on many particular issues. Nonetheless, we will devise a somewhat different path. I will attempt to show that the literary heritage of the apostolic church represented by the books of the New Testament is so closely and organically related to the Eucharist that one can truly say that the whole of New Testament scripture has a eucharistic provenance. Thus, we hope to show that not only does the New Testament offer a doctrine *about* the Eucharist, but it is the product of the apostolic church's eucharistic practice.

This statement does not contain anything extraordinary or unexpected. Historians and scripture scholars have repeatedly recognized that the texts of which the New Testament consists have been both historically and logically preceded by, prepared for, and based upon the Eucharist.

The Apostolic Letters as Eucharistic Documents

The earliest Pauline letters we have were written as early as twenty to twenty-five years after Jesus' death and resurrection. Their purpose and occasion show considerable diversity. But the presence of liturgical formulas (greeting, prayers, blessings, fragments of hymns)[1] are unmistakable signs that they were meant to be presented to communities at assemblies connected with the celebration of the Eucharist.

The clearest view of such early celebrations might be obtained from Acts 20 where Luke narrates an assembly that includes the celebration of the Eucharist. What he describes happening in Troas in the presence of Paul leaves little doubt that the Sunday Vigils of the Christian assembly gave ample time for reading texts even as long as any Pauline letter, like Galatians or even First Corinthians, in its entirety. The reading of such letters served, among other functions, that of substituting for the actual presence of the apostle. After examining many liturgical greetings, doxologies, prayers, and other formulas, Oscar Cullmann arrives at the following conclusion:

> The presence of so much that is liturgical here in the Pauline Epistles connects almost certainly with the fact that the Apostle, while writing his letters, had in mind the community assembled for worship.[2]

Thus one is fully entitled to read Paul's letters in the context of the Eucharist.[3] But the same is true of letters as liturgically charged as First Peter or Ephesians and Colossians, texts that are understood by most exegetes as circular letters extending apostolic presence to various congregations, even if their actual apostolic authorship might be doubtful. The eucharistic context of letters like Second Peter or James or Jude might be more remote, especially because these letters might only imitate the literary form of an apostolic letter without being pieces of actual correspondence. But even if they are not meant to address a particular congregation, the most convenient way of publicizing them was in the context of the Eucharist. So, for example, in James 2:2 the term "your *synagoge*"[4] must be thought of as referring concretely to a gathering of Christians in which the Eucharist is being celebrated, in which the "word of truth" mentioned in 1:18 is being preached to people listening to God's word (1:22), a community formed from people of various social classes (2:5–9). Regardless of this letter's preponderantly exhortative and moralizing tone, its references to the "Parousia of the Lord" (5:7–8) or to prayer of healing in the Lord's name (5:13–18) must be referenced to eucharistic services of the community addressed.

The Eucharistic Context of the Gospel Narratives

Passion and Resurrection Narratives

More intricate than the eucharistic relevance of the texts treated above is the relationship connecting the structure and content of the canonical gospels with the eucharistic celebrations of the early church.

First of all, one must take seriously the fact that the narratives of the institution of the Eucharist in Matthew, Mark, and Luke are not only chronologically linked to each Passion story but serve as their theological overture. Since First Corinthians begins the narration of the institution with the precise chronological indication "on the night he was handed over" (11:23, NAB), this theological link between the institution and the passion story goes back to Paul's first preaching in Corinth in A.D. 50.[5] But, in fact, Paul is only quoting what he himself "received" from those who have been apostles before him.[6] Thus, we are dealing here with tradition that was probably handed down to him about fifteen years after the death of Jesus. In any case, the reference to the institution as an overture to the passion far antedates the composition of the gospels. The use of the verb *paradidomai* (in the form *paredideto*), often translated as "betrayed," has a wider meaning. In fact, this verb became in early Christian Greek a specialized term charged with reference to violent death, accepted and suffered voluntarily, or briefly martyrdom.[7] At the beginning of the institution it signifies not only the betrayal of Jesus by Judas, but his being delivered "into the hands of sinners" (cf. Matt 26:45; Mark 14:41) for the purpose of execution (cf. Matt 27:26; Mark 15:15).[8]

Second, the gospels of Luke and John which have resurrection appearances emphasize that, after the resurrection, the risen Lord and his disciples resumed their table fellowship which had come to an end after the institution of the Eucharist at the Last Supper. To this we need to return later.

But now our main question is: Do the remaining narratives in the gospels manifest a similar eucharistic link in a way comparable to that which the passion narratives show? The question can be answered in two ways.

First, a number of important episodes in Jesus' ministry which are narrated in the gospels seem to have an intentional linkage to the Eucharist. The most obvious examples are the stories of the feeding of the multitude in the desert. Regardless of how one feels about duplications ("doublets") produced in the course of the history of the Synoptic tradition, the fact remains that the multiplication of loaves is an episode narrated altogether six times in the canonical gospels: twice each by Matthew and Mark, once by Luke, and once by John. Little doubt remains about why this story is reproduced with such unparalleled frequency, for the story of the multiplication of loaves seizes that christological and ecclesiological reality which constitutes the core of the Christian faith. It describes the community that Jesus forms around himself as he makes them re-enact and bring to fullness the experience of Israel in the desert with thousands of people miraculously receiving their food and drink. Each of the six narratives has well-known eucharistic overtones: the remarks about looking up to heaven, giving thanks, breaking the bread, and giving it to the disciples (Matt 14:19; 15:36; Mark 6:41; 8:6; Luke 9:16; John 6:11) cannot be explained otherwise. Of course, in John, the discourse at Capernaum makes these allusions quite explicit as it forms a eucharistic commentary on the sign performed by Jesus in the desert. One must add also that, in all the four gospels, these narratives are also connected with Jesus' activity of healing, so that the feeding of the multitude is intimately linked to the dispensation of divine mercy not only through the service of teaching but also by restoring the sick to health.[9]

Once we acknowledge the eucharistic significance of these six narratives, we can easily develop a perspective for seeing the eucharistic relevance of each narrative where either Jesus is involved in common meals with his disciples[10] or the theme of the messianic banquet is being mentioned, as well as in those passages in which the kingdom of God is compared to a meal or a feast.[11]

The Narrative Structures of the Gospels

However, I would like to explore another issue, under the heading of "Eucharistic Features in the Narrative Structures of the Gospels." This has to do with the familiar image of Jesus in his ministry as an *itinerant teacher*, something that we often regard as a merely biographical fact. However, modern criticism has taken issue with this image and called attention to the complexity of the factual background.

Let us here recall a peculiar feature of the literary genre of the gospels. They all describe Jesus' activities as a chain of episodes and thus present him between episodes as being *on the way*. Especially in the Synoptic gospels the usual framework into which an episode is inserted is a voyage, specifically a missionary journey, so that Jesus is always presented as *coming* from somewhere and then moving on— i.e., going to some new geographic location. Although in Matthew and Luke, in parallel passages, we find short sayings about the homelessness of the Son of Man (two in Matt 8:18–22 and three in Luke 9:57–62), other passages clearly indicate that Jesus had a permanent home in Capernaum to which he regularly returned. Matthew 4:13 is quite explicit about this. The three verbs of the sentence mean that (1) Jesus moved away (*katalipon*) from Nazareth, (2) moved over to

(*elthon*) the city of Capernaum, and (3) there he took up residence
(*katokehsen*). In agreement with this interpretation, the phrase *en oiko*
in Mark 2:1 is widely understood as meaning "at home."[12] A similar
interpretation would result from Mark 9:33 which reads: "And they
came to Capernaum. And as they were in the house he asked them…"
(*Kai elthon eis Kapharnaoum. Kai en teh oikia genomenos epehrota
autous…*). Even if this was Peter's house, and even if one wants to
emphasize the fact that they were "indoors," the narrative still carries
the supposition that Jesus had a permanent domicile in Capernaum.[13]

Commentators on Matthew's gospel often point out that in the
structure of the work there appears a geographic outline, a feature
important for the evangelist. They also quickly add that this peripatetic image of Jesus—he travels non-stop from place to place in a
sequence of missionary episodes—is redactionally produced and theologically motivated rather than reflecting historically identifiable
journeys. The form critics of more than eighty years ago insisted on
the conclusions that Jesus' trips outlined in the Synoptic gospels must
not be regarded as actual travel reports but rather the result of super-
ficial links externally connecting the narrative episodes of an oral tradition that carried along and shaped them while keeping them in rela-
tive isolation from each other. This point is central to the famous
contribution of K. L. Schmidt about the "framework of the synoptic
gospels"[14] in which he insists that the original narrators of the stories
about Jesus paid little or no attention to chronological or topographi-
cal links between the individual episodes but "concentrated on the
picture-like independence (*bildhafte Vereinzelung*) of the pericopes as
required for a liturgical celebration." Thus K. L. Schmidt, Dibelius,
and Bultmann initiated the approach that reduced the importance of
the links between the episodes as secondary and historically irrelevant. We know that, due to this approach, Synoptic research became
overly fragmented and the possibility of any biographic approach to
the gospels became methodologically impossible. The next trend,
redaction criticism, went even further as it came to the conclusion that
the links of the Synoptic episodes are mere theological constructs
reflecting what the author of each gospel made of the complexities of
the oral tradition and of the sequencing of the episodes he found in his
sources. From early days of form criticism, conventional wisdom held
that the formation of the gospels was intimately linked to early Chris-

tian cult as the "*Sitz im Leben*" of most Synoptic narratives. However, what remained largely unspecified was how this cultic/liturgical framework impacted the narratives or the way they became linked together. Most important, what remained unanswered was the question of why the narrative units appear connected in the gospels, by means of arrivals and departures, into a loosely yet consistently connected chain of "comings and goings," a constant and apparently artificial missionary meandering.

Any investigation of the compositional outline of the Synoptic narratives results in the realization that the episodes of Jesus' ministry are inserted into a framework of traveling which both connects and separates the individual pericopes while depicting Jesus (and his disciples) as always arriving and leaving, moving in and out of different localities of Galilee, crossing back and forth over the same lake, and meeting randomly all sorts of people and human situations on the way.[15]

These considerations led me to pay more attention to the all too frequent use of the Greek verb *erchesthai* and its derivates at the beginning of so many gospel episodes in Matthew and Mark and the use of the verb *poreuesthai* and its derivates in Luke. For what purpose or in function of what necessity are these episodes so often, one might say, habitually connected by Jesus' movements going to a place or "crossing over the lake," or coming to a town, departing and arriving as if by so many movements of walking onto some stage upon which a particular story is to take place? While in the individual gospels the particular verbs describing the beginnings or the ends of the episodes are not necessarily the same, they appear redactionally chiseled into repeated similarities and even identical formulas. So, for example, the verb preferred by Matthew is *proserchesthai*, "to approach." At least twenty-five times in his gospel, an episode begins with the use of *proserchesthai*, so as to describe someone (a man or a woman in some physical or spiritual need) physically approaching Jesus.[16] In Mark, an episode usually starts with Jesus or more frequently with "them," meaning Jesus and his disciples, coming to a place or simply "coming" so that Jesus could be petitioned or approached or asked a question.[17] Similarly, a number of episodes begin by reporting that people of some sort are congregated around Jesus: either his disciples convoked by him, or crowds hearing about him, or people with some need or intention—

sometimes his enemies, the Pharisees or the Sadducees—gathering around him and giving him the opportunity to address them, reply to them, or begin to teach.[18]

The Eucharistic Origins of the Gospel Genre

Behind all these common characteristics of the Synoptic gospels there stands a basic feature of the gospel genre that needs to be explained. The gospels are collections of episodic narratives about Jesus as their one and only protagonist. Do these narratives, lined up along a fragile string of ongoing physical movements, serve a common purpose and, if so, what is it? The answer lies in a fact that gospel critics have often emphasized for the last hundred years but have failed to connect with questions of genre and composition. We are speaking of the observation that the gospels are based on a tradition formed and formulated in the eucharistic assemblies of the early church. So, for example, Bultmann readily states:

> One may designate the final motive by which the gospels were produced as the cultic (that is, the needs of common worship), if one considers that the high point in Christian life was the gathering of the community for worship, when the figure of Jesus, his teaching as well as his life, was set before the eyes of the faithful and when, accordingly, the gospels served for public reading.[19]

But contrary to what Bultmann and Dibelius habitually presuppose, this feature of the liturgical roots of the narratives does not imply that they were produced and manipulated according to the needs of some worshiping community.[20] Rather, this insight should open us up to the reality that the first Eucharistic assemblies came about as Jesus' original disciples were prompted to meet after experiencing the first evidences of the resurrection and there they were led to begin a process of recalling and retelling the memories of Jesus' ministry. The narrative tradition that stands behind the Synoptics was formed and shaped in this "eucharistic cradle" of early Christian liturgy. From its beginning, the Synoptic tradition stood in live exchange with an audience gathered for hearing about Jesus because they wanted to meet Jesus by means of the liturgical assemblies where they experienced the past encounters as being re-enacted and re-lived. Consequently, the narratives were formed for audiences that identified themselves with those described in the narratives as meeting Jesus, being brought to him, or approaching him for healing, teaching, or some other benefit. In such presentation of episodic material, Jesus is necessarily featured not as a figure of an objective past, defined and isolated in a context of a *mere* historical past, but as the one who, at the beginning of an episode, both arrives and is being approached, encounters a human need or religious problem—a human situation of "crisis"—and brings an experience of salvation, i.e., a manifestation of divine mercy resulting in a solution unexplainable from mere human resources. Therefore, the framework of the Synoptic tradition—to quote the title of K. L. Schmidt's book—is not a chronological segment of time or a geographically arranged missionary project, but the sequence of ongoing encounters in which two features complement each other: Jesus is portrayed as "the one coming," and the people whom he encounters keep on approaching him in their need as he moves from place to place so that a variety of people find their way to him.

Consequently, an important portion of this paper's thesis is that the basic understanding of Jesus' mission and ministry as presented by the Synoptics is best understood in this eucharistic context of early Christian worship and it was in this context that not only the individual episodic pieces were formulated, rehearsed, and fixed but the literary genre of the gospels—the model for assembling, linking, and organizing these units into a composition—took its origin.

I do not claim that, due to their narration at eucharistic celebrations, the episodes about Jesus were *staged* by their first preachers in such a way that their beginnings would narrate a fictitious arrival or coming of Jesus. In fact, quite often the "coming" depicted to introduce a Synoptic episode stands in a redactional passage or sentence, containing clear marks of the evangelist, and thus seems to belong to the written form of the gospel rather than the oral tradition. However, I do claim that the way Jesus is portrayed in the literary compositions of our canonical gospels—this framework of a peripatetic way of life and the fact that, episode after episode, he keeps on coming and being approached as he passes from place to place—is the result of the eucharistic setting in which the Jesus tradition was formed, chiseled into oral patterns, and finally turned into literary compositions which the early church canonized.

That the gospels represent a chain of discrete episodes is well accepted in both older and more recent gospel research. To this I intend only to add that it is no mere coincidence nor the consequence of mere biographic data that the Jesus of the gospels is in ongoing movement. The consistent portrayal of Jesus as the one *coming and being encountered* must have something to do with the way memories about him were recalled, told, and retold to eucharistic congregations: gatherings held for the purpose of re-living and re-enacting anew such encounters. This understanding of Jesus is a common feature, essential and constitutive for both the gospel episodes and the early Christian celebration of the Eucharist. I also claim here that this consistent feature of the gospel narratives not only makes them a perfect fit for serving as pericopes at eucharistic celebrations, but that this feature came about due to the eucharistic setting of the gospel tradition that characterized it at its most primitive oral phase.

We know from Justin Martyr that in the middle of the second century, some eighty years after the first canonical gospels were composed, they were called "the memoirs of the apostles" and were regularly and routinely used for pericopal reading at the eucharistic assembly. Such a use of the gospels at the Eucharist to which Justin testifies as a generally accepted practice (*First Apology* 67) is best explained if we assume that even when still being handed over orally, they fulfilled the function of recalling the past that was to be re-lived and re-enacted at the eucharistic celebration.[21]

Jesus as "the One Who Comes" in the Gospels

Does the Christology of the gospels recognize the eucharistic feature of these compositions? More specifically, do the gospels become explicit about Jesus as he keeps on coming and arriving so as to be approached? I find a positive answer to this question in the way the term *ho erchomenos* or "coming" is applied to him in the gospels.

A generation ago, when it was customary to study the Christology of the New Testament by christological titles,[22] the question was debated whether or not the term *ho erchomenos* was one of such titles and, if so, if it was used by Jesus' contemporaries to designate the Messiah. Although the debate has never been settled, this term is certainly essential for both the Christology and the eschatology of the canonical gospels.

The meaning of the term *erchomenos* becomes fully apparent as we study it in Matthew. John the Baptist is the first to use it when he points to the one coming after him (3:11). The term is re-assumed in Matthew 11:2 by the disciples of John coming to Jesus and asking him if he is identical with "the one to come." Jesus' answer is often read as a catalogue of healings listed in the framework of Isaian passages (mostly Isa 61:1). "Go and tell what you see, for the blind see, the lame walk, the deaf hear and to the poor the kingdom is being proclaimed." But this verse is not just a reference to miraculous healings of bodily ailments. Matthew makes it clear that Jesus fulfills these prophecies also when preaching the kingdom of heaven to the poor (cf. 5:2) and by providing forgiveness as he takes upon himself our sins (8:17 quoting Isa 53:4).[23] These two occurrences of *erchomenos* in 3:11 and 11:2 encompass the first part of Matthew's gospel dealing with Jesus' Galilean ministry. The rest of the gospel consistently follows along the same path, for it demonstrates how Jesus continues to manifest himself as the one who is coming. This happens in peak scenes revealing his power as he walks on the sea (14:25) or reveals his glory in the transfiguration (17:7), scenes that emphasize *his coming* to the disciples.[24] Moreover, throughout the second part of the gospel every major eschatological statement and parable uses the verb *erchesthai* in reference to the Parousia as the *coming* of the Son of Man.[25] Finally, a fullness of meaning for this term is achieved in Jesus' statement before the Sanhedrin: "From now on you will see the Son of Man seated on the right hand of the Power and coming (*erchomenon*) in the clouds of the sky" (26:64). Some commentators focus on the words "from now on," while others insist that the Son of Man is not (or not exactly) a self-designation by Jesus. Yet the term *erchomenon* should not be deprived of its semantic link to its previous crucial occurrences in the gospel at 3:11 and 11:2, nor is it legitimate to take away its syntactic value as a present participle. Used several times throughout Matthew's composition, it means essentially the unfolding character of Jesus' mission. The chain of events that narrate Jesus' ministry in the gospels is nothing but a process of an ongoing coming to people whom he encounters, with his final manifest coming in divine power unfolding at his condemnation, death, and resurrection.

In the Gospel of John, Jesus is also designated as *ho erchomenos*, the one who comes after John the Baptist (see 1:15; 1:27). Yet his coming is shown in its true dimension when it receives a cosmic significance. His "coming" is already the central issue in John's prologue, where the Logos is depicted as the true light "coming into the world" (1:9)[26] in order to become flesh (1:14). Several times in this gospel a physical movement of *coming* has deeper symbolic meaning (cf. Jesus' *coming* to John as he sees him coming from a distance in 1:29). The transcendental meaning of "his coming" is at times explicitly stated as a "coming from above" or a "coming from heaven" (3:31), by reference to "the prophet coming into the world" (6:14) or to "the Son of God coming into the world" (11:27). Thus his coming is in the transcendental sense a *descent*, so that in the explicitly eucharistic text about the Bread of Life it is said to be "coming down from heaven" and becomes semantically linked to the term *erchomenos*. The statements made by believers about "the coming of the Messiah" (*erchetai ho legomenos Christos*) are not only expressions of traditional Jewish messianism, but also of Johannine theology describing Jesus as the subject for a process of arrival into the world reaching fullness in the gospel narratives (4:23–25; 7:41–42). Seen in the light of this usage, the expressions "he came" or "he is coming" in the context of the Johannine resurrection narratives take on an explicit eucharistic meaning with eschatological reference: twice Jesus comes (*ehlthen* in 20:19 and *erchetai* in 20:26) through closed doors, and the meeting ends in physical contact with his body, with the disciples touching the marks of the wounds, while in the third appearance "Jesus comes and takes the bread and gives it to them" (21:13).

This theologically deepened Johannine usage links together Christology, Eucharist, and a sacramentally "realized" eschatology into a unified vision of Jesus' coming in the form of an unfolding process that penetrates cosmos and history. Is John's vision an esoterical specialty or are its roots found in the Synoptic tradition? The reference to the "one who is coming after me" on the lips of the Baptist belongs to the oldest common elements of all gospels. One must say the same about the phrase "blessed is the one coming in the name of the Lord" quoted from Psalm 118:26 and applied to Jesus six times in the gospels, once in each of the four descriptions of the triumphal entry to Jerusalem (Matt 21:9; Mark 11:9; Luke 19:38; John 12:13) and once more in a saying common to Matthew and Luke (Matt 23:39 and Luke 13:35).

Exegetically the following can be said about Jesus portrayed as "the one coming" in the gospels:

- It translates the Hebrew *habba*, the present participle of the verb to come (*labbo*) with the definite article as it appears in the quotations of Psalm 118:26 and Malachi 3:1 that has the meaning of an actual but ongoing and, therefore, also future coming.

- It completes importantly the notion of the "coming of the kingdom" by referring to Jesus as the king coming.

- It connotes the dynamic character of Jesus' mission as a chain of comings. The term depicts his entry into the world, his encountering all sorts of people through the various episodes of teaching and healing, his travel to Jerusalem, his facing death, his return to the Father, and his constituting a new way of presence with the disciples.

- It puts the eschatological dimension of Jesus' mission and message in seamless continuity with his earthly ministry.

The Eucharistic Character of the Book of Revelation

A summary look at the Apocalypse, the only prophetic book of the New Testament canon, can greatly enhance and complete the above considerations.

By its opening vision and general framework, this book is compositionally inserted into a general liturgical framework. On this Fr. Feuillet's comments, made in the 1960s, are still valid:

We should be on guard against the danger of misunderstandings with regard to the Apocalypse's liturgical character. True enough, [this book] is not a specifically and professedly litur-

gical document, but rather a prophecy and an account of
visions. Still we must not lose sight of its liturgical aspects,
which have been emphasized, and placed very much in relief,
although not always very discretely, by modern exegetes.
Most of the great visions of the Apocalypse have some sort of
a liturgical flavor to them, which is basically due to their
essentially eschatological orientation, characteristic of the
Christian liturgy, especially of the Eucharist...[27]

The book itself begins with an apparition of the risen Lord on a
Sunday, the Lord's day. This reference is not just a coincidental piece
of chronology about the day the vision happened, but fits into an
overall liturgical scheme provided for the book.[28] That the visionary
sees the risen Lord on a Sunday (1:10) must be taken in continuity
with the resurrection appearances in the Fourth Gospel, the only passages of the New Testament that emphasize Jesus' appearance on
Sundays (Easter Sunday in John 20:19 and a week later in John
20:26). The risen Jesus appears clothed in priestly garments of a long
white tunic and a golden sash amidst seven lamps (1:12–13)—i.e., he
is clothed as the high priest.[29]

This appearance of the risen Lord must be understood as a coming to the church that the book collectively addresses. In ancient
times the number seven for churches to whom seven letters are
addressed is intentional, expressing the entirety of the church.[30] The
idea of Jesus coming is emphasized at the beginning in the first revelatory statement of the book, introducing the description of the risen
Lord with the following words: "Behold he comes (*erchetai*) in the
clouds and every eye will see him, including those who pierced him
through" (1:7). This reference to the Johannine scene of the crucifixion must not be missed. The Fourth Gospel alone quotes Zechariah's
prophecy stating that "they will see him whom they have pierced"
(Zech 12:10 in John 19:37). The reference is quite important for the
Johannine passion story, for it proves the truly physical suffering and
death of Jesus, witnessed by the Beloved Disciple (19:35–37). Its use
in the Apocalypse aims unmistakably at establishing a link between
Jesus' violent death and his glorious return, the ignominious past and
the glory of the future. The verb "he comes," or *erchetai*, belongs to

an eschatological language, but the use of present tense reveals a sense of actuality just as well.[31]

Quite significant is the connection between the beginning of the Book of Revelation and the apparitions of the risen Lord in John 20. All these apparitions happen on a Sunday. In both books he is described not appearing, but coming: *erchetai*. Also in John 20 he is said to be appearing as the one whom they have pierced, for he invites the disciples to view (and Thomas to touch) his wounds, specifically the wound of his chest (20:26–27).[32] Therefore, the quotation from Zechariah provides an important bridge between a future coming "in the clouds" and the event that took place on the cross. At the eschatological coming, all eyes will see what the eyes of the Beloved Disciple perceived when Jesus was pierced on the cross and what all the eleven disciples saw when Jesus appeared to them on the two Sundays that followed the crucifixion.

It is also important to note that the Apocalypse calls Jesus "the one who is to come" or "the one who is coming" in a phrase repeated three times, sounding like a liturgical formula: "the one who was, who is and who is coming" (*ho ehn kai ho on kai ho erchomenos*).[33] The Hebrew/Aramaic origin of the formula is hardly in doubt. Accordingly, the word *ho erchomenos* is a Hebraism.[34] In Hebrew one uses the present participle of the verb "to come" (*habba*) for the purpose of expressing future existence: the one who will be. But again, it would be incorrect to separate the word *erchomenos* from its etymological root and deny its basic grammatical meaning, thus not realizing that it refers to an actual coming, i.e., a present-time active process of coming near and becoming present.[35]

In spite of the attempts that have been made to separate the Book of Revelation into originally independent parts, the unity of the composition keeps asserting itself and is again recognized in contemporary research.[36] Within the unity of the composition the eucharistic links become visible. We will comment now on two issues that will complement what has been said about the apostolic letters and the gospels.

First, the seven churches are collective addressees of the seven letters, and they also collectively constitute the recipients of the book for whom John is told to write (1:11). Therefore, one must see in the appearance of the risen Lord to the prophetic messenger a visitation intended for all the churches in which John is exercising his prophetic role. In this way the opening vision determines the framework of the whole book as we read in 1:19: "Write down both what there is and what will come about later." In this way the prophet is told to compose a book of two parts, the first being the evaluation of the present-day status of the churches (chapters 2 and 3) and the second their future destiny (chapters 4 through 19). But both parts are addressed to all churches, and are a revelation about the Son of Man's coming: a revelation inspired by the same Spirit.

Consequently, the vision of the heavenly liturgy in chapters 4 and 5 that follows the seven letters is a continuation of the same revelation experience taking place on "the Lord's Day" (1:10). However, now, in verse 4:2 the prophet ascends into heaven, i.e., he falls in ecstasy and obtains divine knowledge that penetrates the future.[37] As the first revelation took place in virtue of a coming of the risen Lord on a Sunday, now the second stage of the revelation makes him present at the heavenly worship. This cosmic liturgy is described in concentric circles around the throne of God (4:3, 5–6) as it is celebrated by twenty-four elders (4:4) and four living creatures (4:7–8) who perform their homage in the first round (5:6–10), then by myriads of angels in the second round (5:11–12), and finally by a redeemed and sanctified universe (5:13–14). This scene is best understood as the fullness of the reality that takes place in the earthly—ecclesial—celebration of the liturgy, a heavenly reality present in a hidden way in Christian worship. The first action that takes place in chapter 5 is the opening of the seven seals of a book by the Lamb who had been slain, signifying the full manifestation of God's salvific will and thus making possible the prophetic visions which follow. This, together with the liturgical scene in chapter 19 where the same assembly sings and worships, constitutes the framework of the revelations about the future.

Most significantly for our topic, after seven letters in the first part and the opening of the seven seals followed by an elaborate chain of apocalyptic signs in the second part, this worshiping heavenly assembly reappears and is now ready to celebrate the wedding feast of the Lamb. The prophet receives another order to write: "Write, happy are those invited to the wedding *banquet* of the Lamb" (19:9).[38] This wedding banquet is called here *deipnon*, the noun used by Paul in First

Corinthians[39] and also by John[40] to designate the Last Supper. As soon as the seer receives the command, he falls prostrate before the messenger[41] who has given the order, but is told by the messenger that he is only a fellow servant and prophet, thus providing testimony on behalf of Jesus, and must not be adored.

At this point there is serious discontinuity in the book. No description of the banquet follows. Instead, a sequence of other visions begins abruptly, most of them about the heavenly Jerusalem, then in 22:8–9 the same scene is repeated, with the seer falling prostrate before the messenger and being told in identical words to worship God alone. My concern is to rescue verse 19:9 from being overlooked or marginalized. It seems to represent the final act in the eucharistic framework of the book, the same framework that started with the coming of Jesus on the day of the Lord resulting first in letters to the churches, then the ecstatic participation in the heavenly liturgy of praise and prophetic testimony accompanying the opening of the book with seven seals, and finally a banquet of the marriage feast to which the seer must invite all the believers,[42] but which—as the Omega Point of sacred history[43]—he otherwise does not intend to describe.

With or without accepting a specific redactional hypothesis about the end of the Book of Revelation, one can easily see 19:11 to 22:8 as if put into parentheses so that the end of John's vision would continue with the command not to seal the book (22:10–11), followed by the repetition of the title "Alpha and Omega" first announced in the prologue (22:12) and three final eucharistic references. The first of these recalls the "tree of life" (22:13), the second excludes the ones in grave sin from communion,[44] and finally, after repeated calls by the Bride, the Spirit, and the faithful for the Bridegroom to come (22:17–18), is the concluding eucharistic exclamation "*Maranatha*." This exclamation closing First Corinthians (16:22) is known also from the *Didache* (10:6) as the concluding line of a eucharistic or (Eucharist-related) agape celebration. Even if one opts for the Syriac translation in perfect tense to represent an authentic understanding of the term, in this book the Greek equivalent is given as *erchou kyrie* (22:20) and must be seen, therefore, as the most explicit eucharistic use of the verb *erchesthai*.

The "*Maranatha*" of the Book of Revelation is not a stray reference to early Christian liturgy. It is of a piece with the opening lines of the book. The survival of its Aramaic form in First Corinthians and the *Didache* testifies to the fact that in regard to the Eucharist Gentile churches were expected to adhere so carefully to the tradition of the first disciples that it mattered little if they risked becoming esoteric by their use of incomprehensible or ambiguous Semitic words. Nonetheless, one may say that the whole of the Book of Revelation is an explanation of *"Maranatha"*: the coming of God in the coming of Jesus, both complete and to be completed.

Conclusion

This paper intended to show that the entire New Testament is of a eucharistic provenance and, therefore, must be interpreteted in a more or less immediate eucharistic context.

One might say that the whole of the New Testament canon is based on the use of three literary genres: the gospel, the apostolic letter, and the Apocalypse as prophetic writing. While the apostolic letters are intended for addressees assembled in liturgical worship, the Book of Revelation was shown to be patterned according to the Sunday assembly of the apostolic congregations. More important, I intended to show that the way the gospels are composed presupposes that the Jesus tradition collected in those episodes were from earliest time on presented to cultic assemblies gathered to witness, experience, and respond to the coming of the Lord.[45] The apostolic memory of the Jesus tradition was exercised in the early church not for the sake of biographical purposes reconstructing or defending a great historical figure's memory, but in order to present episode by episode the salvific encounters his disciples had with him both during his ministry and after his death and resurrection.

The overall impact of these statements goes in two directions. On the one hand, I want to offer biblical foundations for a theology of the Eucharist in which elements of Christology, ecclesiology, and eschatology complement each other and receive equal attention. The dichotomies between these disciplines of systematic theology might be avoided or at least reduced if the eucharistic nature of their scriptural base remains protected. In such a perspective, a "high Christology" is not an added dimension to the historically reconstructed figure of Jesus first ("originally") perceived in the context of merely human terms (tactfully called a "low Christology"), for there is no way of "distilling" a portrait of Jesus independently from a worshiping assembly. Similarly, the church is not merely a faith community with a variety of subjective states of minds and self-expressions, but a eucharistic community in which acts of faith refer to sacramental realities, namely the coming of the faithful to Jesus in response to their perception of the coming of the Lord to his people. Finally, one must not be split and torn between a futuristic or realized eschatology but accept the sacramental (or liturgical) eschatology exemplified in the Book of Revelation. According to this view, eschatology sees the fullness of Christ's arrival in every event of his coming but still consciously anticipates a further completion due to the ongoing character of all history, both individual and collective.

Of great importance was for me to include into these considerations a perspective in which one could approach all scriptural texts by means of an ecclesial and sacramental exegesis. If the gospel pericopes had their *Sitz im Leben* in eucharistic assemblies, then their liturgical actualization does not constitute an intrusion into the text or an undue manipulation of what "truly happened." Rather, the gospel tradition has been formed, formulated, and transmitted due to the early church's perception that what "truly happened" is perceived only when once again Jesus comes, and the blind see, the deaf hear, the lame walk, and to the poor the kingdom is being preached. The eucharistic practice of the church constitutes that medium in which ongoing continuity can be legitimately perceived and claimed between the historical past and the present on its way into the future. The Eucharist is the context in which history does not undergo a *rigor mortis* by becoming both stiff and irrelevant, hopelessly and irredeemably glued to long-past events and states of mind. Instead, in this medium of the church's continued sacramental practice, Jesus' universal mission (Matt 28:16–20) successfully extends the chain of the gospel episodes so as to reach all times and all places and make his journey transcend the limits of history without rendering it ahistorical. This would, of course, mean that, in this way, the last words of Matthew's gospel, "I will be with you always until the completion of the aeon" (*synteleia tou aionos*) becomes a highest expression of eucharistic theology.

NOTES

1. Oscar Cullmann in his *Early Christian Worship* (London: SCM Press, 1953), 20–25, lists "psalms and hymns" formulas of benediction, doxologies, and responses, like *Amen*, to substantiate this claim.

2. Cullmann, 24.

3. Relying on Lietzman's research, Cullmann writes: "the closing formulae of the Pauline epistles correspond to the liturgical phrases which we find at the beginning of the old liturgy of the Lord's Supper especially see (1 Cor 16:21–23). The reason for that is that the Lord's Supper will follow immediately after the reading of his letter" (*Early Christian Worship*, 24). Due to the result of research sponsored by the liturgical movement in the Catholic Church, the missal published after the Second Vatican Council introduced these phrases as currently used formulas for the beginning of the Mass.

4. About the "*synagoge*," meaning here the Christian congregation, cf. Bo Reicke, *Epistles of James, Peter and Jude, The Anchor Bible* 37 (New York: Doubleday, 1964), 27–28.

5. Cf. J. Fitzmyer, "Paul" in *The New Jerome Biblical Commentary* (Englewood Cliffs: Prentice Hall, 1990), 1335.

6. Cf. the expression *tous pro emou apostolous* in Gal 1:17.

7. This usage is clear in passages like Matt 10:17; Mark 13:9, 11; Luke 21:12 about persecuted Christians. The relationship of this expression with Isa 53:6 Septuagint appears clearly in First Clement 16:7, but also in Rom 8:32.

8. The Fourth Gospel, which does not contain the narrative of the institution of the Eucharist, also introduces the passion story by a series of eucharistic themes in the farewell discourses. See the parable of the vine, analyzed for its eucharistic meaning by A. Feuillet, "Le discours sur le pain de vie," *Etudes johanniques* (Paris: Desclée de Brower, 1962), 83–88.

9. Cf. Matt 14:14; 15:29–31; Mark 6:34; 7:37; and 8:2; Luke 9:11; John 6:2. These all belong to the immediate context of the various accounts of multiplication of loaves.

10. Matt 9:10–12/Mark 2:15–17/Luke 5:27–32; Luke 7:36–50; John 2:2–11.

11. Matt 22:2–14; Luke 17:8; 14:15–24; 15:32; 22:17–18.

12. V. Taylor, *The Gospel according to Saint Mark* (Macmillan: New York, 1966), 193, considers it as Peter's house. C. S. Mann translates it as "at home" while admitting the possibility that it was Peter's house: *Mark, The Anchor Bible* 27 (Garden City, N.Y.: Doubleday, 1986), 223.

13. What other meaning could there be for the fact that it is in Capernaum where Jesus is reproached for not paying tax (Matt 17:24)?

14. *Der Rahmen der synoptischen Überlieferung*, orginally published in 1919 (Berlin: Trowitch und Sohn). I use here the excerpts published again by Ferdinand Hahn, *Zur Formgeschichte des Evangeliums* (Darmstadt: Wissenschaftliche Buchgesellschaft, 1985), 118–126.

15. That the evangelist Luke already found the Synoptic tradition in this form appears from the fact that for inserting additional material he simply expanded the travel narrative from Galilee to Jerusalem and placed most of his independent tradition into this section (chapters 9 to 18).

16. The various forms of the verb *proserchesthai* are quite important for Matthew as it is an expression typical of the Matthean redactor. The verb appears altogether as often as forty-eight times in Matthew, while only four times in Mark and nine times in Luke. Yet the similarities and discrepancies between Matthew and Mark are complicated. Of Mark's four uses of *proserchesthai*, only three (Mark 6:35; 12:28; 14:45) have parallels in Matthew; of these, only two are followed by the typically Matthean dative case *auto* (6:35 and 14:45). For the use of the verb in Mark 1:31 there is no (exact) parallel in Matthew. On the other hand, for Matthew's *proserchesthai* + dative, we usually find in Mark *erchesthai pros* + accusative in four places (1:40; 7:1; 11:27; 12:18), and *erchesthai* with no preposition in five places (2:18; 5:27; 6:29; 10:2; 14:66). However, in other instances, there are a few similar constructions that use synonyms like *prosdramon* (10:17), or *prosporeuontai* (10:35), or *eiselthen* (15:43).

17. Jesus "coming": Mark 1:14, 31, 35, 39; 2:1, 13; 3:1, 13, 20, 31; 6:1, 6, 45; 7:17, 31; 8:10, 13, 27; 9:28; 10:1, 17 (twenty-one occurrences); Jesus and the disciples "coming": 1:21, 29, 38; 3:7; 5:1, 38; 6:29, 35; 8:22; 9:14, 30; 10:46 (twelve occurrences).

18. Mark 3:22; 4:1; 6:7, 30; 7:1; 8:1, 34; 10:13, 42.

19. R. Bultmann, "The Study of the Synoptic Gospels" in R. Bultmann–K. Kundsinn, *Form Criticism, Two Essays on New Testament Research*, trans. and ed. C. F. Grant (New York: Harper and Brothers, 1962); original title: *Die Erforschung der synoptischen Evangelien* (1930), 64. The same insistence appears in K. L. Schmidt's work quoted above: "If the origin of Christianity is identified with the coming about of a religious cult—and in the last decades this understanding has been asserted with increasing force—then it is clear that the formation of early Christian literature must take place on the basis of ancient Christian cult. In my opinion for understanding the formation of the gospels one cannot overrate the importance of the early church's liturgical practice. The oldest form of the Jesus tradition is liturgically determined (*"kultisch bestimmt"*) and therefore it is filled with images and transcends history (*"bildhaft und übergeschichtlich"*). *Der Rahmen der synoptischen Überlieferung*, p. 119.

20. In a brief footnote in one of his essays, K. L. Schmidt compares his position with those of Dibelius and Bultmann and remarks that Bultmann went too far by reducing "Christuskult" and "Christusmythos" to the creative activities of Hellenistic Christianity. He thinks that for understanding the oral tradition that antedates the written gospels (*"die Vorstufen der Evangelien"*) one must posit a closer connec-

tion between "cult" and "community." K. L. Schmidt, "Die Stellung der Evangelien in der allgemeinen Literaturgeschichte" in *EUCHARISTEHRION, Festschrift fuer Hermann Gunkel*, 1923, re-edited by F. Hahn, *Zur Formgeschichte des Evangeliums* (Darmstadt: Wissenschaftliche Buchgesellschaft, 1985), 213, n. 177. Now, almost eighty years later, it is fascinating to discover that these most significant figures of this school of thought have succeeded in substantiating the way in which the cultic "*Sitz im Leben*" of the gospel episodes determined the formation of the Synoptic tradition, and what is even more surprising, they reached a consensus in this matter.

21. For this position one obtains support from almost diametrically opposed sources such as O. Cullmann and Karl Ludwig Schmidt. Cullmann states that "in the service described by Justin...we are not dealing with a later development," except, he adds, for a decrease of the role of the prophets and the omission of the *agape* (*Early Christian Worship*, 30). K. L. Schmidt, who elsewhere reproaches Justin for distorting the genre of the gospels for centuries by calling them "memoirs of the apostles," recognizes that both he and his disciple Tatian (and his gospel harmony) stand in the line of a continuous tradition that antedates the composition of the gospels, since "the steps that lead to the formation of the gospels must be enlightened from the liturgical practice of pericopal reading (*schon die Vorstufen der Evangelien müssen von der Perikopenpraxis aus beleuchtet werden*)," "Die Stellung der Evangelien in der allgemeinen Literaturgeschichte," 206. Afterwards, K. L. Schmidt quotes with great approval the "very remarkable" statements of one of his great opponents, Theodor Zahn (*Einleitung in das Neue Testament*, 3rd edition, 1907) who asserts that "all works of early Christian literature of which we know had some relationship—for a shorter or a longer period of time, in wider or narrower circles—with Christian '*anagnosis*,' i.e., some use in the community's liturgy." Ibid., 207, n. 164. He is, indeed, justified to state that the argument about a liturgical "*Sitz im Leben*" for the gospel tradition is not an issue "between right and left wing, conservatives and liberals, orthodox and critics, but the right and wrong practice of philology and theology." Ibid., 218.

22. O. Cullmann's *Die Christologie des Neuen Testamentes* (Tübingen: Mohr, 1957).

23. One must read in this context 9:11–13 in which the equivalence of forgiveness and healing is made explicit.

24. In the episode of Jesus' walking on the sea, first we read that he was "coming" to them (14:25), then the same verb is used three times to describe Peter's "coming" to him (vv. 28–29), until Peter finally exclaims "save me" (the meaning of Jesus' name according to Matt 1:21), and is rescued (v. 31). This episode, consisting of Jesus' coming to the disciples and Peter's coming to Jesus, ends when Jesus enters the boat and the disciples worship him with a confession of faith. One cannot find an episode more "cultic" and thus "eucharistic" in both form and content. However, the transfiguration matches it with Jesus first " bringing" the disciples to the "high mountain" (17:1), then "coming" (*prosehlthen*) to them and touching them (v. 7) and making a statement about the resurrection of the Son of Man from the dead (v. 9).

25. Matt 16:27; 21:9, 40; 24:42–44; 25:10, 19.

26. The theme of Jesus' coming organically expands on the Synoptic sayings about the purpose of Jesus' "coming," the term he uses when explaining his mission. See Matt 5:17; 9:13; 10:34–35; Mark 1:38; 2:17; Luke 12:49; John 1:31; 8:14; 9:39; 10:10; 12:27, 47.

27. A. Feuillet, *The Apocalypse* (New York: Alba House, 1965), 85.

28. "[I]t is not without significance that the Seer mentions that he saw his visions on 'a Lord's day' (1:10), at a time, therefore, when the Christian community was gathered together. Thus he sees the whole drama of the last days in the context of the early Christian service of worship, which, so to speak, has its counterpart and at the same time its fulfillment in the coming aeon, so that all that takes place in the gatherings of the early Christian community, seen from this side, appears as anticipation of that which in the last day takes place from God's side. Hence, the whole Book of Revelation from the greeting of grace and peace in 1:14 to the closing prayer: Come Lord Jesus, in chapter 22:20, and the benediction in the last verse, is full of allusions to the liturgical usages of the early community." Cullmann, 7.

29. Cf. O. Karrer, *Die geheime Offenbarung* (Einsiedeln/Köln: Benziger, 1948), 38.

30. The Muratorian Canon, most often dated around A.D. 200, states this explicitly: "Joannes enim in Apocalypsi, licet septem ecclesiis scribat, tamen omnibus dicit." D. J. Theron, *Evidence of Tradition* (Grand Rapids, Michigan: Baker Bookhouse, 1958), 110.

31. One of the ways this ongoing concept of coming receives emphasis is its double mentioning in the prologue (1:7) and the epilogue (22:13).

32. For both appearances to the Eleven, the Fourth Gospel uses the expression "Jesus came and stood" (*elthen* in 20:19 and *erchetai* in 20:26).

33. The shorter form, *ho ehn kai ho on*, occurs two more times (11:17; 16:5).

34. Authors point out its grammatical irregularities. A. Vögtle considers it as "*eine grammatisch unmögliche Formulierung*" and connects it with Hellenistic formulas of the day (*Das Buch mit sieben Siegeln* [Freiburg-Basel-Wien: Herder, 1981], 20), while J. M. Ford points out that it functions like an expansion on the divine name, YHWH, as meaning "the one who is" (*Revelation, The Anchor Bible* 38 [Garden City, N.Y.: Doubleday, 1975], 376). Most satisfactory is the explanation offered by R. H. Charles: "As for *ho erchomenos*, where our author returns to the participial construction, it is clear that he uses *erchomenos*, instead of *esoomenos*, with a definite reference to the contents of the Book and especially to the coming of Christ, i. 7, ii. 5, 16, iii. 11, xxii. 7, 12 etc., in whose coming God Himself comes also." *The Revelation of St. John*, ICC (Edinburgh: Clark, 1920), I: 10.

35. Very helpful are the remarks by Richard Bauckham: "John has taken advantage of this usage to depict the future of God not as his mere future existence, but as his coming into the world in salvation and judgment. He has in mind no doubt those

many Old Testament prophetic passages which announce that God will 'come' to save and judge (e.g. Ps 96:13; 98:9; Isa 40:10; 66:15; Zech 14:5) and which early Chritians understood to refer to his eschatological coming to fulfill the final purpose for the whole world, a coming he identified with the parousia of Jesus Christ." *The Theology of the Book of Revelation* (Cambridge: University Press, 1993), 29.

36. Quite helpful are in this regard R. Bauckam's remarks about "the First and the Last" as a basic pattern of composition in this book. *The Theology of the Book of Revelation*, 54–58.

37. "Ascend to here and I will show you what is supposed to happen after these. Immediately I fell into ecstasy" (*egenomehn en pneumati*: 4:1–2).

38. Incidentally, the present-day Roman liturgy combines this verse with John's "Behold the Lamb of God" in the Fourth Gospel (1:29) as the form of invitation of the faithful to the eucharistic meal at communion.

39. 1 Cor 11:20: *kuriakon deipnon*.

40. John 13:4; 21:20.

41. One must note, however, that it is not at all clear in front of whom he falls down. Charles's commentary enumerates five weighty reasons for considering 19:9b–10 as an interpolation, one of them being the dative instead of the accusative after *proskunehsai*. But, indeed, one may rather speak of the hand of a redactor who overlooks the fact that the invitation to the Lamb's Supper was made by a voice, not by a messenger, in 19:9a. Throughout the whole vision that begins in 19:9a, no angel is mentioned whom the seer would be adoring. Quite a curious way of combating angel worship, as the explanation of modern commentaries (Ford, Karrer, Harrington) view this passage, since no angel is mentioned throughout the vision! More probably, the original function of 19:10 was to indicate the end of the visionary experience which began with the vision of 1:10–16 and was followed with his first "fainting" as he fell to the feet of the Lord "as if dead" (1:17). Now it seems that, after the invitation to the Lamb's Supper, the same fearful experience repeats, but it signals the end of the whole chain of visions. As John is lifted from the ground, he realizes that no "divine presence" is left, for the one who awakens him identifies himself as only a "fellow-servant" and a "fellow-martyr." Such an explanation would regard the whole section 19:11 to 22:7 as an inserted epilogue to the book and 22:8 as a reprise of 19:9b leading to the concluding passage of the work.

42. The invitation to the marriage banquet is preceded by a command connected with a makarism: "write it down: Happy are…" (*grapson makarioi*). While the command "write" runs through the whole book (in the prologue: 1:11, 19; once for each of the seven letters: 2:1, 8, 12, 18; 3:1, 7, 14), it comes back only three more times, just once again in connection with a makarism speaking of those who have died before the Parousia in 14:13. From such a formal point of view, the command "write" in 21:5 seems to belong to an inserted appendix rather than being an organic part of the main outline.

43. Or is it also because of a *disciplina arcani* that the liturgical pattern does not continue?

44. *[E]xo hoi kunes kai hoi pharmakoi kai hoi pornoi kai hoi phoneis kai hoi eidololatrai kai pas philon kai poion pseudos.*

45. The claim may not have to be made about every gospel pericope. Yet, looking for passages that could not have been formed and used in a eucharistic context brings surprising results. In the Synoptics there are literally only a handful of episodic passages which are not fit for presentation at the Eucharist. Such are, for example, the narrative of the death of John the Baptist in Matthew and Mark, or the story about Judas's suicide inserted in Matthew's passion narrative. In these passages Jesus is not the protagonist. As a consequence, such episodes necessarily become *detours* in the narrative flow of the gospels. They cannot be fully inserted into the main stream of the compositional framework, for they cannot begin with a reference to Jesus' "coming," or someone approaching him, and they do not result in a salvific encounter with him.

But in no way do I claim that *all apostolic preaching* took place in a eucharistic context as its *"Sitz im Leben."* This is most clear about missionary preaching, such as that mentioned in Acts 5:21 in the temple or the various speeches given by Paul in public places (e.g., the Areopagus in 17:22–34 or the school of Tyrannos in 19:9). However, for the gospels, form critical studies revealed not only a pre-existent oral phase but also the presence of a cultic audience which cannot be legitimately separated from the Eucharist. Therefore, in First Corinthians Paul designates "the upbuilding of the church" (using the noun *oikodomeh*, four times: 14:3, 5, 12, 26; plus twice the verb *oikodomeo* in 14:4) as the purpose of "speaking" at assemblies, and writes in the same context about "the body of Christ." For Paul, Christ's ecclesial body to be built up by the gifts of the Spirit (1 Cor 12 to 14) is inseparable from his eucharistic body (1 Cor 11).

A RESPONSE TO DENIS FARKASFALVY ON

The Eucharistic Provenance of New Testament Texts

BY FRANCIS MARTIN

Abbot Denis Farkasfalvy has made a substantial contribution by joining historical research into the provenance of our New Testament texts and research into the origins of Christian worship, most notably eucharistic worship. He looks in turn at the three types of literature found in the New Testament and, basing himself on positions commonly held in New Testament studies, indicates how all three have an intimate relation to communal worship. Briefly, the apostolic letters are addressed to communities who will read them as they are gathered at worship; the early strata at least of the gospels were composed within the matrix of a eucharistic setting; and the Book of Revelation reflects the structure and even the texts used at worship. I will consider each of these in turn, and then offer some reflections, devoting most of my attention to the gospels.

Part One: A Resume of the Paper

The Apostolic Letters

Abbot Denis rightly points to the fact that, with the exception of the Letter to Philemon, all the letters designated as Pauline are destined to be read out in the eucharistic assembly. Much the same can be said about the Letter of James and 1 Peter and, I would think, the

First Letter of John. There is, as many commentators have pointed out, a "liturgical aura" about these letters. They allude to liturgical pieces, hymns, creeds, etc., and they use phrases that are redolent of the eucharistic practice of the early church as we know it. An important example is found in Hebrews 9:20 where, in citing Exodus 24:8, the author changes "Behold (*idou*) the blood of the covenant" to: "This (*touto*) [is] the blood of the covenant," bringing the phrase more into line with the four accounts of the institution of the Eucharist (esp. Matt 26:28/Mark 14:24; see Luke 22:20/1 Cor 11:25). I might add that the remark in 2 Peter 3:15–16 concerning the "letters" of Paul presumes a collection of such letters and therefore a communal effort to assemble them and a communal destination for their reading. While much more could be said on this topic,[1] I would like to dedicate more time to the position elaborated by Professor Farkasfalvy with regard to the gospels.

The Gospels

After recalling the near-unanimous opinion of New Testament historians that the passion narratives of the gospels were elaborated in a liturgical setting, Farkasfalvy points to the fact that the account of the institution of the Eucharist serves as a "theological overture" to these narratives. He then moves on to ask another question: "Do the remaining narratives in the gospels manifest a similar eucharistic link in a way comparable to that which the passion narratives show?" A twofold answer to the question is then proposed. There is first of all the undoubted eucharistic intent to be found in the sixfold account of the multiplication of the loaves and perhaps in other narratives and, second, there is the structure of the gospels themselves.

In regard to the second part of this answer, Abbot Denis points to the fact that all the gospels make what may be called a theological use of geography in structuring their narratives: they portray Jesus as an itinerant preacher and use the change of place that this entails as a means of both dividing the pericopes from each other and of connecting them. This has been a gospel commonplace at least since the work of K. L. Schmidt's *Der Rahmen der synoptischen Überlieferung*, but this observation can be pressed into further service. Jesus is often portrayed as coming or arriving at a certain place, and people are described as approaching or coming up to him. Without denying the evidence that these verbs often reveal the redactional activity of the evangelists,[2] Farkasfalvy sees this rhythm of Jesus coming and being encountered as having something to do with the ways memories were recalled as the community gathered for the purpose of re-living and re-enacting such encounters. I will return to this.

Building on the fact that much of the peripatetic vocabulary used of Jesus includes the notion of coming, the next part of the paper considers not only the title *ho erchomenos* but also all the ways that the notion of coming is applied to Jesus. It is clear from the way this terminology is used that the New Testament saw that there were many ways in which Jesus' coming at the end of the ages is anticipated in the life of the church, most particularly as the community is gathered together. This usage strengthens the eucharistic overtones of many gospel texts and suggests once again that the matrix of the gospel material was the eucharistic communal worship of the early community.[3] I might observe that this part of the study could be enhanced by a closer consideration of the *elthon* sayings and their development in the gospel tradition.

The Book of Revelation

The opening vision of this book, its general framework, and the liturgical hymns cited therein all point to a context of eucharistic worship. In addition, we have once again a multi-layered use of the term *erchesthai*, the use of the term *deipnon* to describe the "banquet of the Lamb" (Rev 19:9), and the community's prayer expression *maranatha*. I would like to point as well to one significant eucharistic allusion that also contains the notion of an anticipated "coming" of the Lord. It is found among the concluding admonitions to the church at Laodicea: "Behold, I stand at the door and knock (see Luke 12:35–38). If anyone hears my voice and opens the door, I will come in with him and I will banquet (*deipneso*) with him and he with me" (Rev 3:20). Jürgen Roland remarks in this regard: "[T]he church's celebration of the Eucharist here and now is an allusion to the imminent coming of the Lord and anticipation of the future meal with him in its perfection."[4]

Part Two: Reflections

I wish to concentrate my remarks on the second section of Denis Farkasfalvy's paper, namely the eucharistic setting for the early stages of the gospel tradition. The remarks will be largely corroborative of the paper, but I would like to raise as well some issues for further consideration. The first reflection has to do with the notion of "encounter" used in the paper, the second with the sacramental nature of the New Testament pericopes, and the third with what I will call the earliest view of the events in the life of Jesus as *mysteria*.

The New Testament Pericopes as Encounter Stories

We have seen that one part of the rhythm discerned by Farkasfalvy is that of "encounter." Strictly speaking, this should designate the pericope as narrative because, under this aspect, it is the literary presentation of a complete action. Allow me to cite here an apt philosophical and literary definition of narrative which I will then apply to a significant percentage of the gospel stories. The definition of narrative is that of Tzvetan Todorov:

> The minimal complete plot consists in the passage from one equilibrium to another. An "ideal" narrative begins with a stable situation which is disturbed by some power or force. There results a state of disequilibrium; by the action of a force directed in the opposite direction, the equilibrium is reestablished; the second equilibrium is similar to the first, but the two are never identical.[5]

In the above definition I wish to put the accent on "the action of a force directed in the opposite direction." The source of this action in the gospel pericopes is always Jesus. Before approaching the texts themselves, it will be helpful to note that they all follow a particular narrative grammar, in that they all portray Jesus encountering a situation, reacting to it, and resolving it.

In the narrative pericopes of the gospel tradition, a significant percentage (about 70 percent) follow a basic plot line, or narrative grammar, whose simplest form is as follows:

Setting: The action is usually given a certain chronological and geographical situation. The significance and extent of this depends upon the work of each author.

Meeting: The action proper begins when Jesus meets up with a situation. This usually occurs because someone approaches Jesus and the situation of "disequilibrium" described by Todorov is initiated.

Response: Jesus reacts to the situation with either a word or a gesture or both. This is Todorov's "force in the opposite direction."

Result: A new situation of equilibrium is either described, as in the case with *transeunt* activity (see below), or implied as is often the case with a narrative of immanent activity (also below). I will explain this distinction momentarily. With the attainment of the result, the action terminates in a new situation of equilibrium.

It frequently happens that, in one or several narrations of the same action, the conclusion of the narrative action is followed by a sequel that does not pertain to the action as such but flows from it. Examples of such sequels, often wrongly adduced as necessary components of miracle stories, for example, would be the wonder of the bystanders, praise on their part, publication of the healing, coming to faith, etc.[6]

In regard to the Result, we have to distinguish between those actions of Jesus that are *transeunt*, in that they pass from him to another, and those which are narratively immanent. In the first instance, the termination of the action is reported explicitly: "the fever left her" (Matt 8:15; Mark 1:31; Luke 4:39); "and her daughter was healed instantly" (Matt 15:28), "so she went home and found the child lying on the bed and the demon gone" (Mark 7:30), etc.

There are other narratives in which the rhythm equilibrium-disequilibrium-equilibrium takes place on an immanent plane. These are conflict stories in which the "force in the opposite direction" is a word of Jesus. No result need be explicitly stated, since the reader can experience personally the restored equilibrium. Examples of such narratives would be: the paying of taxes to Caesar, the debate about divorce, and the debate about resurrection of the dead. In such instances, there is a true action though the movement is illative, taking place in the mind of Jesus and his audience and in that of the recipient of the text: it is an illustration of the fact that, for the ancients, words are actions too. These texts are true narratives and should be distinguished from those texts in which the description of the situation provides a setting for the saying of Jesus but is not the literary presentation of a completed action. Such texts are found primarily among the stories designated as pronouncement stories but also among narratives which present a conflict situation.[7]

The importance of delineating the specific and frequently found narrative form which may be called "encounter story" lies in the fact that it shows us that in the very narrative grammar of a majority of the gospel narratives about Jesus, there is found a rhythm that places Jesus at the center of the action and makes him and him alone the power which is able to bring about a restored equilibrium. Clearly, such a manner of narrating embodies a faith vision of Jesus, not as an important protagonist of the past, but as the Lord still in the midst of his people. This is another indication of the correctness of the position of Abbot Denis's paper which sees the eucharistic milieu of Christian worship as the matrix of the gospel narrative material.

There is a question, however, which still remains: How did this eucharistic matrix contribute to the present state of the gospels? Literary analysis has shown that the gospels as we now have them are not merely a conglomeration of pericopes loosely strung out along a travel narrative, but very closely structured statements which make an overall faith statement concerning the present reality and majesty of Jesus Christ and portray this as refracted in the events of his life. I leave this as a subject for further discussion.

The Sacramentality of the Text

In his study, *The Miracle Stories of the Gospels*, Alan Richardson writes: "They [the miracle stories] are for the Christian no dead records of an age that is past and tales of long ago, but parables of the dealings of the living Christ with those who trust Him and obey His Word."[8] This view echoes that of St. Leo the Great, one of the foremost exponents of what I am calling the sacramentality of the sacred text: "All those things which the Son of God both did and taught for the reconciliation of the world, we not only know in the account of things now past, but we also experience in the power of works which are present."[9] That he intended by this to refer not only to the sacraments of the church but also to the reading of the scriptures is evident from his oft-repeated notion that the gospel text, when received by faith, makes present that which it speaks about.[10]

. The gospels themselves bear witness to the fact that they are disclosure narratives, manifesting and making available the realities mediated by the text. There are, for instance, many phrases that reflect the liturgical life of the community. Thus, in Matthew's account of the storm at sea the disciples cry out "Lord save!" (*Kyrie soson*), "We are perishing!" (Matt 8:25; compare Mark 4:38; Luke 8:24). Again, the phrase "Your faith has saved/healed you," while it occurs in healing stories and elsewhere, probably reflects a baptismal theology (see Matt 9:22 / Mark 4:34 / Luke 8:48; Mark 10:52 / Luke 18:42; Luke 17:19; 7:50).[11] Narratives of the healing of the blind are redolent with baptismal and discipleship themes, as can be clearly seen in John 9, but this is evident as well in the story of the blind man at Jericho who follows Jesus after he has been given sight (Matt 20:34 / Mark 10:52 / Luke 18:43). Matthew and Luke also contain the phrase just discussed linking faith and healing/salvation while Mark adds that the healed man followed Jesus on the way. Another discipleship theme, that of service, is sounded in the sequel to the account of the healing of Peter's mother in law: "she served him (Matt)/them (Mark, Luke)." All of these instances are but selections from a large corpus of gospel usage which clearly indicates the correctness of the view that these narratives were told or read to a community who in faith were reliving and re-enacting the same events on the level of their present existence. These texts, oral or written, were also sacramental in that they rendered the risen Jesus present precisely as the one in whom the event recounted continued to exist in his glorified humanity as a source of life and blessing.

The Mysteries of the Life of Christ

I wish here to touch but very briefly on another aspect of the pericopes in the gospel tradition, namely, that they are told in such a way that the interiority and vertical dimension of the event in Christ's life recounted there is disclosed in its reality and power for those who receive it in faith. Faith must first penetrate to this inner core and then find a way to disclose it to others. This is precisely what Henri de Lubac meant when, in speaking of the interpretation of scripture, he insisted on seeking the inner depth of the events recounted there by reading historical reality spiritually and spiritual reality historically.[12]

One of the most striking ways in which this is accomplished by the gospels is to be found in the manner in which the event is placed within the context of multiple allusions to the Old Testament and other teachings of Jesus. The regularity with which a narrated event will contain the same set of allusions, even in traditions that are not dependent upon one another, points to the fact that there must have been a cadre of Spirit-inspired teachers who established a "canonical" way of mediating the various mysteries of the life of Christ, and presented their narrations in the context of community worship. I will give but one example here: the account of Jesus' temptation just before his passion.

The Synoptic gospels (Matt 26:36–46 / Mark 14:32–42 / Luke 22:40–46) all attest to a moment of crisis in the life of Jesus, just before his arrest and death, when amid great distress and fear he embraced the will of the Father. This same crucial moment is placed by John at a point in the concluding chapter of the first part of his gospel (John 12:27–29). He includes other elements of the Synoptic account elsewhere in his gospel (14:31; 18:11). The Letter to the Hebrews also makes use of this event in order to accent the interior dimension of Christ's priestly self-offering (Heb 5:7–10). All the accounts contain the same key elements, though in different form. Let me illustrate.[13]

First, all the accounts allude to Jesus as the suffering just man of the psalms who is "sorrowful" (Matt 26:38 / Mark 14:34) or "troubled" (John 12:27). These two terms are found as parallel expressions in LXX Pss 41:6, 12; 43:5. (See also Ps 6:3–7.) He prays with "loud cries and tears" (Heb 5:7; see LXX Ps 37:10; 6:3–7, etc.). In addition, all the accounts stress the fact that this prayer is an expression of the filial relation Jesus has with the Father. In the four gospel narratives, Jesus explicitly addresses his prayer to the Father (Matt 26:39 / Mark 14:36 / Luke 22:42 / John 12:27), while in Hebrews 5:8, Jesus is called

"Son." The Gospels frame the actual expression of submission in terms meant to evoke the "Our Father": Matthew 26:39/Mark 14:36/Luke 22:42 (also Matt 26:42) reflect Matthew 6:10 (despite the fact that this petition is not in the Lukan version of the "Our Father"), while John 12:28 echoes Matthew 6:9. This same prayer provides the theme of "temptation" found in the Synoptics (Matt 26:41/Mark 14:38/Luke 22:40, 46; see Heb 4:15). In addition, the gospel tradition concurs in calling this moment "the hour." This is particularly striking in Mark (14:35b [see John 12:27]; 37d; 41c [= John 12:23]), although it also figures in Matthew 26:40, 45 (see Luke 22:53). Such agreement on the key elements in the narration amidst differences in theological orientation and literary genre suggests an intense Spirit-led activity on the part of the "ministers of the word" (Luke 1:2) to find the most effective way of leading people into the mystery at the heart of this event and to see its relation to the present life of the church. It is interesting, in reading the homilies of the fathers of the church, to see how often they are instinctively in tune with this manner of presenting the mystery at the Eucharist.

Conclusion

The theme of Denis Farkasfalvy's paper is the eucharistic provenance of New Testament texts, and we are in his debt. I have attempted to summarize the paper and then to offer three ways, literary, sacramental, and theological, in which the fundamental proposition of the paper might be supported. In addition, I have raised a question concerning a wider context for the redactional level of the gospel texts as we now have them.

NOTES

1. For an extended study of these and other issues related to the early liturgy and the New Testament, the reader will find a helpful orientation in Pierre Grelot, *La liturgie dans le Nouveau Testament*, ed. A. George and P. Grelot, vol. 9, *Introduction à la Bible, Édition Nouvelle* (Proost/Tournai: Desclée, 1991).

2. For a good study of Matthew's use of *proserchesthai*, etc., in this manner see H. J. Held, "Matthew as Interpreter of the Miracle Stories," in *Tradition and Interpretation*

in Matthew, ed. G. Bornkahm, G. Barth, and H. J. Held (London: SCM, 1963), 165–299, particularly 226–230.

3. One can still consult with profit the study by John A. T. Robinson, *Jesus and His Coming: The Emergence of a Doctrine* (New York: Abingdon, 1957).

4. Jürgen Roland, *Revelation*, trans. John E. Alsup, *Continental Commentaries* (Minneapolis: Augsburg, 1993), 65.

5. *The Poetics of Prose*, trans. Richard Howard (Ithaca: Cornell University Press, 1977), 111. It is interesting to observe that a similar description of action as a movement from one equilibrium to another through a state of disequilibrium is utilized by Hardison in commenting on Aristotle's notion of *praxis*: L. Golden and O. B. Hardison, Jr., *Aristotle's Poetics. A Translation and Commentary for Students of Literature* (Englewood Cliffs, N.J.: Prentice Hall, 1968), 140–141.

6. I have discussed the deficiencies of the "classical" structuration of miracle stories by Bultmann, Leon-Dufour, et al. in *Encounter Story: A Characteristic Gospel Narrative Form* (Gaithersburg, Md.: Word Among Us Press, 1979). The critique offered there applies as well to the similar deficiencies in the work by Gerd Theissen, *The Miracle Stories of the Early Christian Tradition*, ed. John Riches, trans. Francis McDonagh (Philadelphia: Fortress, 1983), esp. 142–173. By failing to see the "sequel" nature of what follows the end of the action, "acclamation" is made an essential part of a miracle story when in fact it is treated as one movable part among others to be used or not by the various gospel authors. Compare, for example, the different sequels in Matt 20:34; (9:31); Mark 10:52; Luke 18:43, or in Matt 8:4; Mark 1:45; Luke 5:15–16; etc.

7. It is difficult to assess such stories as: picking grain on the Sabbath, the debate about David's son, the debate about the great commandment, etc. In these and similar stories, the setting is necessary for an understanding of the word of Jesus, as it is not, for instance, in the saying about the foxes and their holes, but there does not seem to be a true action presented literarily. Robert C. Tannehill says of a pronouncement story that it is "a story with narrative tension and movement, not just a saying with a narrative setting." "Varieties of Synoptic Pronouncement Stories," *Semeia* 20 (1981): 101–120; citation is from 117.

8. Alan Richardson, *The Miracle Stories of the Gospels* (London: SCM Press, 1941), 136–137.

9. *On the Passion*, 12 (*Sources Chrétiennes [SC]* 74, 82).

10. *On the Resurrection*, 1 (*SC* 74, 123); *On the Epiphany*, 5 (*SC* 22 bis, 254); *On the Passion*, 5 and 18 (*SC* 74, 41 and 112).

11. The remarkable causality attributed to faith in these stories is such that they are practically the only ones in which the *suppliant's* action resolves the narrative movement. For other instances where *pistis* and *sozein* are so intimately linked, see: Acts 3:16; 14:9; 16:31; Rom 1:17; 3:28; 10:10; Gal 5:6; Heb 11; etc.

12. "God acts *within* history, God reveals himself *within* history. Even more, God inserts himself *within* history, thus granting it a 'religious consecration' which forces us to take it seriously. *Historical* realities have a *depth*; they are to be understood *spiritually: historika pneumatikôs*... and on the other hand, *spiritual* realities appear in the movement of becoming, they are to be understood *historically: pneumatika historikôs* ... The Bible, which contains revelation, thus also contains, in a certain way, the *history* of the world." Ignace de La Potterie, "The Spiritual Sense of Scripture," *Communio* 23, no. 4 (1996): 738–756 at 743; originally in Henri de Lubac, *Catholicisme: Les aspects sociaux de dogme chrétien* (Paris: Cerf, 1938, 1941), 119. For a discussion of this aspect of biblical narrative from the point of view of the "openess of the event," see Francis Martin, "Historical Criticism and New Testament Teaching on the Imitation of Christ," *Anthropotes* 6 (1990): 261–287.

13. The following paragraph is largely taken from Francis Martin, "Literary Theory, Philosophy of History and Exegesis," *The Thomist* 52 (1988): 575–604, at 580–581.

Robin Darling Young

The Eucharist as Sacrifice according to Clement of Alexandria

By the end of the first century and the beginning of the second, Christian writers had already developed a vocabulary describing as a sacrifice their own most important act of worship, the Eucharist. Although no one composition had yet concentrated solely on the ceremony or the meaning of the Eucharist, authors from Paul through Ignatius of Antioch reinterpreted the worship of Israel as sacrifice, now focusing it upon both the memorial meal demanded by Jesus of his followers, and upon Jesus' own death, to which that meal referred.[1]

During the second century, though, Christian authors deepened their understanding of the Eucharist as a sacrifice. They did this for a number of reasons. First, as in the case of the author of 1 Peter, or the Letter to the Hebrews, or Ignatius of Antioch, they had to understand the eucharistic sacrifice in relation to the occasional persecutions of Christians. A martyr's death imitated the death of Christ and extended its effects as sacrifice and example. In addition, these authors had not only to contrast the Eucharist with Jewish sacrifices conducted at the now-destroyed temple; they also had to come to an understanding of how the eucharistic sacrifice was both like and unlike the sacrifices of pagan cult. Finally, as the local traditions of teaching and scriptural interpretation developed, they had to understand the dimensions and layers of meaning within the Eucharist and Christian sacrifice as a central mark of the church.

Against this view certain thinkers later labeled "Gnostics" reacted, both by rejecting the value of the body and by emphasizing that salvation came about by an enlightenment that negated, rather than saved, the material cosmos. On the other hand, the lasting contributions of Gnosticism were a more philosophical understanding of Christian teaching and an allegorical interpretation of scripture, and the response to these contributions gave momentum to numerous thinkers of the late second and early third centuries, including Irenaeus, Tertullian, Clement, and Origen.[2]

Of these four, the late second-century Alexandrian *didaskalos* Clement of Alexandria was the first thinker to understand and describe all the major dimensions of the matter. Deeply immersed in the catechetical training of Christian neophytes for the Alexandrian church, thoroughly involved in the education of Christian *gnostikoi*, or advanced students, and always occupied with the securing of orthodox doctrine against heretics by refuting the determinist dualism of Valentinus and Basilides, Clement was a thinker absorbed in the deepening of Christian thought. He was the first to express fully a philosophical Christian mysticism shaped by desire for union with Christ through the Christian mysteries of baptism and the Eucharist. He understood these mysteries as true sacrifices. Consequently, when he directed his writings toward Christian teachers, the contemplative gnostics, he let them know that they might well be required to offer themselves in the sacrifice of martyrdom.[3]

As the responses to this essay indicate, the above assertions may well seem counterintuitive, or at least surprising in view of the usual treatment of Clement as an author dedicated more to philosophy and poetry than to liturgy. General accounts of the interpretation of the Eucharist among earliest Christian authors often omit any discussion of Clement's thought. Furthermore, since Clement's own writing is elliptical and allusive, it is not easy to trace the strands of his thought. His extended discussions of a topic often shade off into an ambiguity or leave a thought unfinished where—for the purposes of ascertaining his opinion—a flat assertion on his part would have been more helpful.[4]

Yet a close examination of Clement's thought about the Eucharist is extremely rewarding. This essay will propose that the Eucharist both imbued and oriented his writing, and that a kind of sacrificial understanding of human salvation and restoration accompanied and transformed the philosophical and literary themes that he adapted to Christianity from Greek poets, dramatists, and philosophers. If this is true, two consequences are important: first, Clement himself must be re-evaluated and considered as a contributor to—perhaps even as an originator of—the complex Christian understanding of sacrifice in its three dimensions of Christ's death, the Eucharist, and the death of the martyr. And second, Clement's own thought will be seen to be firmly rooted in Christian worship and, therefore, in the communal expression of Christianity, rather than primarily in some elite and separatist form of Gnosticism. Throughout, the form in which the reader encounters this thought is not yet formulaic or closed—it is open, ambiguous, interpretable, fertile, and above all lively in its invitation to the reader that begins in the *Protreptikos* as an invitation to leave pagan rites and join the Christian procession and shades off, in the *Stromateis*, into unspoken hints at the way in which this procession concludes in silent contemplation and praise of the unseen Father made visible in his Son.[5]

Clement was the first to sketch out the main lines of what became the typical description of the Eucharist among later authors like Origen, Athanasius, Cyril of Jerusalem, and their successors among fourth- and fifth-century Greek writers. These authors took the view that the Eucharist is both the atoning sacrifice of Christ and the church's own cultic sacrifice. They thought that the liturgy of the Eucharist itself was a part of the path of understanding by which the human being as a rational creature reorients him- or herself to the intelligible world of supreme beauty, now understood as the Trinity itself and Israel's God. For these authors, the Eucharist recalled the turning point of the divine economy, in which the passion of Christ fulfilled the descent of the Logos and made it possible for life as immortality and incorruption to return to the human race. Real understanding, for which they often used the term "gnosis," is given to participants in the church's ritual; they celebrated not only a founding sacrifice of the church, but also participated in a mystery that communicated understanding. The Greek fathers' broadest interpretation of the liturgy was that of a city of God founded upon the sacrifice of Christ, a city in which the citizens possess real understanding founded upon real discipline; and the witnesses to the city of

peace were those who most fully participated in its defense as martyrs. All of their later themes may be found in the thought of Clement,
and to some of them this essay will turn, after placing Clement in his
proper setting as a theologian.[6] First, however, it is well to recall some
general characteristics of Greek patristic thought on the Eucharist.

Early Christian Thought about the Eucharist

Between 152 and 155, Justin Martyr composed his First Apology
to refute slanders against Christianity and correctly represent its
practices. In the sixty-sixth paragraph he describes concisely the food
that Christians eat in common as a memorial meal of Christ. He
wrote, "We call this food the 'Eucharist'":

> No one is allowed to partake of it except him who believes
> that our teachings are true, and has been cleansed in the bath
> for the forgiveness of his sins and for his regeneration, and
> who lives as Christ commanded. Not as common bread or as
> common drink do we receive these, but just as through the
> word of God, Jesus Christ, our Savior, became incarnate and
> took on flesh and blood for our salvation, so, we have been
> taught, the food over which thanks has been given by the
> prayer of His word, and which nourishes our flesh and blood
> by assimilation, is both the flesh and blood of that incarnate
> Jesus.

Justin adds that the apostles alone were told by Jesus to do this, and
that they had handed on this instruction in the gospels. He makes an
analogy between the incarnation and the eucharistic blessing that
begins with the breaking of bread and continues with a thanksgiving
and a recitation of his words at the Last Supper. In the next paragraph, Justin adds that the Christians hold their common assembly on
"the day of the Sun...because it is the first day. On it God, transforming darkness and matter, created the world; and our Savior Jesus
Christ arose from the dead on the same day" (67). Jesus' resurrection
corresponds, then, to the original creation, illumination, and ordering

of the cosmos; the eucharistic food nourishes Christians' bodies for
their own resurrection.

That short work of Justin's has received extensive attention from
scholars of the early liturgy and of early Christian theology. With its
connection of Eucharist, incarnation, and resurrection, it offers in just
a few lines numerous tantalizing allusions to the self-understanding of
early Christians and their connection of the Eucharist with the salvation of the entire cosmos. Clement of Alexandria, with his open,
ambiguous, fertile, and lively thoughts on the Eucharist, is in agreement with Justin's views, but because of the size and subtlety of his
work is a much better representative of the later theology that developed out of second-century thought.

Exactly this fertility has been discerned, without particular connection to Clement, in some recent scholars' descriptions of authentic
eucharistic theology. Among some Catholic and Orthodox scholars,
in particular, the patristic exegesis of the eucharistic passages of the
Bible has given rise to a renewed understanding of the Eucharist. Of
the liturgy of his own day, the Orthodox theologian Alexander
Schmemann wrote:

> The liturgy of the Eucharist is best understood as a journey or
> procession. It is the journey of the Church into the dimension
> of the Kingdom ... our entrance into the presence of Christ is
> an entrance into a fourth dimension which allows us to see the
> ultimate reality of life. It is not an escape from the world,
> rather it is the arrival at a vantage point from which we can
> see more deeply into the reality of the world.[7]

Trained by Sergei Bulgakov and therefore a beneficiary of the
early twentieth-century Russian revival of patristic studies, Schmemann in his characterization of the Eucharist deliberately avoided the
stale, overly technologized questions of late medieval and modern
eucharistic theology. He also avoided the overspiritualized interpeta-
tion of the liturgy that his colleague John Meyendorff ascribed (too
sweepingly) to the thought of Dionysius, Origen, and Evagrius.[8] He
emphasized that the liturgy was a liturgy of earth and heaven, a cosmic procession toward God instantiated in the church's worship

within the entire sweep of the economy of salvation. But he was doing little more than summarizing, in contemporary words, the central insight of the early church into the liturgy it understood to have been instituted by its Lord.

There is, however, a corollary in early Christian thought which must be raised alongside Schmemann's point of view. And another, very different, contemporary Orthodox theologian has grasped this well. Vasileios of Stavronitika, a scholar of Maximus the Confessor and an Athonite abbot, makes the point that not only does the liturgy result in a "new mind," a perspective or contemplation of the reality of being, but that the very act of theology is liturgy. Vasileios writes:

> The first Christians lived their theology totally and with the whole of their bodies, just as they were baptized with the whole of their body and soul into the new life. Thus their liturgical gatherings were an initiation into the mystery of theology. They would gather with one accord in one place, and make a total offering of themselves... They would open their hearts and confess their hidden pains and their personal struggles in front of all the brethren. And for them "in front of all" meant in front of and in the One, in Christ, whose Body they constituted... So the early Christians, making their confession within the Church, offered up and sanctified within it and confessing their faith with the sacrifice of love, came to have a different understanding of themselves, as persons and as a community.[9]

In short, Vasileios writes, the prayer of the church is the matrix of theology, a theology which is a participant, at the same time, in the liturgy; this liturgy not only constitutes a sacrificial offering, but also provides the ground of self-understanding. In confrontation with the Divine Person, it makes possible the self-understanding of the person.

These modern authors, like their Catholic contemporaries in the *ressourcement* movement of the mid-twentieth century, could be criticized for presenting a harmonizing portrait of early Christian thought, a portrait easily refuted by the evidence of first-century writers. Likewise, the divisive character of the Eucharist could be discerned from the writings of the next generation of writers, who insist so strenuously on unity as a precondition for eucharistic participation. All calls for concord and orthodoxy in the celebration of the central Christian rite, skeptics might say, are signals that no such concord existed. Schmemann and Vasileios represent different aspects of the same naiveté, not only with respect to the historians' plausible reconstruction of the life of the early church, but also with respect to the discourse of contemporary eucharistic liturgy, which therefore distorts their perspective.

There is one good reason, however, why their interpretations are worth considering, even if they downplay the differing accounts that a full historical account would inevitably raise. By the early second century, Christian authors were already drawing a close parallel between the incarnation of the Logos and the presence of Christ in the Eucharist, and they were making a connection between both of these and the understanding that, even at its most basic, is a requirement for the baptized—that is, that if Christ as God had died a sacrificial death for the redemption of man and restoration of the cosmos, then the Eucharist was also a sacrifice that effected those same results.

This view continues, and is given increasing detail in catechetical homilies, from the third through the seventh centuries. The dualist interpretation of certain Christian Gnostic teachers, and their denigration of the benefits of the flesh, led by the mid-third century to a strong, continuous emphasis on both the reality of Christ's incarnation and passion and the reality of his presence in the Eucharist by means of a *metabole* brought about by the Holy Spirit. There is an actual unanimity of the Greek fathers in the view that the Eucharist is both the atoning sacrifice of Christ and the church's own cultic sacrifice. In addition, they agree in varying degrees that the liturgy of the Eucharist is itself a part of the path of intellection by which the rational creature reorients himself to the intelligible world of supreme beauty, the invisible world of the Trinity.

The Eucharist recalls the turning-point of the divine economy, in which the passion of Christ fulfilled the descent of the Logos and made it possible for life as immortality and incorruption to return to the world. Not only these, however, but also that for which the original pair traded their immortality, to be like God or gods. Real under-

standing, for which the term "gnosis" is often used, belongs to participants in the church's ritual; they celebrate not only a founding sacrifice, but also a mystery that communicates understanding. Their ultimate view is of a city of God founded upon the sacrifice of Christ, a
city in which the citizens have real understanding growing from serious personal discipline. The witnesses to this city of peace are the
martyrs, according to second- and third-century authors.

A full survey of the thought of the early Greek fathers on the
Eucharist would have to review with extreme care the letters of
Ignatius of Antioch and Polycarp of Smyrna, the writings of the apostolic fathers, the works of Irenaeus, the Acts of the Martyrs, and the
writings of the major teachers of the church in various locations to
the end of the third century. It would have to explore the ways in
which incarnation, Eucharist, sacrifice, and martyrdom are connected
and develop in the period before the first recorded eucharistic liturgies of the late fourth century. It would require the attentive and close
reading of those texts to discover where the Eucharist was forming
the pattern of theology itself, and guiding the collection and exegesis
of biblical texts. It would also have to attend to a distinction made by
a fifth-century Greek theologian who deliberately placed his theology
in a first-century context and thereby gives his readers a clue to the
meaning of earliest Christian thought on the subject. Dionysius the
Areopagite wrote in a quasi-apostolic letter the following:

> Theological tradition has a dual aspect, the ineffable and the
> mysterious on the one hand, the open and more evident on
> the other. The one resorts to symbolism and involves initia-
> tion. The other is philosophical and employs the method of
> demonstration. The one uses persuasion and imposes the
> truthfulness of what is asserted. The other acts and, by means
> of a mystery which cannot be taught, puts souls firmly in the
> presence of God. (Letter 9.1)

As a partial foray into the survey outlined above, an examination of
Clement of Alexandria's thought on the Eucharist can offer some
interesting indications, *pars pro toto*, of the already deep connection
between catechesis and philosophy, sacrificial Eucharist and theology,
in early Christianity.

Clement of Alexandria as a Theologian

Of all the Christian teachers of the second century, Clement is doubtless the most learned, the most detailed, and the most profound. Yet his skill and his evident intention as a catechist, that is, to aid in the conversion of human beings to the gospel, have not been duly appreciated, doubtless because his writings often have been misunderstood as a collage of philosophical doctrines. In this essay I am trying to demonstrate that Clement's understanding of the Eucharist is both the fullest and earliest statement of the two main aspects of it, according to Christian thought, and that the Eucharist and its significance lie at the center of and thoroughly guide his thought. But to make this demonstration it is first necessary to recall what is known of Clement's life and briefly to indicate why Clement chose to articulate his teaching in the form that he did.

During the second century it was not uncommon for Christians seeking a Christian philosophy to travel from one city to another in search of an appropriate teacher. Justin Martyr gives an account of one such peregrination in the beginning of the Dialogue with Trypho, and similar journeys are known. Clement, like many other Christian teachers of the era, had been born into a pagan family, but once he became a Christian he traveled to study in Greece, southern Italy, Syria, and Palestine. (Such travels are another indication that Christians knew themselves to be part of a catholic church.) His final teacher he found in the city of Alexandria, where an incomparably lively discussion of religious philosophy was being carried out, in a form inseparably literary and philosophical, and from Pantaenus he inherited the direction of the program of catechesis in the Christian church of Alexandria.[10]

Clement may have been the catechist there for more than a decade when, in 202, during a persecution, he left the city for Jerusalem. Perhaps he did not return to Alexandria due to tensions with Demetrius the bishop, or the situation with Origen some years later; at any rate, he was a priest in Jerusalem, his last known activity being a mission undertaken for Alexander the bishop in 212 or 213. He had died by 231, because Alexander mentions the fact in a letter of that year to Origen. It is not difficult to see, from Clement's own remarks about "simple-minded" Christians, that the ambitious, philosophical approach to Christian truth may well have provoked opposition among the other clergy, and even the bishop, of Alexandria.

When he lived in Alexandria, Clement undertook the immense effort of composing a kind of Christian library for the education of the Christian human being. He did no less than re-found Christian thought, by digging deep trenches into the ground of Greek philosophy, culture, and religious practice to build a comprehensive Christian teaching with the materials of Jewish law and cult practice developed before the fall of the temple. But he did not build the edifice of a Christian library for its own sake; he built it for the crafting of Christian beings (living stones), and therefore his writing was always qualified in its permanent value by the superiority of oral communication. In fact, in the three major works authored by Clement in Alexandria, which he composed in genres he specially selected for his purpose, Clement trains his students and readers for appropriating Christian truth by becoming less and less explicit in writing. This evident practice leads his modern readers to assume that most of the deepest truths must have been communicated to them by voice.

Whether or not it is a programmatic collection, the three major works by Clement do constitute a connected curriculum of initiation into Christian philosophy—or, put differently, into Christian communal life, in which philosophy is the motivating force even if only its elemental or moral principles can be appropriated by most. Here Christianity is conceived as a philosophy in the sense of a psychagoge. The beginning of this path of Christian life is described in the *Protreptikos*. Clement deliberately and strategically used the well-established form of the protreptic discourse to recruit to Christian discipleship, and in Clement's hands that discourse also becomes an apologia—an argument against pagan cult and philosophy. As I will demonstrate below, the *Protreptikos* is also a song, pictured by Clement as Christ's living voice calling human beings to know him by means of baptism and liturgical worship. The second book, the *Paidagogos*, presents Christ as the companion in knowledge, a companion who trains rejuvenated human beings, i.e., children in the ethical life that is the bottom step of God's economic pedagogy. Here Clement adapts Paul's reference to the law/Torah as the "Law-Companion-Teacher [who] has guided us" to faith, understanding that a pedagogue is both a slave and a teacher accompanying children to school, only the school is the liturgical church, in which Eucharist is the pattern for Christian life, and the slave (*doulos*)-pedagogue is the humble Christ of Philippians 2:6f.

The third book, *Stromateis*, is often thought to represent Clement's failure to write a promised book, the *Didaskalos*. But the title, given to it by Clement himself, is a clue that Clement wanted to represent the highest level of knowledge, that is, appropriation of the knowledge that Christ gives of the Father and the created invisible world, under another customary Hellenistic rhetorical form, the miscellany. This form was carefully structured to represent an assemblage of topics in a way that apparently lacked organization. As a sequel to the two previous works, both of which are clearer to a cursory examination, the *Stromateis* tries to bring the student, already prepared in the first two books, to an understanding of how God has emptied himself in Christ so that he may be appropriated by the Christian. Again, that self-emptying, self-limiting action on the part of God, an act of love, is characterized and symbolized by the Eucharist, so that the one who appropriates this knowledge does so by means of beginning in the Eucharist and understanding exactly what the meaning of it is. It is crucial to understand that Clement has here reversed both the central tenet of Greek philosophy by making the transcendent, silent source of being itself come down as a man, to man; he has also reversed the traditional direction of sacrifice, by understanding that a divinity now sacrifices himself for humans. It may be argued that he has done no more than follow lines indicated by Paul, but if this is the case, he has (once more) re-founded Pauline theology by purging it of the radical philosophical dualism of Valentinus and Basilides and elaborating it philosophically following the thought of Philo.

A reader of Clement always has to overcome obstacles to gaining a more complete view of his aims. It is true that his instruction proceeded at a high level of sophistication, appropriate to his own learning and his audience's capacity for understanding the pagan literary culture that is his medium. But Clement's ornamented learning does not mean that he disregarded the cluster of Christian religious themes as a temporary and extrinsic veil for the secret truth which contradicted or nullified those themes. Thus in "Who is the Rich Man That Is Going to be Saved?" Clement's only extant sermon, his portrait of the church, built up rhetorically over several paragraphs, is one in which the rich man is part of a mutually dependent society in which offerings are made back and forth in view of the preparation for entering into the kingdom of God. All this culminates in a discussion of the incarnation and its consequences, namely the relativization or abandonment of riches in a Christian society.

The foundation of this new society, Clement thinks, is the sacrificial death of Christ. In the following quotation, the three introductory *dia touto* clauses build to the conclusion that the Word came to equalize human beings with himself. In fact, the rich man is analogous to Christ only inasmuch as he spends his wealth in imitation of the Logos; and the liturgical side of this deed is the way in which the Word himself transforms the material riches of the rich man. This makes his action, also, a material reflection of an event within the immaterial, therefore indescribable, Godhead. Clement writes:

> For this also he descended
> For this he put on man
> For this the things of man he willingly suffered—
> In order that toward our weakness, to us whom he loved, he
>   reduced himself to enlarge us to his own power.
> And about to be poured out on an altar of sacrifice and giving
>   himself as a ransom he left for us a new covenant: "My
>   love I give unto you."
> And what and how great is it? For each of us he laid down his
>   soul as an equivalent for all. This he requires of us for
>   each other. (37)

The Eucharist in the *Protreptikos*

Although Clement employed a set genre in composing the *Protreptikos*, he casts it as an appeal to join the Christian liturgy by posing to the reader a choice between participation in false rites and joining the song of Christ. This means that Clement has to criticize the bloody sacrifices of pagans at the same time that he celebrates the rites of Christians. He does this on a moral and an aesthetic level.

While this contrast between pagan and Christian liturgy is most clear in the final two chapters of the work, throughout the *Protreptikos* Clement identifies Christ as the one who sings the "celestial song" of the liturgy, instead of the songs of the mysteries. Christ, and for him Clement, here clearly function as catechists in preparation for baptism and Eucharist. In the opening chapter of the work he writes:

> Let us bring truth out of heaven above, with wisdom in all its brightness, and the holy choir of prophets, down to the holy mountain of God. Truth will shine its light to the limits, and cast its rays all around on those in darkness, and deliver men from delusion, stretching out its highest right hand, wisdom, for their salvation. And let them raise their eyes, look above, abandon Helicon and Cithaeron, and begin to live in Zion. "For out of Zion shall go forth the law, and the word of the Lord from Jerusalem" (Is.2.3): the heavenly Word, the true athlete crowned in the theater of the whole cosmos. What my Eunomos sings is not the meter of Terpander, or of Capito, or of the Phrygian, Lydian or Dorian, but the immortal meter of the new harmony which bears the Name of God—the new and Levitical song...The charm of persuasion that blends with this tune is sweet and true.

Clement here is not merely using the image of Christ as Orpheus to contrast Christian and pagan truth, or Christian and pagan ceremony. He is referring to the way in which the Word incarnate in Christ has descended to fit human beings for his liturgy. Here he alludes to the Word's creation of humanity as a "universe in miniature" and "free citizens under heaven," and to the fall of humanity that requires the Word's incarnation as man. Following upon his incarnation, humans must receive him:

> This was indicated by the dumbness of Zachariah, which awaited fruit in the person of the harbinger of Christ (John), that the Word, the light of truth, by becoming the Gospel, might break the mystical silence of prophetic enigmas.

Receiving him, Clement writes, requires ritual purification beginning with righteousness and temperance. For Clement, these dispositions allow the worshiper to enter Christ's kingdom, pictured always doubly in the *Protreptikos*, as both church and heaven.

Although Clement devotes the long middle section of the *Protreptikos* to a refutation of pagan worship and particular errors of pagan philosophy, he does not neglect the liturgical context of his discourse. Speaking directly against pagan rite, he exclaims "Cease singing, Homer!" If the pagan song leads to adulterous mingling, the Christian ritual song must drown it out, because it offends against Christ, God's image in man. Here Clement evidently has in mind the indwelling of Christ in the Christian, because he writes that Christ the inner image of God

> feels with us, feels for us. We have become a consecrated offering to God for the sake of Christ: we are the chosen generation, the royal priesthood, the holy nation, the peculiar people . . . who have learned to walk in newness of life. (4)

Here Clement employs the theme of the church, and of Christians, as temples. At this point it would be easy to say that Clement is merely alluding to the spiritualized notion of Christians as sacrifice. Indeed, at the end of chapter 9 Clement calls for unity among those who are converting to Christianity (and probably among those already Christian):

> [L]et us hasten to salvation, to *regeneration* (i.e., baptism); let we who are many hurry to be gathered into one love, according to the union of the essential unity . . . [which] becomes one symphony out of a medley of sounds and division, following one *choregos* and teacher, the Word, arriving to and resting in the same truth, and crying Abba, Father. This the true utterance of his children, God accepts with gracious welcome, the first-fruits he receives from them.

In the final three chapters of the *Protreptikos*, Clement begins to draw a sharper contrast between the shape and consequence of pagan cult and the requirements for participation in Christian worship. To readers who may be hesitating in departing from paganism he writes, "The only thing you make a subject of question is, whether God should be worshipped, and whether this wise God and Christ should be followed." Those who are going to be Christians should not be bothered by shame attaching to the name of Christian, but should "openly strip for the contest, and nobly strive in the arena of truth, since the holy Word is the Judge and the Lord of the universe has set the contest." Perhaps there is a double meaning here, and the passage should be seen as referring both to baptism, with which the *Protreptikos* is concerned, and to martyrdom, which will occupy Clement in book 4 of the *Stromateis*. Certainly baptism is meant: Clement writes, "[R]eceive the water of the word; wash, polluted ones; purify yourselves from [pagan] custom by sprinkling yourselves with the drops of truth."

But Clement also makes direct reference to the suffering of Christians, and particularly of the Christian leader who trains others. Contrasting the speech of a Christian man to the cries of birds, he writes:

> [T]he man of God, who neither croaks nor chatters, but speaks rationally and instructs with love, they persecute; and while he is inviting them to cultivate righteousness, they try without humanity to kill him, neither welcoming the grace from above nor the penalty. (10)

At the end of chapter 10 and the beginning of 11, the discourse begins to speak in a more concerted way about the pattern of salvation brought by Christ, which Clement of course characterizes as philosophy, and about the response of the catechumen to it. Here he refers to baptism as enlightenment, and the baptized as children, rejuvenated when they had "grown old in superstition." Continuing his characterization of the baptismal liturgy as a drastic contrast with pagan rites, he uses the term *ta mysteria*:

> Oh truly holy mysteries, oh stainless light! My path is lit with torches, and I can see the heavens, and God; I become holy while I am being initiated. The Lord is the hierophant, and

seals while illuminating him who is initiated...If you want,
be initiated, too, and you will join the choir along with
angels, around the unbegotten, incorruptible and only true
God, the Word of God, raising the hymn with us. This Jesus,
who is eternal, the one great High Priest of the one God and
of his Father, prays for and exhorts human beings. (12)

Clement concludes the *Protreptikos* by comparing the baptismal
procession as antitype to the type of Christ in procession into
Jerusalem, being borne by a colt who is a type of humanity. The fulfillment of both type and antitype Clement says is the heavenly
liturgy: "[Christ] directs his chariot to immortality, hurrying to
clearly fulfill, by driving now into heaven, what he shadowed forth
before by riding into Jerusalem"(12).

If the *Protreptikos* can be seen as a clarification delivered to the
newly baptized of their new condition as friends of God conducted in a
new rite, singing and being sung by Christ, then it can be seen how the
Paidagogos is a sequel to and an expansion upon the *Protreptikos*.
Clement once again approaches the Christian life from the point of
view of liturgy, and once again contrasts Christian rite with pagan rites.
However, in the *Paidagogos* Clement is giving instruction as to the kind
of action that Christians must undertake to ensure their stability in the
deepening understanding and appropriation of God. Although in the
Protreptikos Clement has little to say about Christian gnosis, in the
Paidagogos he begins to describe how Christian habits of behavior are
established precisely for the purpose of securing gnosis. He does this by
making the eucharistic celebration a model for all meals that Christians
attend, and showing how, now that Christians are in the position of
being living temples, they must exercise care with their bodies in order
not to betray the Word who dwells in the temple.

Paidagogos and Sacrifice

The *Paidagogos*, the sequel to the *Protreptikos*, no longer exhorts
its readers to depart pagan rites for Christian ones. In this book,
pagan rites as such fade into the background and disappear from view
as Clement moves his readers more centrally into the process of prac-

ticing a Christian manner of life in the midst of a city culturally pagan. He assumes that Christ the teacher accompanies his students invisibly as they participate in the culture of Alexandria, and, as any reader of the work knows, Clement lays out for new Christians a code of conduct unmatched by any other second-century Christian author for its specificity and detail.

Two things are important to note here: first, Clement is engaged in a training exercise: he is trying to work out the consequences of his students' baptism and their reception of the Eucharist prefatory to the appropriation of Christian knowledge. Second, he is trying to communicate, again, the truth expressed philosophically to those who are assumed to be at a higher stage than the audience of the *Protreptikos*. His readers are now inside the church and participants in the liturgy; but they also had to go outside the church, carrying Christ inside themselves, aware that their lives were not unendangered.

The consequences of Christian baptism, according to Clement, and the truth that Christians were beginning to learn because of it, is that Christians now participated in the divine economy. They were to "philosophize," as he puts it in book 1. But this philosophizing entailed being conformed to the presence of Christ, and, possibly, to being slain as a sacrifice for God, and for the salvation of the world. In this way, imitating the life of Christ, they were also to consider that they might well imitate his death. This is the eucharistic pattern of Clement's thought brought to term: having been drawn into the true temple by the blood of Christ, they were now in the position to stand as Christ to others, revealing the truth that he reveals. As Clement will make clear in the *Stromateis*, the Gnostic who appropriates and participates in the knowledge of truth will make it possible for others, not so advanced, to do the same—he will become their pedagogue, that is to say, their Christ. Yet this Gnostic may well do so by means of her death. And this death, in imitation of the pattern of Christ's passion, participates in his atoning sacrifice expressed both in the Eucharist and on the cross.

The rhetoric of the *Paidagogos*, again, suits a treatise that depends upon its readers' self-understanding as newly born children of the Word. Book 1 carries an extensive description of how the readers are children. Clement is most interested to gather instances of disciples being called children in biblical quotations, and combining these creates an image of Christians as human beings who have returned to simplicity and are prepared to be led by the hand by Christ as teacher. Nevertheless, Clement also uses this characterization as a description of how Christians may be martyrs: "[B]y Moses, [Christ] commands 'two young pigeons or a pair of doves to be offered for sin (Lev 15.29),' thus saying that the harmlessness and innocence and peaceable nature of these tender young birds are acceptable [as an offering] to God, and explaining that like is an expiation for like."

At the end of *Paedagogos* 1.5, in the middle of another demonstration of exactly how Christians might be called "children," Clement develops a remarkable spiritual interpretation of Genesis 26:8f., in which "Abimelech king of the Philistines looked out of a window and saw Isaac fondling Rebecca his wife." The principle of his interpretation is the incarnation of Christ, and he understands the patriarch and his wife to signify "[t]he Father of the universe [who] cherishes affection toward those who have fled to him." The mutual love of God and man is an erotic one here, and it is God's love that assists Christians in endurance. Clement also gives an alternate explanation, one corresponding to the spiritual and ecclesiastical interpretation of the Song of Songs in Origen and later exegetes: the signification of the text could also mean

> our rejoicing for salvation as Isaac, he also, delivered from death, laughed, sporting and rejoicing with his spouse, who was the type of the helper of our salvation ... and the witness of those that have endured to the end [i.e., martyrs] and the rejoicing on their account, is the mystic love, and the salvation accompanied with sober solace, which brings help to us.

But Abimelech is Christ too: "[T]he King who beholds our laughter from above, looking through the window, looks at the thanksgiving, the blessing, the rejoicing, the gladness, and moreover the endurance which works together with them and their embrace." In other words, Christ is lover and spouse of the church, but also the king of the universe. Next, Clement ties the image of Isaac, married and sporting with his wife, to that of Isaac bound as a child in sacrifice by Abraham. This passage shows how the spouse of the church, Christ, is also sacrificed for her:

And where, then, was the door by which the Lord showed himself? The flesh by which he was manifested. He is Isaac [also]... who is a type of the Lord, a child as a son for he was the son of Abraham, as Christ the Son of God, and a sacrifice as the Lord, but he was not immolated as the Lord. Isaac only bore the wood of the sacrifice, as did the Lord the wood of the cross. And he laughed mystically, prophesying that the Lord would fill us with joy, who have been redeemed from corruption by the blood of the Lord. Isaac did everything but suffer, as was right, yielding the precedence in suffering to the Word. Furthermore there is a hint of the divinity of the Lord in his not being slain. For Jesus rose again after his burial, having suffered no harm, like Isaac released from being sacrificed.

The entire *Paidagogos* is devoted to showing how the Christian must act after being released from corruption by entering the church. Understanding the Christian as a body-and-soul in need of nourishment for her or his obedience to Christ the teacher, Clement allows his entire discussion of the Eucharist as physical and spiritual food to be guided by Exodus 3:8 with its reference to the land of promise as a land flowing with milk and honey, through which he understands Paul's distinction in 1 Corinthians 3:2 between milk and meat. According to Clement, Paul is calling himself a wet nurse:

As nurses nourish newborn children on milk, so do I also by the Word, the milk of Christ, instilling into you spiritual nutriment. Thus, then, the milk that is perfect is perfect nourishment, and brings to that consummation which cannot cease; that is why also the same milk and honey were promised in the [eternal] rest.

The Word of nourishment, however, is also the Eucharist; Clement quotes here John 6:55, "My blood is true drink." Paul, says Clement, understands that "I have given you milk to drink" means "the knowledge of the truth, the perfect gladness in the Word, who is the milk." And what follows next, "not meat, for you were not able," may indicate the clear revelation in the future world, "Like food, face to face." For the present life, however, Christ's milk is also his blood,

because both are the Word. The blood of Abel witnesses that the
blood is the Word, "the righteous interceding with God." Yet Christ
is also portrayed as a woman and a mother, and here perhaps Clement
has in mind the way in which Christ also bears children through the
church and its baptism:

> For if we have been regenerated to Christ, he who has regen-
> erated us nourishes us with his own milk the Word; for it is
> fitting that the one who is procreated should immediately sup-
> ply nutrition to the child. And as the regeneration was spiri-
> tual, so also was the nutrition of man spiritual. In all respects,
> therefore, and in everything, we are brought into union with
> Christ, into kinship through his blood, by which we are
> redeemed, and into sympathy, because of the nourishment
> which flows from the Word, and into immortality, through his
> guidance...The same blood and milk of the Lord is therefore
> the symbol of the Lord's passion and teaching. (4)

For Clement, as for other early Christian authors, the term "symbol"
was a precise word that indicated not merely a shorthand reference to
a larger truth, but rather an object, person, or act that mediated, and
participated in, the truth that it indicated. Only for this reason would
it be logical to exclude anyone from the Eucharist for other than
external, disciplinary reasons; when Clement calls the Eucharist "the
medicine of immortality," he, like Ignatius, means that it is what it
signifies, and also that in it, because of the indwelling of Christ, is the
power to condemn as well as to bless.

For this reason, Clement spends the rest of the *Paidagogos* in
demonstrating what kind of eating, drinking, and sexual coupling the
baptized Christian must avoid. And in Clement's highly allusive way,
it is quite clear that it is the Eucharist as rite and the eucharistic word
as immanent in the Christian that forbids him from any but the most
sober and watchful attendance at non-Christian feasts. Although
Christ turned water into wine at Cana, he does not allow drunken-
ness. Rather,

> He gave life to the watery element of the meaning of the
> law, filling with His blood the doer of it who is of Adam,

that is, the whole world; supplying piety with drink from the vine of truth, the mixture of the old law and of the new word, ordered to the fulfillment of the predestined time. The Scripture has thus named wine the symbol of the sacred blood...(2.2)

Clement takes up this theme again at the end of the chapter, showing that Christ himself drank wine and himself imparted all the symbolic meanings possessed by the drink. Clement even adds a humorous note in favor of moderate wine-drinking, though not departing from his counsel that a Christian could smile but not snicker or guffaw—by adding that his readers should "strongly maintain against the Encratites" that Christ referred to himself as "a glutton and a wine-bibber, and a friend of tavern-keepers" (Matt 11:19).

Clement makes a similar connection between Christian rite and sumptuous pagan meals throughout the rest of his instructions in the *Paidagogos*. Christians adhering to Christian practice had to adopt a modesty befitting the righteousness of their Lord when he ate and drank—with his disciples and his followers, but most importantly in the Last Supper. Because "the humble God, and Lord of the universe...did not bring down a silver footbath from heaven," but ate from a common bowl, lying on the ground, and washed their feet.

The use of scented ointment at banquets should be understood and used discerningly, because of the associations of oil with the life and passion of Christ. The oil "that the woman brought to the mystical supper" in Matthew 26:7 may have been "a symbol of the Lord's teaching, and of his suffering. For the feet anointed with fragrant ointment mean divine instruction traveling and becoming known to the ends of the earth." The oil was a symbol of his passion, Clement wrote, for two reasons: first, because oil (*elaion*) points to the word mercy (*eleos*), and second, because the sweet smell of oil is reminiscent of the Lord's sacrifice. "If, then, we say that the Lord, the great High Priest, offers to God the incense of sweet fragrance, we should not imagine that this is a sacrifice and sweet fragrance of incense," i.e., incense offered at a pagan altar, "but understand it to mean that the Lord lays the acceptable offering of love, the spiritual fragrance, on the altar" (2.8).

A final example of Clement's symbolic interpretation of pagan banquets through the lens of the Eucharist comes in his discussion (in

Paidagogos 2.9) of the use of crowns. Here Clement can deploy the New Testament symbol of the crown as *athlon*—as a prize for Christians who have suffered for Christ and have a heavenly crown awaiting them. Against the wearing of flowery garlands on the head, Clement writes, "It would be irrational for us, who have heard that the Lord was crowned with thorns, to crown ourselves with flowers, insulting thus the sacred passion of the Lord." Two lines of interpretation contribute to Clement's understanding of the crown. The first is a negative one: like those who crucified Christ, those who wear garlands wear them to their own condemnation. Although Clement does not often mention the rejection of Israel—in fact, he generally treats the incarnation as an extension and intensification of the covenant with Israel—in this passage Clement makes one of the relatively few references to the rejection of Christ by Israel, which placed a crown of thorns on Jesus' head; they are

> the people which erred, which was not circumcised in understanding, whose darkness was not enlightened, which knew not God, denied the Lord, forfeited the place of the true Israel, persecuted God, hoped to reduce the Word to disgrace; and Him whom they crucified as a malefactor they crowned as king.

In other words, Christ's passion turns the tables on those who refuse to acknowledge him as Lord. The crown refers also to those who follow Christ in martyrdom. Christ's diadem defends "those who make up the church. This crown is the flower of those who have believed in the glorified one, but covers with blood and chastises the unbelievers." It also symbolizes Christ's atonement for sins and the ensuing freedom.

But, Clement adds, "I can also show you another mystic meaning." The crown then becomes a cosmic symbol, a kind of trope for the beginning and end of time. He considers the burning bush to have foreshadowed Christ's crown of thorns, thus locating it at the beginning of the history of salvation, and he considers the crown of thorns also to be the path of return to the Father.

> For when the Omnipotent Lord of the universe began to give the law by the Word, and wanted his power to be displayed to

Moses, a divine vision of light that had assumed a shape was shown to him in the burning bush, a thorny plant. But when the Word concluded giving the law and ended his abiding with men (*epidemia*), the Lord was again mystically crowned with thorns.

He was shown in both ways, Clement adds, so that he could show that the "work of one power" lay behind all of it, since he is one Son of one Father, "who is truly one, the beginning and the end of time."

The *Paidagogos* concludes with a summary of the laws governing the Christian life. Notably, this summary gives another description of Christ as ruler of the universe by listing all the laws given in the Old Covenant and those given by Christ himself, ending with an image of Christ as the tamer of wild beasts and human beings. Clement tells his readers: "[N]ow...it is time for me to cease instructing, and for you to listen to the Teacher; he, receiving you who have been trained in excellent discipline, will teach you the oracles [i.e., the scriptures]." These oracles, hidden or ambiguous meanings of scripture, belong to the *gnostikos* to interpret. Clement conceives of the elementary teaching he has concluded as a song, just as he did in the *Protreptikos*. Such a song is a song of good counsel, wisdom, knowledge, and propitiation (3.12). In fact, Clement ends the treatise by appending his own song, a poetic list of Christ's titles, which at the end recalls Christ's image as a mother whose breasts yield "rational food" for Christians. Clement wrote in the first chapter of the work that it was a discourse regarding practice in order to provide training for *theoria*, or contemplation; but it is interesting that the discourse ends in a doxology, which links it to the liturgical context of the *Protreptikos*.

Eucharistic Thought in the *Stromateis*: The Gnostic Martyr

The *Stromateis*, cast in the form of a miscellany, takes a more oblique view of the Eucharist, but nonetheless it draws on the previous two works to show how the life of the Gnostic can be seen as sacramental: the Gnostic is prepared to be a martyr, and is also like the high priest in entering the heavenly tabernacle, and thus offers two sacrifices under each aspect.

In the *Paidagogos*, Clement had argued extensively that Christian men and women were directed by the Word to "philosophize," meaning to train themselves in practice that prepared them to receive knowledge. Clement returns to this matter in the first book of the *Stromateis*, further elaborating how the Christian teacher was to use philosophy to prune the vine of scripture. He "protects the faith against an assault," that is, responds to attacks from pagans and heretical Christians; and distinguishes what is useful from what is deceptive in philosophy. Clement cites as his authority Christ's temptation after his baptism. "How useful it is to distinguish expressions which are ambiguous, and which are used synonymously in the testaments. For the Lord, at the time of his temptation, cleverly matched the devil by an ambiguous expression" (1.9). The ability to distinguish ambiguous expressions and to sift philosophy Clement puts squarely in a Eucharist context: "The Savior, taking the bread, first spoke and blessed. Then breaking the bread, he offered it, that we might eat it, according to reason, and that knowing the Scriptures we might walk with obedience" (2.10). The rest of the first book Clement devotes to describing Greek philosophy and showing how the revelation to Moses was its antecedent. But in the second book, Clement begins his discussion of the true Gnostic, as distinguished from Valentinians who wrongly appropriate the term.

Here, and throughout the rest of the *Stromateis*, Clement sometimes says that the Gnostic's knowledge is directed, not to his own salvation primarily, but to the instruction and salvation of those in the church. A long passage shows their destiny. Having insisted that faith is the beginning of knowledge, Clement alludes to Zeno in acknowledging that a martyr's death is the most effective demonstration of philosophy:

> But we have exhibited before our eyes every day, abundant sources of martyrs who are burned, impaled, beheaded. All these fear inspired, by the law—leading as a pedagogue to Christ, trained so as to manifest their piety by their blood. "God stood in the congregation of the gods; He judges in the

midst of the gods" (Ps. 132:1). Who are they? Those who are superior to pleasure, who rise above the passions, who know what they do—the Gnostics, who are greater than the world.

Like Christ's, martyrs' deaths have an epideictic purpose. But, as others have noted, Clement's discussion of martyrdom in the fourth book of the *Stromateis* threads its way between the views of opponents who see little value in martyrdom and certainly did not regard it as a redemptive sacrifice, and those who were all too enthusiastic about it. Therefore, Clement does not applaud or encourage martyrdom to the degree that Tertullian or Origen did, nor does he connect it with Christ's passion as obviously. However, traces of a similar approach are easily visible. At the beginning of his discussion of the Gnostic martyr, Clement writes:

> With good courage, then, he goes to the Lord, his friend, for whom he voluntarily gave his body, and, as his judges hoped, his soul, hearing from our Savior the words of poetry, "dear brother," because of the similarity of his life. We call martyrdom perfection, not because the man comes to the end of his life as others do, but because he has exhibited the perfect work of love. (4.4)

This "perfect work of love," however, has already been described by Clement as the Word's death for the world; and given the martyr's imitation of Christ, and the beneficence Clement ascribes to him elsewhere, it is unlikely that martyrdom was not, in his view, salvific as well as epideictic. And this salvation is not only for himself; it benefits others, too.

Perfection, says Clement comes "when the Gnostic martyr has shown the perfect work, and rightly exhibited it, and having shed his blood with thanksgiving, has yielded up the spirit: blessed then will he be, and truly proclaimed perfect." The parallels Clement draws here between Christ's Last Supper and crucifixion, and the death of the martyr, can hardly be missed. Yet finally the Gnostic's life passes beyond a desire for salvation for himself or others, and broadens beyond its likeness to the passion and ascension of Christ. Clement clearly states that if the Gnostic had to choose between salvation and truth, he would choose truth, because in adhering to truth he becomes like God. Clement does not abandon, here, the comparison between the Gnostic and the true priesthood, and he makes the Gnostic martyr's priesthood his asceticism and knowledge:

> The perfect propitiation is that propitious faith in the Gospel which is by the law and the prophets, and the purity which displays itself in obedience in everything, along with the abandonment of the things pertaining to the world, ordering a grateful surrender of the tabernacle, which results from the enjoyment of the soul. (4.25)

Once again, this priesthood of the Gnostic is connected to the priesthood of Christ foreshadowed by Melchizedek, "priest of the most high God, who gave bread and wine, furnishing consecrated food for a type of the Eucharist" (4.25). And in book 7 of the *Stromateis*, where Clement again turns to a description of the Gnostic, the author states that although the Gnostic prays at all hours, not just on the third, sixth, and ninth, he also intercedes for others "as the Lord prayed, giving thanks for the completion of his service; so the Gnostic prays [with] thanksgiving, and petition for the conversion of those near us … that as many as possible might come to knowledge" (7.7).

What Clement has done, in the *Stromateis*, is to consider the passion of the martyr and the priesthood of the Lord, as well as the Eucharist itself, from the angle of the incorporeal world. From that angle, symbols that were closely connected with the realities toward which they point look less vivid and correspond less exactly to their realities than they did when Clement was, in the *Protreptikos* and *Paidagogos*, looking directly into and through them toward the realities. That is why, I think, Clement can in *Stromateis* 5.11 reinterpret baptism and its consequent illumination as a sacrifice that yields immediately to that mental stability possessed by the Gnostic. He writes there:

> [T]he sacrifice which is acceptable to God is unswerving abstraction from the body and its passions. This is the really true piety… [Moses] commands holocausts to be skinned and

divided into parts (Lev 1.6). For the Gnostic soul must be consecrated to the light, stripped of the material hides, without bodily frivolousness and passions...

It is in this context that Clement "spiritualizes" the interpretation of Old Testament sacrifices and is often said to "spiritualize" the sacrifice that constitutes the Eucharist.

Clement's understanding of the Eucharist, like his interpretation of the Christian Gnostic as martyr, shifts, then, depending upon his angle of vision. On the one hand, in the Excerpts from Theodotus, Clement contradicted the view that regarded the Eucharist as an empty ritual. He wrote:

The Son is the living bread that was given by the Father to those who wish to eat. "And my flesh is the bread which I will give," he says, that is, to him whose flesh is nourished by the Eucharist, or better still, the flesh is his body, "which is the church," "heavenly bread," a blessed assembly.

But in *Stromateis* 5.10 Clement wrote:

The flesh and blood of the Word is the comprehension of the divine power and essence. "Taste and see that the Lord is Christ," it is said. For so he gives from himself to those who receive such food in a more spiritual manner...For the knowledge of the divine essence is the meat and drink of the divine Word...

Here the ritual of the Eucharist, so important in the *Protreptikos* as the entry into salvation, and in the *Paidagogos* as the pattern of Christian life, becomes transparent to what it itself communicates—the knowledge given in the breaking of bread. After Clement's work, such a dual interpretation of the Eucharist becomes common among early Christian authors. It is understood both as atoning sacrifice and as the sacrifice that, participating in the one sufficient sacrifice of Christ, replaces the sacrifices of the old covenant, refutes pagan sacrifice, and leads to the illumination outshining both philosophy and law.

Notes

1. For general studies of the developing understanding of the Eucharist, see among others L. Bouyer, *Eucharist* (Notre Dame: Notre Dame, 1968); C. O. Buchanan, ed., *Essays on Eucharistic Sacrifice in the Early Church* (Bramcote, Notts.: Grove Books, 1984); R. Daly, *The Origins of the Christian Doctrine of Sacrifice* (Philadelphia: Fortress Press, 1978); J. Daniélou, *The Bible and the Liturgy* (Notre Dame: Notre Dame, 1956); J. Jeremias, *The Eucharistic Words of Jesus* (New York: Scribner, 1966), H. J. Schulz, *The Byzantine Liturgy* (New York: Pueblo, 1986); and E. Mazza, *The Celebration of the Eucharist* (Collegeville, Minn.: Liturgical Press, 1999). See also E. Osborn, "Clement of Alexandria: A Review of Research, 1958–1982," *Second Century* 3 (1983): 219–244.

2. For the origins of this approach in Hellenistic Jewish thought, see J. Laporte, *La doctrine eucharistique chez Philon d'Alexandrie* (Paris: Beauchesne, 1972).

3. A survey of the scholarly literature on Clement of Alexandria yields the striking result that there are few general studies of his thought. Rather, scholars have concentrated upon his use of philosophy, in particular his use of middle Platonism and Aristotelianism; his arguments against the Gnostics; and his use of Philo. Perhaps because Clement quotes earlier sources so frequently, he has not received the serious study he deserves as a Christian thinker. Classic studies are: W. Voelker, *Der wahre Gnostiker nach Clemens Alexandrinus* (Leipzig, 1952); E. Osborn, *The Philosophy of Clement of Alexandria* (Cambridge: The University Press, 1957); S. Lilla, *Clement of Alexandria: A Study in Christian Platonism and Gnosticism* (London: Oxford University Press, 1971); E. A. Clark, *Clement's Use of Aristotle: The Aristotelian Contribution to Clement of Alexandria's Refutation of Gnosticism* (New York: Edwin Mellen Press, 1977); A. Van den Hoek, *Clement of Alexandria and His Use of Philo in the Stromateis* (Leiden, New York: E. J. Brill, 1988); R. Mortley, *Connaissance religieuse et hermeneutique chez Clément d'Alexandrie* (Leiden, New York: E. J. Brill, 1973). More recently, there has been an examination of the matter of teaching authority in Clement's thought: D. K. Buell, *Making Christians: Clement of Alexandria and the Rhetoric of Legitimacy* (Princeton, N.J.: Princeton University Press, 1999).

4. On the matter of Clement's treatment of the Eucharist, see A. Mehat, "Clement of Alexandria," in *The Eucharist of the Early Christians*, ed. W. Rordorf (New York: Pueblo Pub. Co., 1978), 99–131.

5. The standard critical edition of Clement is that of O. Staehlin, ed., *Die griechischen christlichen Schriftsteller*, vols. 12, 15, 17, and 52 (Leipzig: J. C. Hinrichs, 1905–1980). Some of his writings have been published in *Sources Chrétiennes* (Paris, 1940–); see also M. Marcovich, ed., *Clementis Alexandrini Protrepticus* (Leiden, New York: E. J. Brill, 1995). The standard English translation is in the *Ante-Nicene Fathers*, vol. 2, ed. W. Wilson; reprinted (Peabody, Mass.: Hendrickson, 1995); see also R. Casey, ed., *Excerpta ex Theodoto of Clement of Alexandria* (London: Christophers, 1934).

6. A. Van den Hoek, "Clement of Alexandria on Martyrdom," *Studia Patristica* 26 (1993): 324–341, and A. H. C. Van Eijk, "The Gospel of Philip and Clement of Alexandria: Gnostic and Ecclesiastical Theology on the Resurrection and the Eucharist," *Vigiliae Christianae* 25 (1971): 94–120.

7. A. Schmemann, *For the Life of the World: Sacraments and Orthodoxy* (Crestwood, N.Y.: St. Vladimir's Seminary Press, 1973), 26. See also his *The Eucharist: Sacrament of the Kingdom* (Crestwood, N.Y.: St. Vladimir's Seminary Press, 2000).

8. J. Meyendorff, *Byzantine Theology: Historical Trends and Doctrinal Themes* (New York: Fordham University Press, 1974), 56. Meyendorff names Gregory of Nyssa in the *Great Catechetical Oration* as well as Basil of Caesarea in his *Letter 93* as sources for fourth-century teaching on the Eucharist.

9. Vasileios of Stavronikita, *Hymn of Entry: Liturgy and Life in the Orthodox Church* (Crestwood, N.Y.: St. Vladimir's Seminary Press, 1984), 29.

10. See the standard studies of Clement's education and position in E. de Faye, *Clément d'Alexandrie* (Paris: E. Leroux, 1896); C. Mondesert, *Clément d'Alexandrie, Introduction à l'étude de sa pensée religieuse à partir de l'Ecriture* (Paris, Aubier: Editions Montaigne, 1944); and A. Méhat, *Etude sur les Stromates de Clément d'Alexandrie* (Paris: Editions du Seuil, 1966); and for the school of Alexandria, A. Knauber, "Katechetenschule oder Schulkatechumenat," *Trierer theologische Zeitschrift* 60 (1951): 213–266.

The Eucharist as Sacrifice
according to Clement of Alexandria

BY BRIAN DALEY

Surprise can often be the first step in the process of learning
something new. I must confess that I was a little surprised, as I suspect many of us were, to discover that Professor Robin Darling
Young had chosen to make her contribution to this conference, under
the general heading of the "Eucharist in the Greek Fathers," a reflection on the role of the Eucharist in the theology of Clement of
Alexandria. Most handbooks on the history of doctrine do not spill
much ink over the eucharistic theology of Clement; aside from a few
references to the liturgical "sacrifice" of the Christian community,
which Clement tends to interpret as a symbol of the more sublime
and lasting nourishment of spiritual contemplation, his works offer us
frustratingly few clear affirmations of the importance of what we
would think of as eucharistic liturgy in the Christian life, and even
fewer hints of what that liturgy might have looked like in late second-
century Alexandria. His identification of "the actual flesh and blood
of the Logos" with the Christian's "contemplative understanding of
the divine power and the divine essence," in *Stromateis* V, 66, struck
the modern Catholic scholar Johannes Betz as nothing less than "a
downgrading of the liturgical celebration of the Lord's Supper"—a
"spiritualization" that in Betz's view "represents the real Heleniza-
tion of the sacrament."[1] Most historians of the early church, in fact,

92

tend to assume that neither Clement nor his fellow Alexandrian Origen had much time for sacraments in their version of the Christian life; the church certainly gathered regularly for worship and used rites that by now were both traditional and distinctively Christian, but for these two Alexandrian intellectuals, it is often argued, sacraments and external rituals were beginner's fare, food for spiritual children. The intellectually mature, the spiritually sophisticated, encountered God primarily in the head and in the heart, rather than at the font or the table.

The central contribution of Professor Young's fascinating paper, I think, is to move us beyond this over-simple distinction, and to show us, by means of Clement's elusive but challenging way of speaking of the Eucharist, a wider context for understanding the sacramental theology of at least one major and influential strand of patristic thought, perhaps even an entry into a fruitful way of conceiving of the sacraments ourselves. Drawing on the writings on Eucharist and liturgy of a number of twentieth-century Orthodox theologians—writers such as Pavel Florensky, Alexander Schmemann, and the Athonite Abbot Vasileios—Professor Young is suggesting, it seems to me, that the approach to the Eucharist as a mystery of revelation, an encounter with the divine beauty that transforms the mind and ravishes the heart, while uniting the believer personally with the Word of God who became flesh and who always touches us through fleshly things, which is the approach that Clement first articulated for the theological tradition, may well be more fruitful and less divisive as a way of understanding Christ's eucharistic presence than the opposing categories of symbol and reality that have preoccupied Western discussions since Carolingian times. As a thoroughly ecclesiastical theologian who (in Professor Young's phrase) was also "the first to express fully a philosophical Christian mysticism shaped by the desire for union with Christ through the Christian mysteries,"[2] Clement understood both the sacraments of the church and the incarnation of the Logos as the self-communication of God, a gift that took shape both in revelation to the mind and in the sacrificial offering of humanity to God that reconciled our race, by God's redeeming initiative, to its creator. Stressing the continuity between the transformation of human reality in the incarnation and the continuing, analogous transformation of the eucharistic elements, both by the power of the Holy

Spirit, Clement and the Greek fathers after him came to agree, as Professor Young puts it,

> that the Eucharist is both the atoning sacrifice of Christ and the church's own cultic sacrifice. In addition, they agree in varying degrees that the liturgy of the Eucharist is itself a part of the path of intellection by which the rational creature reorients himself to the intelligible world of supreme beauty, the invisible world of the Trinity.[3]

Moment of revelation as well as cultic offering, an instrument of gnosis that both purifies the soul and reunites it to God, the Eucharist was seen by this early Greek tradition, in Professor Young's view, as "not only a founding sacrifice, but also a mystery that communicates understanding." The ultimate vision of these authors, beginning with Clement, "is of a city of God founded upon the sacrifice of Christ, a city in which citizens have real understanding growing from serious personal discipline. The witnesses to this city of peace are the martyrs, according to second- and third-century authors."[4] Worship, witness unto death, the understanding that unites and transforms in response to scriptural revelation, incarnation, and ultimately the atoning sacrifice of the Son of God: this is the rhythm of divine gift and human response Professor Young detects as the underlying structure of faith that for Clement of Alexandria is also the foundation of eucharistic theology.

In my judgment, Professor Young is on to something centrally important about early Greek theology here. What she is on to is an aspect of the early Greek fathers' way of conceiving the created world and the presence in it of the redeeming God that may offer even to us, in the midst of our own uncertainties about God's knowability and accessibility, new avenues of understanding the role worship plays in our lives and new chances for moving beyond the polemical questions on eucharistic reality that have divided Christians since the Reformation. My only reservation is that her claims about Clement's influence, as stated here, may need nuancing. Without wanting to rewrite her paper, let alone to sketch out the history of later Greek patristic thought on the Eucharist, let me simply add a few suggestions.

The first and most obvious heir to Clement's way of thinking about the Eucharist is Origen, his younger contemporary from Alexandria. In Origen, it seems to me, one sees more clearly what Clement's way of referring to traditional forms of liturgy is meant to do: not to devaluate them but to recontextualize them in what he understood to be the real divine strategy for healing humanity—the contemplative enlightenment of the mind and the moral transformation of the heart. In Origen's works, the main change of emphasis is his continual insistence that the gnosis which is redeemed humanity's real food is the understanding of the message of salvation conveyed, and partially hidden, in the text of scripture. Just as the real "priest" of the new law is the person who can "cut up" the text of difficult biblical passages and lay them open on the church's altar for the nourishment of the people,[5] so the food of the Christian people, the true "bread of life," is for Origen above all the text of scripture understood in its deepest meaning as revealing the saving mystery of Christ. Origen puts this theme boldly in a well-known passage from his "Serial" Commentary on Matthew, in which he interprets Jesus' words of eucharistic institution at the Last Supper:

> For God the Word did not say that that visible bread, which he was holding in his hands, was his body, but rather the word in whose mystical celebration (*mysterio*) that bread was to be broken. Nor did he say that visible drink was his blood, but the word, in whose mystical celebration of that drink was to be poured. For what else can the "body" or the "blood" of God the Word be, but the word that nourishes and the Word that "gladdens the heart" (see Ps. 104.15)?[6]

Numerous other passages, however, make it clear that Origen is not so much intending to substitute a "spiritual" or figural understanding of the eucharistic food and drink for the more "realistic" understanding that seems to have been common in the Caesarean church, as to open his reader's eyes to what he considers the most fundamental kind of "real presence of Christ" in the community of faith, his life-giving presence in the word of scripture, and of the liturgy in which that scripture is proclaimed. In his Sixteenth Homily on Numbers, for instance, Origen comments on a verse of Balaam's canticle, "He will not sleep until he consumes his prey, and drinks the blood of the wounded," as a reference to the double "feeding" that takes place in the eucharistic gathering:

> For we are said to "drink the blood of Christ" not only in the celebration of the sacrament, but also when we receive his words, in which life is present; just as he says, "the words which I have spoken are spirit and life" (John 6:63)...So also when we read the words of the Apostles and draw life from them, we "drink the blood of the wounded."[7]

In other homiletic passages, Origen insists that his hearers should show at least the same reverence in hearing every crumb and droplet of the scripture that they show in receiving the eucharistic food,[8] or that they should show the same care to purify their spiritual "garments" for the banquet of the word that they do in preparing to "eat of the flesh of the Lamb."[9] His own interests, however, seem to be most sharply focused on the spiritual "garments" for the banquet of the Word.[10]

Later Greek theologians assimilate the tradition of Clement and Origen in a variety of ways. The fourth- and fifth-century biblical interpreters of the Antiochene school, for instance, always concerned to draw a clear line between God's transcendent being and the historical, materially circumscribed order in which we live, tend to speak of the Eucharist and the other sacraments largely in typological terms, as a "memorial" of the sacrifice of Christ offered once on the cross and as a "kind of image of the heavenly liturgy" which Christ continues to offer on our behalf in heaven.[11] Theodore of Mopsuestia went so far as to connect various elements in the liturgy with people and events in the gospel passion narratives,[12] and to see the eucharistic meal as a type of the fullness of salvation that still lies ahead, for the Christian, in the resurrection.[13] Pseudo-Dionysius's discussion of the Eucharist, in his Ecclesiastical Hierarchy, treats the central prayer and actions of the eucharistic liturgy, including the narrative of institution and the sharing of the elements with those present, as primarily a revelation of the descent of the Word from the divine unity into our own fractured world, in order to draw us into a share of the divine life.

> By bringing Jesus Christ before our eyes in this way (Diony-
> sius writes), he depicts in sensible fashion and in images the
> One who is the life of our soul, and who came out of the hid-
> denness of divinity for love of man... He came to our divided
> condition without any departure from his essential unity and
> called the human race to association with himself and his own
> good gifts out of his beneficent love for man, provided we
> unite ourselves to his most divine life by an assimilation to it
> according to our ability. Thus we should become truly perfect
> sharers in God and divine things.[14]

For Dionysius, the main function of all liturgy is to reveal a communication of transcendent life that restores intellectual creatures to
their rightful place in an ordered universe; although that communication has already been set in place by the coming of the Word into the
world, its revelation in the Christian mysteries is a key step in our
coming to share the rhythm of this gift of divine life.

Following, by his own admission, in the direction of Dionysius's
interpretation, a century and a half later Maximus Confessor's dense
little treatise, "The Church's Mystagogy," undertakes a figural reading of all the physical and verbal elements of the eucharistic liturgy—
the church building, the scriptures, the assembled congregation, the
ministers, all the prayers and gestures of worship—to discover there
an image of the interior process of transformation in the Holy Spirit
that is the heart of human salvation: a transformation from unbelief
to faith and growing knowledge, from sin and passion to virtue, from
mortality to unending life, which is already under way.

> For we believe that in this present life we already have a share
> in these gifts of the Holy Spirit through the love that is in faith,
> and in the future age, after we have kept the commandments to
> the best of our ability we believe that we shall have a share in
> them in very truth in their concrete reality... Then we shall
> pass from the grace which is in faith to the grace of vision,
> when our God and Savior Jesus Christ will indeed transform us
> into himself by taking away from us the marks of corruption
> and will bestow on us the original mysteries which have been
> represented for us through sensible symbols here below.[15]

Although Dionysius and Maximus are much more inclined than either Clement or Origen were to see the sacraments, especially the Eucharist, as a privileged channel of the transforming life of God to those who receive them in faith, it is still the revelatory aspect of the mysteries, their ability to represent God's creative and saving activity among us in material terms, which dominates these two authors' understanding of sacramental reality.

Another branch of this same tradition of eucharistic interpretation, less explicitly typological but no less focused on the Eucharist's place within the wider contours of the story of salvation in Christ, appears in the writings of Gregory of Nyssa and Cyril of Alexandria at the turn of the fourth and fifth centuries. In many of his works, Gregory of Nyssa emphasizes that change is a fundamental quality of all creatures, and that growth or change toward the good, which is God, is the underlying dynamism of redeemed human life.[16] Gregory's Christology centers on his argument that the transformation God's grace must accomplish in each of us—a transformation from passion and ignorance to virtue and knowledge in this life, which will ultimately result in the transformation of our whole composite nature at the resurrection of the dead—has already been accomplished in the person of the Incarnate Word,[17] and flows from him into us through the sacramental and kergymatic life of the church. In his most extended discussion of the place of the liturgy in this process, toward the end of his Catechetical Discourse, Gregory argues that along with the shape of the cross and the visible ascent of the risen Christ, the "washing" of baptism and the food of the Eucharist are visible things that communicate to the believer the deeper, invisible reality of redemption and transformation.[18] It is important to note that Gregory explains the efficacy of baptism and of the Eucharist in slightly different ways: baptism involves us in the death and resurrection of Christ by the mimetic sign of our descending into water and emerging again;[19] the eucharistic food, on the other hand, which has become "the body of God the Word" by the transforming invocation of the words of institution, achieves in our own body the same life-giving union with the Savior that faith works in the soul.[20] Yet both mysteries, as Gregory understands them, reveal in a material way what they achieve by grace, and so point to a much larger process of the transfiguration of human creatures beyond the limitations of material reality. The meaning of both sacraments is the single meaning of the gospel: that God the Word has entered the world of fallen humanity to communicate an incorruptible life which is essentially an ever-growing share in the inconceivable goodness and life of God.

Like Gregory, Cyril of Alexandria also emphasizes the physical bodily presence of the Incarnate Word of God in the eucharistic bread and wine, to a degree that Clement and Origen might have found excessive. In all his writing—even before the eruption of his controversy with Nestorius over the unity of Christ's person—Cyril constantly stresses the life-giving, embodied presence of the Word in the human world as the source of human salvation. In the Commentary on John, for instance, which seems to have been completed before the Nestorian controversy, Cyril explains Jesus' eucharistic words in the sixth chapter as a promise of renewal—of a "transformation of our elementary structure" (*metastoicheiosis*) through physical contact with the body of the Incarnate God. When Jesus raised the dead during his earthly ministry, Cyril observes,

> the Savior can be seen as active not simply in his words, in his Godlike commands, but he was also eager to use his holy flesh as a kind of co-worker: mainly for this purpose, to show that it was able to give life, and that it had already become one with him. For it was certainly his own body—not something different from himself.[21]

The implications for Cyril's eucharistic theology are clear: "If what was corruptible was made to live simply by a touch of the holy flesh, how can we fail to profit still more richly from that life-giving holy bread (*eulogia*), when we even make it our food?"[22] The act of eating and drinking the bread and wine that Jesus, in the sixth chapter of John, refers to as his flesh and blood actually mingles his holy and life-giving flesh with our own. Alluding to Paul's metaphor of leaven in the dough in 1 Corinthians 5:6, Cyril argues:

> So the smallest portion of the Eucharistic bread (*eulogia*) leavens our entire body with itself, and fills it with its own energy; and so Christ comes to be in us, and we in Christ. For it is

true to say that the yeast is in the whole mass of dough, and the dough—to the same degree—comes to be in the whole measure of yeast. Here you have, in the simplest terms, the meaning of Jesus' words![23]

In Cyril's view, this understanding of the immediate presence of Jesus in the eucharistic species as healer and life-giver is not simply the conclusion of a process of theological reflection, but rather part of the immediate, primary contact the Savior makes with the human mind and heart. Jesus does not explain, in John 6, how it is that he gives human beings his flesh to eat, Cyril insists; "he calls them to see the necessity of believing before making that investigation."[24]

For faith had first to take root in them, and then an understanding of the things they did not grasp could be brought into play; investigation was not seen as anterior to faith.[25]

For Cyril, too, as for Clement and Origen, the Eucharist was the door to a wider understanding of the way Christ saves and transforms the human person.

These scattered observations about Greek theologians after Clement hardly suffice to sketch out a coherent tradition of theological reflection on the Christian Eucharist in the patristic era. It may be enough to show traces, however, of a kind of continuous trajectory of eucharistic interpretation that makes its first appearance, as Professor Young has argued in her paper, in Clement's allusive, often enigmatic philosophizing about the life of Christian faith. In conclusion, I would like to suggest at least a few salient features of this common theological thread.

These early Greek writers' approach to the Eucharist, for all the differences among them, represents what Professor Young here calls a "mystagogical" way. In other words, they tend to think of the Eucharist not so much in specifically ontological or biblical terms (even if there is usually an implied ontology and a clear reliance on biblical texts), but rather as an integral part of the Christian community's progressive integration into the all-encompassing mystery of salvation in Christ.

This salvation in Christ is usually understood by Greek patristic writers in terms of human participation, by God's gift, in the inner life and relationships of the triune God—a participation that gradually transforms the whole human person, body and spirit, into a radiant image of the risen Christ.

Participation in the life of God, for the Greek patristic tradition, has a strong intellectual or cognitive aspect, which itself is always affective, as well: the more we hear the gospel in faith and become like Christ in virtue, the more fully we know God and cleave to him in love. But it also is expressed and nourished now through our bodily experience and our symbolic acts, and will eventually be fully experienced in the incorruptibility of our bodies. This is so because the body and the material world are generally understood to be a metaphor, a revelatory sign, of God's creative and healing purpose.

So the Greek patristic tradition, from Clement to Origen to Maximus and beyond, tends to understand the Eucharist as all of a piece with spiritual exegesis of the scriptures, a virtuous life, and a public witness of martyrdom or ascetic withdrawal: all reveal the breaking of God's transforming grace into our world, all express the desire of alienated creatures to find their way back to God. Along with scripture and a life of dedicated witness, the Eucharist is a type of salvation, an earthly means of encounter with the God who calls us on into the journey of transformation. As the Christian community's central act of worship, and its most explicit memorial of what Professor Young calls the "founding sacrifice" of Jesus' death, the Eucharist remained for the Greek fathers the church's chief window open to the light of God, and its main door for beginning its procession toward the transformed life of the kingdom.

Notes

1. Johannes Betz, *Eucharistie in der Schrift und Patristik*, Handbuch der Dogmengeschichte IV/4a (Freiburg: Herder, 1979), 47.

2. Robin Darling Young, "The Eucharist as Sacrifice according to Clement of Alexandria," p. 64 this volume.

3. Ibid., 69.

4. Ibid., 70.

5. See, for example, *Hom. Lev.* 1.4.

6. *Comm. ser. Matt.* 85. Similarly, in his *Homilies on Numbers* 23.6, Origen interprets the lamb of the Jewish Pasch, as well as the flesh of Jesus, which he commands us to eat in John 6:53–57 if we are to "have life" and "abide in him," as the speech of orthodox, scripturally anchored Christian teaching: "If we say perfect, substantial, strong things, we are placing the flesh of the word of God before you to eat. For wherever mystical speech is found, wherever the language of teaching, solid and full of faith in the Trinity, is served up, wherever the mysteries of the text's spiritual law are laid open, with the veil of the world to come removed, wherever hope turns from the earth and flings itself towards heaven, to rest on those things 'which eye has not seen nor ear heard, nor have they yet ascended into the human heart' (I Cor 2:9)—all these things are the flesh of the Word of God. Whoever can feast on these things with perfected mind and purified heart, he truly offers us the sacrifice of the Paschal feast, and celebrates the festival with God and his angels."

7. *Hom. Num.* 16.7.

8. *Hom. Exod.* 13.3.

9. *Hom. Exod.* 11.7. In *Hom. Lev.* 13.5–6, interpreting the Levitical rule that the priests are to eat sacrificed meat "in a holy place," Origen insists that both the "food of the Word of God" and the "sacraments of the body of the Lord" must be consumed in a heart purified of all sin.

10. See also Origen's *Commentary on John* 10.13, an extended passage in which he comments on the Passover lamb as a type not only of the flesh and blood of Jesus, given as our food, but more basically still of "the mysteries of Scripture," from "the principal and most essential doctrines about heavenly things" (= the "head" of the lamb) to the things scripture can tell us about the earth and the underworld (= the "feet"). "For we ought not to suppose," he concludes, "that historical things are types of historical things, and material things of material, but that material things are typical of spiritual things, and historical things of intellectual" (trans. Allan Menzies: *Ante-Nicene Fathers* 9.391). The most important aspect of the mystery of Christ is, in Origen's view, always the intelligible aspect, to which human and material things point us by means of ecclesiastical interpretation.

11. Theodore of Mopsuestia, *Catechetical Homily* 15.15, 20; cf. Theodoret of Cyrus, *Comm. Hebr.* 8.4.5.

12. *Cat. Hom.* 15.25–26.

13. Ibid. 5.6–7; 16.12.

14. *De Hier. Eccl.* 3.13, trans. Thomas L. Campbell (Lanham, Md.: University Press of America, 1981), 47–48.

15. *Mystagogia* 24, trans. George C. Berthold (New York: Paulist Press, 1985), 207–208.

16. See, for instance, *De Perfectione* (GNO VIII/1, 173–214, esp. 205.22–206.14); *Vita Moysis* Prologue 5–10; II, 225–242.

17. See my article, "Divine Transcendence and Human Transformation: Gregory of Nyssa's Anti-Apollinarian Christology," *Studia Patristica* 32 (1997): 87–95, for further references.

18. *Orat. Cat.* (GNO III/4, 80.8–81.24).

29. Ibid., 86.6–89.14.

20. Ibid., 93.1–97.12.

21. *Comm. Joan.* 4, (on John 6:54) Patrologia Graeca 77.577 C4–10.

22. Ibid., 577 D 8–12.

23. Ibid. (on John 6:55) 584 C11–D3.

24. Ibid. (on John 6:54) 576 D 8–577 A 2.

25. Ibid., 576 D 5–8

A RESPONSE TO ROBIN DARLING YOUNG ON

The Eucharist as Sacrifice
according to Clement of Alexandria

BY EVERETT FERGUSON

I applaud the choice of Clement of Alexandria as a representative of the eucharistic thought of the early Greek Christian writers. He is a thinker not given enough attention on this topic,[1] and he is one with whom I feel a kinship on many aspects of his attitudes. However, the choice immediately raises questions. There is no passage in Clement that has the Eucharist primarily in view; there are several allusions to it in passages discussing something else. And Clement's allusive style makes associations that a literal-minded person such as I has difficulty following.

Clement was a "man of the church," but I suspect that Professor Young has made him represent a more realistic sacramentalism than is the case. She is right to look for eucharistic associations where these may not be explicit, but may it be that instead of Clement providing the foundation for later Greek patristic thought, Professor Young has read later thought into Clement? I want to sketch a reading of Clement that supplements her treatment and offers an alternative interpretation. It seems to me that Clement assumed the Eucharist as part of Christian practice and used it as a basis for the spiritual teaching that was his primary concern. Clement understands the Eucharist primarily in terms of receiving the Spirit of Christ through faith and acquiring the heavenly knowledge that leads to immortality.

Clement found Old Testament anticipations of the Eucharist. There is a liturgical allusion to the prayer of consecration in his interpretation of Genesis 14:18: "[Melchizedek] gave bread and wine [to Abraham] as sanctified food for a type of the Eucharist."[2] He twice refers to Genesis 49:11 ("Binding his foal to the vine and his donkey's colt to the choice vine, he washes his garments in wine and his robe in the blood of grapes"). The first reference gives this interpretation:

> He bound this simple and childlike people to the Logos, whom he allegorizes as a vine. For the vine produces wine, as the Logos does blood, and both are a drink for the welfare of human beings, the wine for the body and the blood for the spirit.[3]

The basis of the statement is obviously the association of wine with the blood of Jesus in the Eucharist, suggested by the parallelism in the biblical text of wine and the blood of the grape. It is characteristic of Clement that he sees a reference to both the physical and the spiritual. The other quotation is incidental to a larger treatment of John 6, to which we shall come shortly. It is to be noted that the most popular Old Testament text applied to the Eucharist in the second century, Malachi 1:10–12 (the pure offering made by the Gentiles), is quoted by Clement only once and that without reference to the Eucharist.[4]

There are several incidental references to liturgical practices. Clement mentions standing with head looking up and hands upraised in prayer. This was the common posture of prayer in the ancient world and so not necessarily eucharistic,[5] but was a practice noted by Christian authors specifically in connection with the *sursum corda* preceding the Eucharist.[6] The eucharistic elements were bread (Clement uses the ordinary Greek word *artos*, as does the New Testament) and wine mixed with water.[7] A Eucharist with bread and water alone he identifies (in interpreting Prov 9:17) with heresies (Encratites and Marcionites) who do not follow the rule of the church.[8] Clement refers to the custom at the distribution of the Eucharist that the people are entrusted individually to examine their consciences when they take a portion.[9]

Clement refers in one passage to those who have been to church having heard a discourse about God and having hymned immortality.[10] He appears to give a fuller list of activities in the assembly of Christians in a passage where he characteristically says these things are to be done always.

> The soul that is always giving thanks (*eucharistousa*) in all things to God by righteous hearing and divine reading, by true inquiry, by holy offering, by blessed prayer, praising, hymning, blessing, and singing Psalms is never separated from God at any time.[11]

It is characteristic of Clement that he gives prominence to vocal musical activities, but that would be another paper.[12] If Clement was thinking of the worship assembly in this listing, the "offering" might be a reference to the Eucharist, but the pairing of items could as well link it with prayer. Liturgical activities would seem to be often in Clement's mind. And, granted that the heart of the liturgy is the Eucharist, we nonetheless must ask if everything that is liturgical is eucharistic. Professor Young appears to have assumed the Eucharist was in Clement's mind and then proceeded to interpret the texts accordingly.

Clement makes fairly frequent use of sacrificial language.[13] There is no doubt that his spiritualizing of sacrifice gives prominence to prayer.[14] One might think that sometimes the Eucharistic Prayer is in mind, but this would be an assumption to be tested in each case. Clement's little treatise on martyrdom uses the phrase "to drink the cup" for martyrdom.[15] The uniting theme is sacrifice, but the phrase is biblical (Matt 20:22).

If Clement gives sacrificial connotations to the Eucharist, we must still ask what kind of sacrifice. The Eucharist is of course associated with Jesus' sacrifice on the cross. Professor Young wants to connect the sacrificial theme in Clement with that atoning sacrifice. The prevailing association in the early church was of the Eucharist with a thank offering.[16] And that seems to be true for Clement as well.[17] Here we have continuity with Rabbi Stern's paper.

Clement makes two references to the institution narratives, both as part of a discussion of something else. In defense of drinking wine in moderation he cites Matthew 26:27–29, and in this instance he explains the phrase "This is my blood" as "the blood of the vine, which is the Logos poured out for many for the forgiveness of sins."[18] In support of the need to speak well and to act well, Clement says, "The Savior taking bread, first spoke and gave thanks, and then breaking the bread, he presented it so that we might eat with reference to the Logos."[19]

For Clement, as for the later Greek Fathers, the principal eucharistic text was John 6.[20] The first extensive treatment comes in Clement's discussion of new Christians as children, who are to be fed on milk. It is plausible to think that the new converts' initial experiences with the Eucharist suggest Clement's development of the theme. He refers to one interpretation of milk and meat (1 Cor 3:2) according to which the "milk" is the proclamation of the gospel and meat is faith given substance by instruction (*katechesis*). He then explains John 6:53 ("eat my flesh and drink my blood"). Jesus is

> describing allegorically through the symbols of eating and drinking what is the outward manifestation of faith and the promise, by which the church, like a human being composed of many members, is given drink and grows..., the body by faith and the soul by hope."[21]

Then Clement follows the medical theory of the day on the blood of the mother becoming milk.[22] He returns to John 6:53–54 and comments that, since the Lord offered his flesh and poured out his blood, nothing more was needed for the growth of his children. "Oh, marvelous mystery!" He presents the following as the "more common" or "more general" understanding:

> He speaks allegorically to us of the Holy Spirit as flesh, because the flesh was created by him, and he hints obscurely to us of the Logos as blood, for the Logos as rich blood has been poured out for life... The Lord is Spirit and Logos. The food, that is the Lord Jesus, the Logos of God, is the Spirit who became flesh, the heavenly flesh sanctified. The food is the milk of the Father, by which alone we children are nourished.[23]

Clement here equates the Logos and the Spirit. The Holy Spirit is allegorically the flesh, and the Logos is blood. Clement's concern is not with flesh and blood, but with the invisible realities to which they refer.[24]

Later in the passage Clement affirms, "For us little children who suck as milk the Logos from heaven Christ himself is food."[25] Shortly thereafter Clement may be thought to make a liturgical reference to dipping the bread in the chalice of wine, but the word he chooses makes this doubtful:

> Since [Jesus] said, "The bread that I will give is my flesh" [John 6:51] and flesh is given drink by blood and the blood is spoken of allegorically as wine, therefore one must know that as bread crumbled [*n.b.*] into the mixture of wine and water seizes on the wine and leaves the watery portion, so also the flesh of the Lord, the bread of heaven, absorbs the blood and nourishes what is heavenly in human beings for immortality and leaves only the fleshly lusts for destruction.

Clement continues:

> Thus the Logos is spoken of allegorically in many ways— meat, flesh, food, bread, blood, milk. The Lord is all these for the enjoyment of us who have believed in him. No one should consider it strange that we speak allegorically of the Lord's blood as milk. Is it not spoken of allegorically as wine? Scripture says, "He washes his garment in wine and his cloak in the blood of the grape" [Gen 49:11].[26]

The repeated use of the word "allegorically" makes clear that Clement is not thinking literally. Moreover, he makes the application, "The very blood and milk are a symbol of the Lord's passion and teaching."[27] The incarnation and the necessity of feeding on Christ are clearly present throughout the passage. There seem to be eucharistic overtones. Given a mind that associates Logos with milk and blood with wine, we should be careful about being too specific about what his thought is. However, all the images—bread, wine, flesh, blood, milk—serve for Clement to describe believing in Christ and growing in spiritual knowledge of him, which will lead to immortality. Whatever is said about bread and wine, however, one must be prepared to say about other food and milk.

Another passage that starts from the contrast of milk and meat (1 Cor 3:1–2), this time between catechesis and contemplation of the highest mysteries, may allude to John 6:53–54. "The flesh and blood of the Logos are the apprehension of the divine power and sub-stance... The knowledge of the divine substance is the eating and drinking of the divine Logos."[28] Eating and drinking are for Clement an image of acquiring divine knowledge.[29]

This conclusion is consistent with what Clement says in another reference to the discourse on the Bread of Life in John 6. The context is the discussion of drinking wine, following after a discussion of eat-ing that included instructions about an agape.[30] This discussion of wine includes what is considered the most important eucharistic text in Clement.[31] That it comes shortly after the discussion of the agape would be consistent with Bigg's argument that the agape and the Eucharist were not separated in Clement's Alexandria.[32] Bigg does not persuade me; Clement draws on many associations that he can relate to whatever he is discussing.

The text is introduced by reference to the water from the rock (Exod 17:1–7) and the cluster of grapes brought back from the promised land by Joshua and the other spies (Num 13:23–24). It con-tinues as follows:

> The great cluster was a sign to those being guided from error into rest, the Logos who was oppressed for us, since the Logos desired the blood of the grape to be mixed with water, as also his blood is mixed with salvation. The Lord's blood is twofold: the blood of his flesh by which we have been ran-somed from corruption, and the blood of his Spirit by which we have been anointed. To drink this [latter] blood of Jesus is to partake of the Lord's incorruptibility. The Spirit is the strength of the Logos, as blood is of the flesh.

In a comparable way as the wine is mixed with water, the Spirit is with a human being. The former mixture of wine and water nourishes us in faith, and the latter (the Spirit) leads to incorruption. Both mixings, that of the drink and that of the Logos, are called Eucharist, which means grace that is praised and beautiful. Those who participate by faith are sanctified in body and soul, when the Father's will mystically mixes together the divine mixture, a human being with the Spirit and the Logos. For truly the Spirit is akin to the soul it bears and the flesh is akin to the Logos, on account of which "the Word became flesh" [John 1:14].[33]

Once more the Logos and the Spirit are identified. Four different mixtures appear in this passage: wine and water, the Logos's blood and salvation, the Spirit with a human being (the Spirit conveyed in the Eucharist, not the incarnation), and by implication the Logos with flesh in the incarnation.[34] Partaking in faith sanctifies body and soul.

Another commentary on John 6 that appears to represent Clement's own view is found in his *Excerpta ex Theodoto* 13.1–4:

> [The Son] is "heavenly bread" and "spiritual food" furnishing life by food and knowledge, "the light of human beings," that is, of the church. Therefore those who ate the heavenly bread died [those who ate the manna in the wilderness—John 6:49], but he who eats the true bread of the Spirit shall not die [John 6:50]. The Son is the living bread which was given by the Father to those who wish to eat. "And my flesh is the bread which I will give" [John 6:32, 51], he says, that is to him whose flesh is nourished by the Eucharist; or better still, the flesh is his body, "which is the church" [Col 1:24], "heavenly bread," a blessed assembly.[35]

The technical use of Eucharist seems clear. There is once more the double reference to food that nourishes the flesh and to knowledge, the "true bread of the Spirit," that gives life to the church, the real body of the Son of God.[36] Later in the document (82.1), bread and oil are cited as analogies to the water of baptism that has a material effect and by the Spirit an immaterial effect:

> And the bread and the oil are sanctified by the power of the Name, and they are not the same as they appeared to be when they were received, but they have been transformed by power into spiritual power.[37]

The language of John 6 appears to shape the following statement in which Clement presents the Savior as speaking:

> I am the one who nourishes you, giving myself as bread. No one who has tasted of this bread experiences death any more. I daily give the drink of immortality. I am the teacher of supercelestial lessons. I contended with death on your behalf and paid in full for your death.[38]

Here is found the by now familiar combination of feeding on the Savior as on bread and taking his drink, receiving his teachings and the benefits of his death, all resulting in overcoming death.

The intellectualizing and spiritualizing interpretation found in the major works of Clement is found also in his *Hypotyposeis* preserved by Cassiodorus. Thus on 1 John 1:7, "The doctrine of the Lord... is called his blood."[39] And on 1 John 4:8, the Spirit is interpreted as life, water as regeneration and faith, and the blood as knowledge.[40]

Professor Young is right to emphasize that for Clement (and for other writers under the influence of Platonism) a symbol mediates and participates in the truth it indicates. But a symbol was still not identical with what was symbolized. I doubt that Clement had a thought-out theology of the Eucharist; it was simply part of his church experience. If I were to characterize his eucharistic thought as exemplified in his treatment of John 6, I would do so by the view that has been called "dynamic symbolism." The Eucharist is symbolism because it participates in the reality symbolized; it is dynamic, for in this instance it conveys the power of the reality that it symbolizes.[41] Clement sees the power or effects of the body and blood of Jesus as conveyed by the taking of the eucharistic elements. They remain bread and wine and so nourish the human body, but there is a heavenly dimension, a spiritual reality that is received by the working of the Logos and the Spirit.[42] In other words, there was a realism of the effects of the Eucharist and a symbolism of the elements, which are associated with the body and blood of Jesus.[43] And, typically for Clement, these effects are described in terms of a heavenly knowledge associated with immortality.

Clement is one of the first to use the language of the Hellenistic mysteries for Christian initiation to any extent.[44] This was part of his general program of borrowing terms familiar to educated Hellenists and using pagan concepts and practices to make Christianity intelligible and acceptable to them. I doubt that we should see in his "mystagogy" more than that. As the terminology became more common, the ideas behind it influenced Christian self-understanding (certainly in the fourth century), but to read Clement in terms of these ideas raises again the question of whether Clement was a Christian who used pagan concepts or a Hellenist not completely immersed. I think Professor Young would join me in voting for the former characterization.

NOTES

1. Representative of this neglect is Enrico Mazza, *The Celebration of the Eucharist: The Origin of the Rite and the Development of Its Interpretation* (Collegeville, Minn.: Liturgical Press, 1999), who does not mention Clement (the liturgical focus of the book does not exempt Tertullian and Cyprian from full treatment). Notable exceptions include Charles Bigg, *The Christian Platonists of Alexandria* (Oxford: Clarendon, 1913), 136–142; R. B. Tollinton, *Clement of Alexandria: A Study in Christian Liberalism*, vol. 2 (London: Williams and Norgate, 1914), 137–139, 147–164; and especially André Mehat, "Clement of Alexandria," in *The Eucharist of the Early Christians*, ed. Willy Rordorf et al. (New York: Pueblo, 1978), 99–131.

2. *Stromateis (Str.)* 4.25.161. The passage is followed by a statement "The Savior initiates us into the mysteries"—4.25.162.3.

3. *Paedagogos (Paed.)* 1.5.15.3–4.

4. *Str.* 5.14.136.2. References to second-century usage in my *Early Christians Speak*, 3rd ed. (Abilene: ACU Press, 1999), 117–118.

5. *Str.* 7.7.40.1.

6. Everett Ferguson, "The Liturgical Function of the 'Sursum Corda,'" *Studia Patristica* 13 (1975): 360–363.

7. For wine mixed with water in ordinary as well as eucharistic usage, see Everett Ferguson, "Wine as a Table Drink in the Ancient World," *Restoration Quarterly* 13 (1970): 141–153.

8. *Str.* 1.19.96. The mixture of wine and water is also mentioned in *Paed.* 2.2.19.3, a passage discussed below, and later in the same passage the use of wine is defended against the Encratites.

9. *Str.* 1.1.5. There follows a quotation of 1 Cor 11:27–28.

10. *Paed.* 3.11.80.4.

11. *Str.* 6.14.113.3.

12. Everett Ferguson, *A Cappella Music in the Public Worship of the Church*, 3rd ed. (Ft. Worth: Star, 1999), 19–23, 46.

13. Everett Ferguson, "Spiritual Sacrifice in Early Christianity and Its Environment," in *Aufstieg und Niedergang der Römischen Welt* (Berlin: De Gruyter, 1980), II.23.2, 1179–1183. Like other Christians, Clement affirmed that Christ was the whole burnt-offering and offering without fire made for human beings and that the Logos prohibited all building of holy places and all sacrifices—*Str.* 5.11.70.4 and 5.11.74.5. An example of his spiritualizing of sacrifice is the reference to offering incense in a meal context: "If one should say that the Lord, the great High Priest, offers the incense of fragrance to God, we do not understand this as a sacrifice and fragrance of [literal] incense, but let us receive this as the Lord offering the acceptable sacrifice of love, the spiritual fragrance, on the altar"—*Paed.* 2.8.67.

14. *Str.* 7.6.31.7; 7.6.31.8 (the altar is the congregation at prayer); 7.6.32.4 (prayer is incense); 7.6.32.6; 7.6.34.2 (prayer is incense); 7.7.49.4; Frg. 61 from *Sacr. Par.* 300 (Stählin III, 227, 28); *Hyp.* on 1 Pet. 2:9 (Stählin III, 204, 21–25).

15. *Str.* 4.9.75.1. He refers to Jesus' calling his passion "a cup"—*Paed.*1.6.46.1.

16. Willy Rordorf, "Le sacrifice eucharistique," *Theologische Zeitschrift* 25 (1969): 335–353; repr. in Everett Ferguson, *Worship in Early Christianity*, Studies in Early Christianity 15 (New York: Garland, 1993), 193–211.

17. Note the association of thanksgiving with prayer in *Str.* 7.7.35.4, 6; 7.7.41.6–7 and with psalmody in *Paed.* 2.4.43.3. The offering of the "firstfruits of food and drink" with thanksgiving in *Str.* 7.7.36.4 reminds one of Irenaeus, *Adversus Haereses* 4.17.5.

18. *Paed.* 2.2.32.2. Cf. *Quis dives salvetur?* (*Q.D.S.*) 29.4, "He poured on our wounded souls wine [Luke 10:34], the blood of the vine of David." Not every reference to "blood" is eucharistic—*Q.D.S.* 34.1.

19. *Str.* 1.10.46.1.

20. The main texts are well studied by A. H. C. van Eijk, "The Gospel of Philip and Clement of Alexandria: Gnostic and Ecclesiastical Theology on the Resurrection and the Eucharist," *Vigiliae Christianae* 25 (1971): 94–120.

21. *Paed.* 1.6.38.1–3.

22. *Paed.* 1.6.39–40; Plutarch, *On Affection for Offspring* 3 (*Moralia* 495D–496A).

23. *Paed.* 1.6.42.3–43.3. Edward Engelbrecht, "God's Milk: An Orthodox Confession of the Eucharist," *Journal of Early Christian Studies* 7 (1999): 509–526 (esp. 512–516).

24. Van Eijk, 111.

25. *Paed.* 1.6.46.1.

26. *Paed.* 1.6.47.1–3.

27. *Paed.* 1.6.49.4. Clement's subsequent reference to mixing milk and honey may allude to the practice of giving milk and honey to the newly baptized at their first Eucharist—so argued by van Eijk, 113–114.

28. *Str.* 5.10.66.1–3, a passage with references to pagan sacrifice, the sacrifice of Christ (our Passover), and Christian spiritual sacrifice as separation from the body's passions, may support the case for an association with the Eucharist, as van Eijk, 108–109, argues. Milk and meat are referred to in another passage followed by this statement: "By the 'blazing wine' [Thespis] teaches the perfecting gladness of instruction, the blood of the vine of the Logos"—*Str.* 5.8.48.8.

29. Van Eijk's comment is à propos, "Clement is less interested in the (sacramental) symbols themselves, than in what is communicated by them" (p. 109).

30. *Paed.*2.1.4–8 and 16 on the agape.

31. Mehat, 113.

32. Bigg, 137, n.1.

33. *Paed.* 2.2.19.3–20.1. Cf. the statement that "Scripture names wine the mystical symbol of the holy blood"—*Paed.* 2.2.29.1.

34. Van Eijk, 111–112, and Marrou in Claude Mondésert and Henri-Irénée Marrou, *Clément d'Alexandrie Le Pédagogue* II, *Sources Chrétiennes* 108 (Paris: Cerf, 1965), 48, give differing lists of the mixtures in the passage, both importing into the passage a mixing of the Logos with the eucharistic elements that is not explicitly there.

35. Robert Pierce Casey, *The Excerpta ex Theodoto of Clement of Alexandria*, Studies and Documents 1 (London: Christophers, 1934), 50–51, whose translation I follow, slightly modified. A fragment ascribed to Clement, but not included in Stählin, from a sermon on Luke 15 is translated in *Ante-Nicene Fathers*, II, p. 582: "He is both flesh and bread, and has given Himself as both to us to be eaten."

36. Cf. *Str.* 1.1.7.2 on nourishment received through bread and words. The statement may be inspired by the Eucharist, but I question that it is.

37. Casey, 88–91.

38. *Q.D.S.* 23.4.

39. Stählin III, 211, 7–9.

40. Stählin, III, 214, 24–25.

41. Walter Völker, *Der wahre Gnostiker nach Clemens Alexandrinus*, Texte und Untersuchungen 57 (Berlin: Akademie, 1952) in a long note (pp. 598–600) surveys Roman Catholic interpretation of Clement that defends the real presence and transubstantiation and Protestant interpretation that advocates symbolism. He agrees with Tollinton's middle position between spiritualizing and realism. His own exposition

(pp. 598, 600–602) emphasizes the close relation for Clement of the Eucharist with the church and with Christ and its function of bringing spiritual life, overthrow of corruption, and immortality. Without using my terminology, his brief statement is consistent with my interpretation.

42. There may be a continuity with David Bentley Hart's characterization of the Byzantine view of the Eucharist as the *site* or *locus* where spiritual reality is received.

43. We may compare Origen, *Contra Celsum* 8.33—"We give thanks to the Creator of all, and with thanksgiving and prayer for blessings received we eat the loaves presented to us that become by the prayer a holy body and sanctify those who with sound intentions partake of that body."

44. H. G. Marsh, "The Use of ΜΥΣΤΗΡΙΟΝ in the Writings of Clement of Alexandria with Special Reference to his Sacramental Doctrine," *Journal of Theological Studies* 37 (1936): 64–80; Harry A. Echle, "Sacramental Initiation as Christian Mystery—Initiation according to Clement of Alexandria," in A. Mayer et al., *Vom Christlichen Mysterium* (Düsseldorf: Patmos, 1951), 54–65. Marsh notes Clement's frequent use of mystery terminology but its rarity with reference to the sacraments and concludes that although there was a tendency to surround the sacraments with concepts from the Hellenistic mysteries, the time for that practice had not yet arrived in Clement's Alexandria (p. 80).

D. Jeffrey Bingham

Eucharist and Incarnation: The Second Century and Luther

Introduction

As the title indicates, this paper focuses upon a narrow issue in the history of the contemplation of the Eucharist. Themes other than "incarnation" could have been selected for the periods and persons studied. Eucharistic liturgy, Eucharist as sacrifice, Eucharist as offering, Eucharist and prayer, Eucharist and church unity, Eucharist and the agape, Eucharist and real or symbolic presence all would be worthy topics. I have chosen Eucharist and incarnation, however, in an attempt to address one particular historical question suggested by the committee: "How is the whole mystery of Jesus (from birth to passion—resurrection—ascension—parousia) present in the Eucharist?" I also have sought to broaden the question through the insights of those studied. As will be seen, one could ask, "How is the whole of the grace of redemptive history present in the Eucharist?" For both the second century and Luther, the Eucharist summarizes and anticipates the parts and the whole of a salvation history which has the incarnation of God the Son at its center.

I have chosen to study the second century and Luther because of my ecclesiological and professional associations. I am an Evangelical Southern Baptist whose major area of research is the second century. I thought I could best serve the conference by linking my Protestant heritage (although Luther is somewhat distant from the Baptists) with my early Christian interests. We will find remarkable continuity. This continuity should encourage future contemplation of the Lord's Supper to reconsider the Eucharist's relationship to all of the history of salvation through the focus of incarnation. Incarnation, for these Christians, is a window into the grace shown to the human creature by the Creator throughout history. In their belief, the Eucharist is the contemporary event of grace which brings to the foreground this history of redemption by manifesting the act of God's becoming human.

The Second Century

Ignatius of Antioch

"For Ignatius, therefore, the Eucharist was first the sacrament of the incarnation. Without the incarnation, the Eucharist would not have been the sacrament of Redemption."[1]

In this way Eugene LaVerdiere summarizes his discussion of Ignatius and the Eucharist. With this summary he conveniently directs us to our topic and first theologian. In Ignatius, when we encounter the idea of incarnation we find him emphasizing the actual revelation of the Son of God in the flesh, with blood. In his letter to the Smyrnaeans the bishop of Antioch develops a pattern from features of this revelation which takes us to the Eucharist and beyond.

In the first paragraph of his epistle to the believers in Smyrna Ignatius praises them for their faith in the Lord as David's descendant according to the flesh, Son of God, born of a virgin, baptized by John, crucified in the flesh. The next paragraph emphasizes the reality of his suffering and resurrection against the docetists, while the third highlights his existence in flesh after the resurrection. This third paragraph has him quoting a saying of Jesus with a parallel in Luke 24:39, which admonishes his disciples to handle him in order to validate his fleshly existence. Immediately, Ignatius proclaims, "they touched him and believed being united with his flesh and spirit" (*Smyrn.* 3.2; L, 226.23–24).[2] In the same discussion he also alludes to the gospel records that "after his resurrection he ate and drank with them as one who is flesh, although spiritually he was united with the Father" (*Smyrn.* 3.3; L, 226.25–26).

In *Smyrnaeans* 1–3, then, Ignatius develops a story of the revelation of the Lord Jesus Christ, in the flesh, from virgin birth to the post-resurrection appearances. The proof of his resurrected flesh and blood as well as the unity of his disciples with him, the fleshy son of David, came in handling him and eating and drinking with him. Spiritually, after resurrection, he was with the Father. But he also was sensibly present in flesh and blood at meals.

In the fourth paragraph of the epistle Ignatius next emphasizes that none of the instances of Christ's fleshly revelation were merely apparent. Ignatius believes that it is Christ, the "perfect man" who empowers him in martyrdom, a true sharing of the Lord's suffering in flesh (*Smyrn.* 4.2; L, 228.10). Anyone who denies that the Lord "was clothed in flesh," he says in paragraph five, is "clothed in a corpse" (*Smyrn.* 5.2; L, 228.16–17). Even the spiritual beings who deny the blood of Christ will be judged (*Smyrn.* 6.1; L, 21–25).

It is in *Smyrnaeans* 6.2 that his christological discussion turns particularly eucharistic. The argument thus far has been that, from cradle to post-resurrection meal, Christ was flesh and blood. Those who deny this are condemned. In the first line of 6.2 (L, 228.25–230) Ignatius reminds the reader that such persons are contrary to God's mind. Also, he magnifies the concept that it was in the fleshly revelation of Christ that the "grace of Jesus Christ" came to humanity. Then 7.1 (L, 230.5–9) describes those who deny that fleshly grace as abstaining from "the Eucharist and prayer because they do not acknowledge that the Eucharist is the flesh of our Savior Jesus Christ which suffered for our sins and which the Father by his goodness raised up."

The heretics, the docetists, avoided the communal meal which included the Eucharist. In doing so they denied Christ's real fleshly presence in passion and resurrection meals. For the bishop of Antioch, there is a pattern of christological presence in flesh from death to resurrection to Eucharist. Each is a pivotal moment in the revelatory history of the presence of Christ.

This suggests Ignatius's understanding of Luke 24:28–35. There, at the post-resurrection meal, the disciples recognized and came to know Jesus in "the breaking of the bread." In the very next paragraph he challenges them to handle him in order to prove that he is flesh and blood (Luke 24:39). Ignatius alludes to this saying in *Smyrnaeans*

3.2. The Lucan account offers a paradigm for receiving knowledge of Christ in his flesh. Such knowledge comes, for the church, through the Eucharist. For the community of the ascended Christ, the eucharistic meal serves the same purpose as the post-resurrection meals. In this light Ignatius announces in *Smyrnaeans* 3.1 (L, 226.20–21), "For I know and believe that he was in the flesh even after the resurrection."

The pattern, however, does not cease with the Eucharist. It continues also in the community's concrete acts of love on behalf of the oppressed. Between the first and last lines of 6.2 (L, 230.2–4) is the following indictment against the heretics:

> They have no care for love, none for the widow, none for the orphan, none for the oppressed, none for the prisoner or the one freed from prison, none for the hungry or thirsty.

As Schoedel points out, two implications follow from this list which occurs within the discussion of the Eucharist. First, since the love-feast was where ministry to the needy took place, in avoiding the meal the heretics avoided love. Second, Ignatius is teaching that the Eucharist anticipates concrete acts of love founded upon the concreteness of the Lord's flesh known in the meal. Failure to embrace the revelation of the incarnate Lord leads to failure in love. But by loving in tangible ways, the community continues to reveal Christ in his flesh. The Eucharist becomes "the sign of the inestimable importance"[3] of such acts. But, in the same way that the post-resurrection meals provide the moments of knowledge prior to the Eucharist, the Eucharist also provides the moment prior to the deed of love. It both continues and anticipates the knowledge of Christ as flesh and blood.

But there is still another moment within the sequence for Ignatius. Following Eucharist and deeds of love is bodily resurrection. The resurrection of loving believers, too, is an instance of the revelation of the flesh and blood of Christ. In regard to the heretics, he writes that it "would be more to their advantage to love, in order that they might also rise up" (*Smyr.* 7.1; L, 230.9). And in regard to the believers, earlier he had spoken of the fleshly passion of the Lord as "our resurrection." This followed his characterization of the heretic who denies the flesh of Christ as one who is "clothed in a corpse," that is, one who does not share in bodily immortality. The believer's bodily resurrection is in continuity with Jesus Christ's fleshly existence, and like the virgin birth and crucifixion manifests again the reality of that existence. The Father who raised the fleshly Son of David will raise those who believe in him (*Trallians* [*Tral.*] 9.2).

In Ignatius's thought the Eucharist plays a pivotal role in this sequence. In *Ephesians* 20.2 (L, 190.14–16) he refers to the breaking of the one bread at the Eucharist as "the medicine of immortality, the antidote so we do not die, but live forever in Jesus Christ." Ignatius is probably thinking here of the word of Jesus in John 6:51: "I am the living bread which came down from heaven; if any one eats of this bread, he will live forever; and the bread which I shall give for the life of the world is my flesh" (cf. *Rom.* 7.3, RSV).[4] Ignatius teaches a quickening, an energizing, of believers by the Lord in flesh through the Eucharist. He whose flesh is the bread of life is known in the Eucharist and he will raise the one who partakes of him "up at the last day" (John 6:54), for "he who eats this bread will live forever" (John 6:58, RSV). But such quickening comes only to those who receive the bread with true christological faith and true ecclesiological love founded upon unity.[5] One must agree with John 6 that Jesus is both from the Father and true flesh and blood. And one must love the members of the body and its unity.

Although there is realism in Ignatius's understanding of the association of the elements with Christ's flesh and blood, there is also a symbolism, or spiritualizing.[6] So when we find him using the flesh and blood of Christ as representative of the virtues of faith and love (*Tral.* 8.1; *Rom.* 7.3), we are to understand that the Eucharist is the event where the members proclaim their faith and practice their love.[7] The Eucharist stands as the witness to the truth announced by Jesus concerning his heavenly origin and fleshly state. Even in its symbolism, it produces life, for faith and love are life's beginning and end (*Eph.* 14.1; cf. *Philadelphians* [*Phil.*] 9.2).

The Bishop of Antioch does associate the Eucharist with the altar, but the emphasis appears to be on the *one* altar around which the faithful gather in recognition of the *one* Eucharist, the *one* flesh, the *one* cup (*Phil.* 4.1). This annunciates his theme of ecclesiological unity. His overwhelming interest, nevertheless, is the Eucharist as the locus of all things Christian, that is, all things christological. Participation in the Eucharist proclaims a unified faith in the flesh and blood of Christ which manifests itself in love and bears fruit for eternal life. It is the center point of Christian existence. Between his resurrection and the resurrection of his followers, Christ manifests himself *in the flesh* by the Eucharist. Ultimately, Ignatius focuses not upon the metaphysics of the Eucharist. Rather, he focuses upon what it says about Christ's human nature and the ramifications of that nature for love, unity, salvation, and redemption history.

Justin Martyr

In his *Dialogue with Trypho* (70.2–3) Justin cites Isaiah 33:13–19 and concludes that

> this prophecy also alludes to the bread which our Christ gave us to eat in remembrance of his incarnation (*somatopoiusasthai*) for the sake of those who believe in him and for whom he suffered, and to the cup which he taught us to drink with thanksgiving in remembrance of his blood. (*Dial.* 70.4; M, 192.23–27)[8]

He is thinking here of Isaiah 33:16: "Bread shall be given him, and his water shall be sure." It is not strange that we find Isaiah 33 as a source of eucharistic teaching in Justin. Earlier, *Barnabas* (11) had listed Isaiah 33:16–18 as a source of baptismal teaching. The sure and trustworthy waters of baptism placed the faithful one upon the firm mountain of salvation as the believer ascended above chaos with Christ in his glory.[9] The fuller context of the prophecy is necessary for understanding this reading:

> He should dwell in a high cave of a strong rock. Bread shall be given him, and his water shall be sure. You shall see a king with glory; your eyes shall behold a land far off.

So Christians of the second century read Isaiah 33 as pertaining to the fundamental rites of baptism and Eucharist. Justin turns our attention to the latter and to that rite's theological focus on the incarnation. This focus can be further appreciated by Justin's additional allusion to Isaiah 33:16 in *Dialogue* 78.6. There he teaches that the prophet told of Christ's birth in Bethlehem in a cave. Against the mysteries of Mithras, the cave of Isaiah 33 is not the cave of initiation, but the cave of Christ's incarnation.

We assume, then, that when Justin speaks of Isaiah 33 as alluding to the bread eaten in memory of the Lord's incarnation, he connects the cave of incarnation, of embodiment, with the provided bread of the Eucharist. The prophet links Christ's birth with the church's eucharistic table. Justin continues the pattern seen already in Ignatius. He remembers at the table the miracle of Bethlehem in the cave. Note that for Justin the Lord both becomes flesh for the sake of the faithful and suffers for them. The incarnation itself, not only Christ's bloody sacrifice, is pivotal to his soteriology. We see this, for instance, in *1 Apology* 63.16 (M, 123.41–46):

> And before he appeared in the form of fire and in the image
> of a spirit being to Moses and to the other prophets; but now
> in the times of your rule, as we said before, he became human
> by a virgin according to the will of the Father for the salva-
> tion of those who believe in him and he endured both con-
> tempt and suffering, that by dying and rising again he might
> conquer death.

The incarnation culminates a long history of the Logos in communion with humanity who is manifested to reveal the one, true God, Creator, and Father.[10] He presents the incarnation itself as the event that brings salvation and victory over demons (cf. *1 Apol.* 63.10; *2 Apol.* 6.5), but one is not to imagine that the Logos has not been known before. The Logos has had an enduring presence. Creation, nature, and reason are all manifestations of the Logos who is Christ. Even before the incarnation, some philosophers had known him in part through the seed of the Logos implanted in all humans (*1 Apol.* 46; *2 Apol.* 8.1; 10, 13).[11] In both theophanies and the prophets the Logos revealed the transcendent God to the Jews (*1 Apol.* 63.14; 36.1–3).[12] But the pinnacle of this history is the incarnation. Explaining the relationship of the incarnation to the universal manifestation of the Logos to the Greeks, he says (*2 Apol.* 10.1; M, 151.1–3):

Our teaching, then, appears to be greater than all human teaching because the whole rational principle became Christ, who appeared for our sake, as body, reason, and soul.

And so, as in Ignatius the Eucharist serves as the place where the believer meets the fleshly Christ of the resurrection after his ascension, in Justin the Eucharist is the place where the incarnate Logos is remembered. The Eucharist is another event in the pattern of the manifestation of Logos to humanity. For Justin, this pattern long precedes the event in the cave.

This becomes more poignant in the *First Apology*. There in chapter 66.1–2 Justin speaks of the Logos continuing to manifest himself in the Eucharist in response to the word of prayer. The elements are consecrated through a prayer of thanksgiving after the pattern of Jesus' prayer at the Last Supper.[13] For him, the consecration yields a transformation of the food and drink into the flesh and blood of Jesus in the same way in which the incarnation occurred through the Logos of God. Finally, there is a third transformation in the sequence. The transformed food feeds and transforms the bodies of the faithful. Here is Justin's text:

> For we do not receive these things as ordinary bread and drink. But just as Jesus Christ our Savior was made flesh by God's Logos and took flesh and blood for our salvation, so also we have been taught that the food which has been consecrated through a prayer of thanksgiving after the pattern of Jesus becomes the flesh and blood of the incarnate Jesus, by which our blood and flesh are nourished by transformation. (*1 Apol.* 66.2; M, 127.4–10)

This text implies that in the same manner in which the Logos effected his own incarnation, he effects the transformation of the bread and wine into Jesus' flesh and blood in response to prayer, and effects through the changed elements the transformation of the bodies of the faithful unto resurrection.[14] As the divine Logos manifested himself in ages past, most critically in the incarnation, he continues his self-manifestation in Eucharist and salvific resurrection. Again, as in

Ignatius, the manifestation of Christ, a knowledge of him, comes in events prior to the Eucharist, the Eucharist itself, and the resurrection of believers. In both the bishop and the martyr, the Eucharist continues the sequence of christological revelation. But it is now the revelation of the Word *become flesh*. Post-ascension believers find him and anticipate that next great moment, their revivification, in the Eucharist.

Justin strengthens the continuity of the sequence by linking both the incarnation and the Eucharist to changes empowered by the same Logos. How the changes occur does not concern him. His interest is the actuality of flesh and blood in both christological moments and the association of both moments with the one Logos. That actuality and that one agent provide foundation for corporeal salvation. Justin looks forward to believers receiving back their own bodies when the Son of Man comes from heaven to raise them and impart to them incorruption (*1 Apol.* 18.16; 52.3).

Irenaeus of Lyons

Eucharist and World

With Irenaeus, the sequence in which the Eucharist has part moves beyond the presence of the Son with humanity. Now, in addition to preserving the sequence so important to Ignatius and Justin, the Eucharist validates the one true God and his cosmological values. Against Marcion who sets forth two different gods, one of the creation and the other of the heavenly kingdom, he writes (*Adv. Haer.* 4.33.2 [*SC* 100.2: 37–50]):[15]

> How, if the Lord is from another Father, could he without injustice declare that the bread which belongs to our creation was his body and affirm that the mixture of the cup was his blood? And why did he declare himself the Son of Man if he had not undergone a human birth? How could he forgive us our sins which make us debtors to our Creator and God? And how, if he was not flesh, but only appeared as a human, was he crucified and how could blood and water flow forth from his pierced side? And what body was it that was buried by those who delivered it to the tomb? And what was that which rose again from the dead?

With these rhetorical questions, the Eucharist is joined to the issues of Christ's human birth, the identity of the offended God as Creator, and the actuality of Christ's flesh, blood, death, burial, and resurrection. The words of the Lord, which unite the bread and wine with his body and blood, Irenaeus understands as a polemic against a docetic Christology and a Gnostic-Marcionite theology. The Father of Christ, the Son of Man, is the Creator who originates the physical world, including the flesh and blood body of Christ which underwent birth, death, burial, and resurrection. Inherent in the Lord's words is the Christian doctrine of the one God, Father and Creator; the Christian doctrine of Christ, flesh, blood, mortal and immortal; and the Christian doctrine of the created, physical world, good and godly. These doctrines are professed by the spiritual disciple indwelt by the Spirit (*Adv. Haer.* 4.33.1 [*SC* 100.2: 802.1–5]). Irenaeus takes us from the Eucharist's implications for Christ's incarnation to its implications for theology and cosmology. Incarnation is now seen as a member of the redemptive sequence beginning at God's initial union with the world at creation. Eucharist, for the bishop of Lyons, reveals more than just the continuity of the history of Logos with humanity. It also reveals the enduring compatibility of the Father with the creature.

This connection comes forth forcefully in *Adversus Haereses* 3.11.5 (*SC* 211: 154.125–31). The wine produced by Jesus from water at the wedding in Cana and the multiplied loaves for which he gave thanks both indicate that the Lord employs created, tangible substance in satisfying human need. In Irenaeus's mind this shows that

> the God who made the earth and commanded it to bring forth fruit, who established the waters and produced the fountains, he in these last times, by his Son, bestowed upon humankind the blessing of food and the grace of drink. The Incomprehensible acted by means of the comprehensible and the Invisible acted by means of the visible, for the Son is not beyond him, but exists in the bosom of the Father.

The point is clear. The Creator who is also the incomprehensible, invisible Father designed human need to be met through created substance. The incarnate Son himself validates this design as he reveals

the Father and as he upholds the design in his own nourishing ministry. Some see in the passage an allusion to the Eucharist. On this
reading, the food and drink through blessing and grace become the
flesh and blood of Christ, spiritual food and drink for human need,
after the manner of John 6:55.[16] The food and drink may refer only to
the multiplied loaves and changed water, however. Nevertheless, a
central Irenaean thesis is established. He who is invisible nourishes
his visible creation by means of the visible creation: bread, wine,
incarnation.

Clearly Eucharistic is *Adversus Haereses* 4.18.4 (*SC* 100.2:
608.104–610.109). Confronting the Gnostics who separate the spiritual Father from the Creator of "degenerate" physical substance, he
points out the contradiction between their belief and the Eucharist. A
true view of the Eucharist involves rejection of a docetic Christology
and acceptance of Jesus Christ as the Son of the Creator. He writes:

> But how can they be consistent saying that the Eucharistized
> bread is the body of the Lord and that the cup is his blood; if
> they do not believe that he is the Son of the Creator of the
> world, that is his Word, through whom the trees bear fruit
> and the fountains gush forth, and the earth produces "first
> the blade, then the ear, then the full grain in the ear" (cf.
> Mark 4:28)?

Here Irenaeus identifies the eternal Word as the *Creator's* Son and the
agent of the Father's creation and links that identity to the dynamic of
the Eucharist and the reality of the incarnation. Consistent faith affirms
that the Word made flesh is the Son of the Creator of the world and
that what transpires in the Eucharist is in necessary continuity with
both the Creation and the actual incarnation. The sequence of orthodoxy for Irenaeus is Creation–Incarnation–Eucharist. This sequence
gives unity to God and integrity to the creation, whether grain or flesh,
loaf or Incarnate Word.

Eucharist and Economy

The orthodox viewpoint is linked to Irenaeus's understanding of
the "universal economy of God" which the heretics pervert. God's
economy of redemption includes both body and soul, flesh and spirit.

He employs the term "universal" in the sense of "total, entire" in order to include both corporeal and incorporeal elements. There is a "universal resurrection" of both body and soul (*Adv. Haer.* 5.31.1) and a universal economy which both values humans as embodied souls and includes each aspect in salvation as the Spirit imparts incorruptibility to the flesh (*Adv. Haer.* 5.10.1; 13.2).[17] With this in mind, in *Adversus Haereses* 5.2.2 (*SC* 153: 30.18–21), the bishop rebukes the senseless vanity of the heretics who in their rejection of this economy "deny the salvation of the flesh." From here he takes the discussion in a eucharistic direction.

He argues that there is no integrity in redemption through Christ's blood and no integrity in the church's communion in his blood and body through the wine and bread if the flesh is not saved. The essential connection is threefold: the Eucharist which is founded upon the Lord's taking and shedding blood anticipates and sows the salvation of the flesh. The Eucharist has meaning only because the divine economy includes the corporeal. Christ's incarnation and death clearly display this economy. In the bishop's own words (*Adv. Haer.* 5.2.2 [*SC* 153: 30.21–32.25]):

> Now if there is no salvation for the flesh neither did the Lord redeem us with his blood, nor is the cup of the Eucharist a communion (*communicatio*) in his blood, nor is the bread which we break communion (*communicatio*) in his body (cf. 1 Cor 10:16).

The allusion to 1 Corinthians 10:16 at the end of this passage is important. Earlier in *Adversus Haereses* 3.18.2 (*SC* 211: 344.14–346.34) he had cited it in support of his thesis that the Son of God had become truly human.[18] Against the heretics who suppose that an impassible "Christ" from above descended into the "Jesus" from below who suffered, Irenaeus cites Paul speaking of the church's participation in the *blood of Christ*. The death of Christ, the pouring forth of his blood, in which the church participates at the Eucharist, verifies, along with his burial and resurrection, the incarnation of the Word of God. The incarnation, then, is the ultimate object of participation in the Eucharist. And when one reads a passage just above this last occurrence of 1 Corinthians 10:16, it becomes clear why it is so crucial for our bishop. The incarnation provides for humanity's recovery of its lost image and likeness. The Word of God in the last days by the Father's design

> was united to his own creation and was made a man capable of suffering... when he was incarnate and made human, he recapitulated in himself the long history of humanity and procured salvation for us in short work, of the kind [of salvation] we had lost in Adam, that is, being in the image and likeness of God, that we might recover it in Jesus Christ. (*Adv. Haer.* 3.18.1 [*SC* 211: 342.1–344.13])

When the cup is taken, the believer participates in this miracle of recovery. And if one considers how Irenaeus reads the first twelve verses of 1 Corinthians 10, further depth is added to the notion of recovery through incarnation. 1 Corinthians 10:1–12, of course, constitutes Paul's warning to the Corinthians against idolatry through the example of the misfortunes of the people of Israel. Verse eleven, which reads, "Now these things happened to them as a warning, but they were written down for our instruction," figures centrally in his thought. Furthermore, verse fourteen, which reads in conclusion, "Therefore, my beloved, shun the worship of idols," summarizes the example's implication for the church, and although not cited by Irenaeus, must be informing him. In the fourth book of *Adversus Haereses* where the citation and discussion of 1 Corinthians 10:1–12 occurs, Irenaeus argues through explanation of the words of the Lord for the unity of the one true God. These words, he concludes in the final chapter, "proclaim one and the same Father, Creator of this world" (*Adv. Haer.* 4.41.4 [*SC* 100.2: 992.78–80]). In *Adversus Haereses* 4.27.3 (*SC* 100.2: 744.119–45), he works through the Pauline text in order to prove, under the guidance of an ecclesial predecessor, that there are not two gods. One should not assume that a god of the Old Covenant judged the ancients while another god relates differently to those of the New Covenant. One God judged the ancients and judges transgressing believers today. He makes this conclusion from the full citation of Paul's passage given in *Adversus Haereses* 4.27.4 (*SC* 100.2: 746.145–59). The teaching of Paul which unifies the two economies, in this case, is 1 Corinthians 10:11: the judgments of God in the Old Covenant were for the instruction of those in the New. Therefore Christians ought not to commit idolatry by splitting the one God in two (1 Cor 10:14).

All of this then leads us back to his reading of 1 Corinthians 10:16. The cup and the bread signify that Christ had become a passible human. And, more than this, they signify that Christ and Jesus are not two, but one. Yet, there is still more. The cup and bread take us to the One true God of both covenants who has the One Christ Jesus as his Son. In a communion with the flesh and blood of Christ through a sincere partaking of the bread and cup, there takes place a communion with the One true God, Father and Creator. In the Eucharist, a true believer shows herself to be a true worshiper, one who in obedience to Paul's teaching shuns "the worship of idols." For the bishop of Lyons, the incarnation of the One Christ and the church's participation in it has critical foundations in the doctrine of God. And this doctrine of God necessitates a peculiar understanding of Christ, salvation, and communion to which Irenaeus turns his attention in the remainder of *Adversus Haereses* 5.2.2–3.

The economy of God upholds the integrity of both the corporeal and incorporeal. Such an economy provides for the salvation of the flesh. Such an economy provides redemption through Christ's blood and communion with his blood and body by means of the cup and bread. These are the bishop's points in *Adversus Haereses* 5.2.2 thus far. From here he develops the notion that communion (or participation) in Christ's blood and body through the Eucharist brings renewal and redemption to the bodies and blood of believers.

Following is a key selection and brief summation from the rich paragraphs of *Adversus Haereses* 5.2.2–3:

> For blood comes only from the veins and flesh and from the rest of human substance. All this the Word of God truly became and thereby redeemed us by his blood as the Apostle says: "In whom we have redemption through his blood, the remission of sins (Eph 1. 7)." And since we are his members and are nourished by the creation . . . he declared that the cup, filled from the creation, is his blood by which our blood

receives renewal and he proclaimed that the bread, taken
from the creation, is his body from which our bodies receive
renewal. (*Adv. Haer.* 5.2.2 [*SC* 153: 32.25–36])

He goes on (*Adv. Haer.* 5.2.3 [*SC* 153: 34.37–38.61]) several more
times to state that the mixed cup and baked bread upon receiving the
word of God become the Eucharist, the body and blood of Christ.
This body and blood is actual; it is true human substance. And
humans receive nourishment in body and blood from them. For Irenaeus the renewing nourishment is fulfilled eschatologically in resurrection. Although buried and decayed, the bodies nourished by the
Eucharist will be raised through the Word, immortal and incorruptible, to the Father's glory.

In the selection quoted from *Adversus Haereses* 5.2.2, "blood"
serves as a metonymy for human nature. But it goes beyond that association to indicate, as well, creature. So when Irenaeus speaks of
redemption through Christ's blood, he speaks of redemption through
the Word's humanity, creatureliness, corporeality, and the church's
communion with it through participation in wine and bread. His biblical source for the connection between Christ's blood and redemption is Ephesians 1:7 to which he alluded already in the previous
chapter of *Adversus Haereses* 5.1.1–3.[19] Significantly, in one place the
"blood" of Ephesians 1:7 becomes "flesh and blood," indicating the
fullness of Christ's identity with the first human:

> For he would not have had the blood and flesh in actuality by
> which he redeemed us, if he had not recapitulated in himself
> the ancient formation of Adam. (*Adv. Haer.* 5.1.2 [*SC* 153:
> 24.56–58]).

This attention to the full humanity reflects no disinterest in the passion and sacrifice of Christ. He gave "his soul for our soul and his
flesh for our flesh" in redeeming us "through his blood" (*Adv. Haer.*
5.1.1 [*SC* 153: 20.33–35]). Redemption was accomplished through the
shed blood of Christ in his real suffering after the manner of Romans
6:3–4; 5:6–10; 8:34 (*Adv. Haer.* 3.16.9 [*SC* 211: 322.283–326.329]).
But the emphasis upon the true incarnation connects with his understanding that redemption involves the reconciliation of human flesh

(and blood) to God by means of Christ's carnal body.[20] Christ saves the original though lost constitution of Adam, made in the image and likeness of God, by taking it unto himself in the incarnation (*Adv. Haer.* 5.14.2–3 [*SC* 153: 186.32–192.77]). He thus "reintroduces it into friendship with God" (*Adv. Haer.* 5.14.2 [*SC* 153: 188.56]). In his understanding, God, in the incarnation, forms a new human (Christ) so that Adam, the old human, might be renewed after God's image and likeness (*Adv. Haer.* 5.1.3 [*SC* 153: 28.87–89]). In his incarnation he unites the (new) humanity to God and bestows incorruption by that communion of humanity with God (*Adv. Haer.* 5.1.1 [*SC* 153: 20.37–40]).[21] With this idea of the communion with God through incarnation in mind, he cites Ephesians 1:7 in both *Adversus Haereses* 5.2.2 and 5.14.3. Christ must have actual flesh, blood, veins in order for human communion with God to take place. Christ did not redeem corporeal humanity by his own blood, the bishop says, if the incarnation as the means of restoring the image and likeness did not occur (*Adv. Haer.* 5.2.1 [*SC* 153: 28.5–30.10]).

Therefore, in *Adversus Haereses* 5.2.2–3 we see him linking the cup and bread to the redemption of the blood and bodies of believers, their corporeality. The Word has become actual creature, actual human, with actual corporeal blood and flesh. The seed of his renewing corporeality comes to the believer in the Eucharist and finds consummation in resurrection. The Eucharist, which is communion in his blood and body, imparts the communion of God and human realized in the Word's incarnation. Such is to be expected in God's entire economy, where spirit and flesh, soul and blood are both saved and in unity.

Our final text from Irenaeus on the topic of Eucharist and economy occurs in *Adversus Haereses* 4.18.5. Again, the issue in his polemic is the salvation of the flesh. He begins, and we are not surprised, by rhetorically stating that human flesh is nourished by Christ's body and blood, and therefore cannot be left to corruption and death. Next, he affirms that the position of the church on the salvation of the flesh through Christ's flesh and blood is established by the Eucharist and establishes the Eucharist. The relation between the Eucharist and the church's faith is symphonic because the Eucharist proclaims the unity between flesh and spirit. There is communion between the two. Here, once more, is the harmony within God's economy. He explains:

> Just as bread which comes from the earth, after having
> received God's invocation, is no longer ordinary bread, but the
> Eucharist constituted of two things, the earthly and the heav-
> enly, so also our bodies when they participate in the Eucharist
> are no longer corruptible, because they have the hope of the
> resurrection. (*Adv. Haer.* 4.18.5 [*SC* 100.2: 610.117–612.122])

As Y. de Andia argues, Irenaeus has a two-point parallel structure
which complements the two earlier points on symphony and communion. The bishop addresses the *constitution* of the Eucharist and the
participation of believers' bodies in the Eucharist unto resurrection.
The constitution of the elements, as a result of their becoming the
Eucharist, is that of two elements.[22] The one is earthly, that is the
bread. The other is heavenly, the glorious body of Christ, the bread
of life who is present in the eucharistic bread, which is his body. Irenaeus supplies no particular metaphysical explanation. The constitution of the Eucharist is next carried forth to the question of the
believer's participation in it. The same two elements, heavenly and
earthly, are true of the bodies that receive the Eucharist. Such bodies
are composed of the earthly, corruptible substance, but also through
participation, a heavenly, incorruptible one which comes from God
and ends in eternal life. Irenaeus speaks already of the body as incorruptible, but he does so in hope, in expectation. Through the nourishing Eucharist, Christian bodies "become 'spiritual' and eventually
imperishable through the resurrection, now possessed in hope."[23] As
the bread actually changes, so also the body is spiritualized, made fit
for the kingdom by the Spirit in promise of resurrection.

The incarnation of the Word binds together for all times the two
realities of flesh and spirit. Although in the one God's economy they
have always been compatible, the incarnation seals their compatibility
in continuity with other events, but more brilliantly. This unity is
revealed also in the Eucharist and finally in the redemption of bodies.
The sequence, which has the Eucharist as its linking pin, is once
again Incarnation—Eucharist—Resurrection. And, then, as we know
from our earlier discussion, prior to Incarnation, for our bishop, is
Creation. The Eucharist captures for the church the whole reality of
God's relationship with the creature. It proclaims the integrity of God
the Creator by employing the fruits of the created field. It announces

the essential unity of Jesus Christ, Incarnate Word from the Father, given to us creatures for salvation in body and soul. It declares God's renewal, rather than his rejection, of the human creatures who exist in physical substance, for he will raise them from the grave.

In the second century we have encountered a rich, fertile field. The prevailing common theme of our interest has been the Eucharist's attestation to the incarnation of the Word and the believer's participation in its blessings. It conveys the post-resurrection presence of Christ. It continues now in supreme form, the gracious ministry the Word has always had within the world. It authenticates the integrity of the creation and particularly the flesh. It maintains the unity of God, his economy, Christ, and human nature. It takes its place as one other crucial, merciful act of God through Christ by the Spirit in the world on behalf of his creatures. Once again, at the Eucharist, for the second century, the Father embraces the physical substance which he created and which he united with his Son, provides once again the presence of his Son with us, and imparts to us the redemption of our bodies.

Martin Luther

In his response to the views of Karlstadt and the Swiss on the Lord's Supper, Luther composed an important work early in 1527. *This Is My Body*, a writing which reflects Luther's developed thought, has a three-part structure.[24] The first portion argues that Zwingli's troublesome, fanatical position bears the burden of proving that the Lord's words are figurative, and that Christ's ascension does not prohibit Christ's presence in the Supper. The second part asserts that the Swiss have misunderstood John 6:63, "the flesh is of no avail," if they apply it to the presence of the Lord's flesh at the Supper. Flesh, in this text, is fleshliness, the orientation toward self and the works of the devil. One must not confuse flesh with "physical" or "bodily," for the Spirit opposes wickedness, not things corporeal. Third, Luther gathers testimony from the fathers in order to combat the ideas of the Swiss.

Like the second-century fathers before him, Luther's doctrine of the Lord's Supper is derived necessarily from his doctrine of Christ, the Incarnate Word of God. His Christology nourishes his understanding of the sacrament. The controversy over the latter, however, certainly drove him further to develop and highlight features within his Christology.[25] Our interest here, as we shift our focus from the second to the sixteenth century, is, for the most part, the second part of *This Is My Body*. We will see how the contemplation of Eucharist and incarnation brings Luther to conclusions similar to those we have seen in Ignatius, Justin, and Irenaeus.

We begin with Luther's conviction about the unity between the physical and the spiritual, the corporeal and the presence of God in Christ. The translator of our text describes the concept in this way:

> Because God uses earthly means in and through which to come to us, faith must cling to them, not as objects but as the signs of his potent presence, the points at which he has told we shall find him. That this is actually the manner of God's revelation we see supremely in Jesus Christ, who is God and man in one person, incarnate on the plane of history. The only Christ we know is this one Jesus, God in human flesh. Therefore his humanity cannot be called useless to our salvation.[26]

For Luther, the redemptive activity of God has always been associated with the bodily presence of the Lord, just as before the incarnation, redemptive blessings were associated with physical things.[27] These instances of bodiliness and physicality, however, were always accompanied by the spiritual belief of the faithful produced by the Spirit. The Spirit and the physical form a unity in the history of salvation. In particular he mentions: (1) the Virgin Mary who bore Christ physically from her womb and spiritually in her heart by believing the angel's words; (2) the shepherds who saw the infant both physically and spiritually; (3) the woman with the hemorrhage who touched Christ in both ways; (4) Abraham who possessed the land physically in faith; and (5) Abraham who begot Isaac first in the belief that God would provide and then physically (*LW* 37:89–91). In this theology, "Nothing can be so material, fleshly, or outward, but it becomes spiritual when it is done in the Word and in faith" (*LW* 37:92).

But Luther insists that these ways of contact with God's blessings and his Christ were for those ancient people. For those of the contemporary church, God has ordained a mode of contact specifically for them. The faithful of the church are charged with eating and drinking the Eucharist. In so doing they, too, encounter Christ physically in continuity with the antique pattern of redemptive history:

> But we trust our God, who has willed to be born of Mary spiritually and physically but not to be eaten and drunk by her physically or spiritually. By the shepherds and Simeon he wanted to be seen spiritually and physically but not born and not eaten. So, according to his good pleasure, he has permitted himself to be physically and spiritually handled, seen, heard, born, suckled, carried, touched, and the like by whomever he willed. But here in the Lord's Supper he wants to be neither born nor seen nor heard nor touched by us but only eaten and drunk, both physically and spiritually. (*LW* 37:94)

The unique place for the church to participate in the repetitive grace of the history of Christ's meeting with his creatures is the table. God in Christ is present everywhere, but he makes a particular promise of presence to the limited creature at the table. There he presents himself for the faithful, there he can be grasped in a way not possible in his regular presence everywhere. The precedent for the presence at the Supper is the presence made possible in incarnation:

> Because it is one thing if God is present, and another if he is present for you. He is there for you when he adds his Word and binds himself, saying, "Here you are to find me..." This God's right hand does, however, when it enters into the humanity of Christ and dwells there. There you surely find it, otherwise you will run back and forth throughout all creation, groping here and groping there yet never finding, even though it is actually there; for it is not there for you...He also now exceeds any grasp...unless he binds himself to you and summons you to a particular table by his Word, and he himself gives meaning to the bread for you, by His Word, bidding you to eat him. This he does in the Supper, saying, "This is my body..." (*LW* 37:69)

Now the particulars of metaphysical mystery are not to be the
believer's focus. Rather, the crucial fact is the believer's physical participation in Christ's true body and blood. According to Luther, the
evangelists demonstrate this concern when they record Christ's saying
of institution:

> Now, here stands the text, stating clearly and lucidly that
> Christ gives his body to eat when he distributes the bread.
> On this we take our stand, and we also believe and teach that
> in the Supper we eat and take to ourselves Christ's body truly
> and physically. But how this takes place or how he is in the
> bread, we do not know and are not meant to know. God's
> Word we should believe without setting bounds or measure
> to it. The bread we see with our eyes, but we hear with our
> ears that Christ's body is present. (*LW* 37:22–29)

All pivots around Luther's conviction that Christ's flesh does avail
and that it avails in the Supper. On this point we return to the pattern
of Christ's bodily ministry. Arguing with sarcasm against his opponents, Luther insists that the creed and the gospels must be mistaken.
The virgin, if the flesh is of no avail, did not bodily carry the Son of
God or bear him bodily through her flesh. Meaningless was his bodily form in the manger, his bodily baptism in the Jordan, and his bodily ministry in the wilderness, towns, and on the sea. Without avail,
too, is the Lord's bodily presence at the Last Supper, his physical
speaking, his physical foot washing, and his bodily session in heaven
at the Father's right hand. With further sarcasm he insists that in each
of these circumstances "he certainly was not bodily present, but only
spiritually" (*LW* 37:83).

Stringing out his sarcasm a bit more and then departing from it,
he goes on positively to state his point. There is no difference
between the significance of the encounter of the faithful with Christ's
flesh in those circumstances just mentioned and in its presence at the
Supper as the faithful eat it. Addressing the "fanatics" he says,

> Even if you proved it—which you cannot do—I would like to
> hear exactly why Christ's flesh is of no avail when it is physi-
> cally eaten, and not also when it is physically conceived and

born, laid in the manger, taken up in one's arms, seated at table at the Supper, hanging upon the cross, etc. All these are outward modes and uses of his flesh as truly as when he is physically eaten. Is it better when it is in his mother's womb than when it is in the bread and in the mouth? If it is of no avail here, it can be of no avail there either; if it avails there, it must also avail here. *For nothing more can be made out of this than that Christ's body is dealt with physically and outwardly, whether it is eaten or conceived, born or carried, seen or heard...And I must continue to maintain what I have said, that Christ's flesh either must avail in the Supper or must be of no avail whatsoever whether in heaven or in the spirit.* (*LW* 37:85, emphasis added)

Here, then, we encounter one of the great themes of the second century. The Eucharist is a moment in redemptive history when God graciously sets his incarnate Son before his faithful. While in continuity with previous instances of the incarnate Son's presence with humanity, this moment maintains its distinctiveness within God's economy. The Eucharist is the occasion when the faithful come into fellowship with the Christ who is not only spirit, but also flesh. It annunciates the integrity of flesh and denies that it is of no avail.

A second theme, highlighted most brightly in Ignatius, is the correlative relationship between the Eucharist and the community's virtue of love. In another text, *The Sacrament of the Body and Blood of Christ—Against the Fanatics* (1526), Luther lists two central principles of doctrine that are found in the Eucharist. The first is that "Christ has given his body, flesh, blood on the cross to be our treasure and to help us receive forgiveness of sins, that is, that we may be saved, redeemed from death and hell." For Luther, in the Eucharist, Christ's "body and blood are given to us to be received corporeally as a token and confirmation of this fact." The second principle concerns love. First of all it puts before the faithful the example to be followed:

The second principle is love. It is demonstrated in the first place by the fact that he has left us an example. As he gives us himself for us with his body and blood in order to redeem us from all misery, so we too are to give ourselves with might and main for our neighbor. Whoever knows this and lives

accordingly is holy, and has not much to learn, nor will he
find anything more in the whole Bible. (*LW* 36:352).[28]

In second place, along with example there exists "figure or symbol."
The loaf, in accordance with Paul's teaching (1 Cor 10:17), and the
wine as well both symbolize the common unity of true Christendom.
"That is," he says, "how a Christian acts. He is conscious of nothing
else than that the goods which are his are also given to his neighbor.
He makes no distinction, but helps everyone with body and life,
goods and honor, as much as he can (*LW* 36:353).

The final theme we will mention is the ancient Christian attestation to the association between Eucharist and resurrection.[29] Repeat-
edly in *This Is My Body* Luther refers to this association. Although the
body is unaware it is being nurtured ("the uncomprehending body
does not know that it is eating a food by which it will live forever"),
the soul comprehends that "the body will live eternally because it has
partaken of an eternal food which will not leave it to decay in the
grave and turn to dust" (*LW* 37:93–94). He brings forward this patristic emphasis in his polemic in the third part of the treatise within his
discussion of Irenaeus. With the bishop of Lyons he opposes any who
would hold to the Valentinian denial of the salvation and resurrection
of the flesh and body. Citing *Adversus Haereses* 4.18.5 and 5.2.2–3, he
takes three features of the Eucharist from Irenaeus: (1) through God's
word, the bread becomes a twofold thing, earthly and heavenly, not
ordinary bread; (2) this heavenly portion imparts to the body, though
hidden in faith and hope until the Last Day, the promise of resurrection in fulfillment of John 6:55, 58; and (3) the flesh, therefore, physically nourished by Christ's blood and flesh, inherits eternal life (*LW*
37:115–20).

The resurrection of the body through participation in the
Eucharist, in the Reformer's mind, means that the body has been
transformed into that which is spiritual. The flesh as that which is evil
and mortal has become "alive and blessed forever" after 1 Corinthians
15:44:

So when we eat Christ's flesh physically and spiritually, the
food is so powerful that it transforms us into itself and out of
fleshly, sinful, mortal men makes spiritual, holy, living men.

This we are already, though in a hidden manner in faith and hope; the fact is not yet manifest, but we shall experience it on the Last Day. (*LW* 37:101)

Conclusion

For the second century and for Luther, to exclude the flesh from salvation and the fleshly Son of God as its agent was not Christian. And, for the second century, as for Luther, any conference on the Eucharist must begin and end with this concern. The Eucharist, for these Christians, casts a dazzling light upon the miracle of grace which is the incarnation. The remembrance of Christ's death is still central, the Eucharist as an offering to the Creator-Father is still emphasized. But with these aspects appears the Word of God made flesh who conveys salvation to flesh and calls upon his faithful to love flesh in deed and truth. The whole economy of the Creator of the physical realm, who is also its Redeemer, is set before the worshiper through the bread and the wine which is the body and blood of the incarnate One. The Eucharist proclaims (and in it the Christian embraces) the unity of redemptive history: Creation–Presence of the Pre-Incarnate Logos–Incarnation–Eucharist–Resurrection.

NOTES

1. E. LaVerdiere, *The Eucharist in the New Testament and the Early Church* (Collegeville: Liturgical Press, 1996), 191.

2. "L" refers to the critical edition of *Die Apostolischen Väter*, ed. A. Lindemann and H. Paulsen (Tübingen: J. C. B. Mohr [Paul Siebeck], 1992).

3. W. R. Schoedel, *Ignatius of Antioch* (Philadelphia: Fortress, 1985), 21.

4. G. Dix, *The Shape of the Liturgy* (London: Adam and Charles Black, 1975), 137–138.

5. R. Johanny, "Ignatius of Antioch," in *The Eucharist of the Early Christians*, ed. W. Rordorf et al., trans. H. J. O'Connell (New York: Pueblo, 1978), 62.

6. Cf. S. M. Gibbard, "The Eucharist in the Ignatian Epistles," *Studia Patristica* 8.2 (1966) [TU 93]: 214; H. B. Swete, "Eucharistic Belief in the Second and Third

Centuries," *Journal of Theological Studies* 3 (1902): 168; reprint in *Worship in Early Christianity*, ed. E. Ferguson (New York/London: Garland, 1993), 116; Schoedel, 21, 24.

7. C. C. Richardson, *The Christianity of Ignatius of Antioch* (New York: Columbia University, 1935), 56, 59.

8. "M" refers to the following critical editions of Justin: *Justini Martyris Dialogus cum Tryphone*; *Justini Martyris Apologiae pro Christianis*, Patristische Texte und Studien 47, 38, ed. M. Marcovich (Berlin/New York: De Gruyter, 1997, 1994).

9. Cf. P. I. Lundberg, *La typologie baptismale dans l'ancienne Église*, ASNU 10 (Leipzig: A. Lorentz, 1942), 178–184; P. Prigent, *L'Épitre de Barnabé I–XVI et ses sources* (Paris: Gabalden, 1961), 94–95; O. Skarsaune, *The Proof from Prophecy*, NovTSup, no. 56 (Leiden: E. J. Brill, 1987), 378.

10. Cf. C. Munier, *L'Apologie de saint Justin Philosophe et Martyr* (Fribourg, Switz.: Universitaires Fribourg Suisse, 1994), 106.

11. Cf. H. Chadwick, *Early Christian Thought and the Classical Tradition* (Oxford/New York: Oxford University, 1984), 16–17; Munier, 104–105.

12. Munier, 104.

13. Cf. A. Gelston, "*Di euchehs logou* (Justin, *Apology* i.66.2)," *Journal of Theological Studies* 33 (1982): 172–175.

14. Cf. *St. Justin Martyr, The First and Second Apologies*, Ancient Christian Writers, 56; trans. L. W. Barnard (New York/Mahwah: Paulist Press, 1997), 181, n. 407; M. Jourjon, "Justin," in *The Eucharist of the Early Christians*, 76.

15. *SC* refers to the following critical editions of Irenaeus: *Irénée de Lyon: Contre les hérésies*, Livres 3, 4, 5, ed., trans., and annot. A. Rousseau, L. Deutreleau, B. Hemmerdinger, and C. Mercier; 6 vols., *Sources Chrétiennes*, nos. 210, 211, 100.1, 100.2, 152, 153 (Paris: Cerf, 1974, 1965, 1969).

16. Cf. Rousseau, *SC* 210: 282–283; D. Unger, "The Holy Eucharist according to St. Irenaeus," *Laurentianum* 20 (1979): 113–114; Centre d'Analyse et de Documentation Patristiques, *Biblia Patristica: Index des citations et Allusions Bibliques dans la Litterature Patristique*, vol. 1, *Des origines à Clement d'Alexandrie et Tertullien* (Paris: CNRS, 1986), 395.

17. A. Orbe, *Teología de San Ireneo: Commentario al Libro V del "Adversus haereses,"* 3 vols. (Madrid: La Editorial Católica, 1985–1988), 1:130–131; Y. de Andia, *Homo Vivens* (Paris: Études Augustiniennes, 1986), 243.

18. Rousseau, *SC* 210: 194–195.

19. Rousseau (*SC* 153: 33, n.c) and *Biblia Patristica* (1:502) both identify the citation with Col. 1:14. In view of Irenaeus's citation of the text again in *Adv. Haer.* 5.14.3 (*SC* 153: 190.69–71) with credit to Ephesians, it seems best to concur with Orbe (1:64).

20. Cf. A. Orbe, "S. Ireneo y la doctrina de la reconciliación," *Gregorianum* 61 (1980): 5–50.

21. Cf. Rousseau, *SC* 152: 202.

22. Cf. de Andia, 242–243; Unger, 137. See de Andia (254–255) and Unger (127–137) for complete bibliography and discussion.

23. Unger, 130.

24. R. H. Fischer, "Introduction," in *Luther's Works*, American edition, vol. 37, *Word and Sacrament, III*, ed. R. H. Fischer (Philadelphia: Fortress, 1961), 5–7. Henceforth *Luther's Works* will be referred to as *LW*.

25. P. W. Gennrich, *Die Christologie Luthers im Abendmahlsstreit 1524–1529* (Königsberg: Buch und Steindruckerei von O. Kümmel, 1929), 129.

26. R. H. Fischer, "Introduction to Volume 37," *LW* 37:xviii–xix.

27. P. Althaus, *The Theology of Martin Luther*, trans. R. C. Schultz (Philadelphia: Fortress, 1966), 393–397.

28. *Luther's Works*, vol. 36, *Word and Sacrament, II*, ed. A. R. Wentz (Philadelphia: Fortress, 1959).

29. The similarity between Luther and Ignatius's idea of the "medicine of immortality" has been noted. Cf., e.g., B. Lohse, *Martin Luther's Theology: Its Historical and Systematic Development*, trans. R. A. Harrisville (Minneapolis: Fortress, 1999), 311; H. Sasse, *This Is My Body* (Minneapolis: Augsburg, 1959), 183, cf. 248.

D. Bentley Hart

"Thine Own of Thine Own": Eucharistic Sacrifice in Orthodox Tradition

I should say, before all else, that a single essay can in no way adequately address the issue of the Eastern Orthodox understanding of the Eucharist in its relation to Christ's sacrifice, as either a historical or a theological topic. I trust, therefore, that I will be forgiven if my treatment of the matter is occasionally somewhat broadly synoptic, as well as slightly loose in its approach to questions chronological. And I hope that my attempt to draw together various strands of Orthodox tradition in a single, internally consistent theological reflection will be seen as at most synthetic, and not in any sense Procrustean. I want to argue that, whatever variations in terms and emphases have marked the evolution of Eastern eucharistic theology, from the patristic to the high Byzantine to the modern age, there has persisted all along a more or less unified vision of what is accomplished in every celebration of the Divine Liturgy, what its relation is to the saving life, death, and resurrection of the incarnate God, and what light it casts upon our understanding of how God acts in Christ to draw all things together to himself. Byzantine Christianity cannot boast a quite intricate and elaborate history of scholastic and dogmatic interrogations of eucharistic doctrine as can the Western Church (which makes my task slightly easier, perhaps, than would be a Roman Catholic theologian's attempt to summarize his tradition's eucharistic speculations), but I hope to show that its vision of the eucharistic oblation—its understanding of how it is an oblation—is one not only of consider-

able theological coherency, but also of exceeding profundity and
beauty.

First, though, it would be well to determine in what sense that
almost infinitely plastic term "sacrifice" is to be used. Perhaps no
word serves better to capture the intuition that governs the Orthodox tradition's reflections on sacrifice (whether in relation to the
self-offering of Christ or the offering of bread and wine in the
liturgy) than the Hebrew "*qurban*," with its connotation of "drawing
nigh," or "coming into the Presence." I say this not only because of
the prominence the Letter to the Hebrews has traditionally enjoyed
in Orthodox texts as a heuristic of the eucharistic oblation, and the
consequently frequent resort of Orthodox theologians to the language of Israel's Day of Atonement offering as part of their sacramental grammar, but because the word *qurban* (or *qurbana*, as Christians who worship in Syriac call the Eucharist) points to an
understanding of sacrifice as not, obviously, a simple propitiation of
the Divine (crudely conceived) or an attempt to importune God
under the shelter of an ingratiating tribute, but as a miraculous reconciliation between God, who is the wellspring of all life, and his
people, who are dead in sin. Sacrifice, in this sense, means a marvelous reparation of a shattered covenant, and an act wherein is
accomplished, again and again, that divine indwelling, within the
body of his people, that is God's purpose in shaping for himself a
people to bear his glory. If it is indeed always the will of God to
"tabernacle" upon the earth, indeed ultimately to make the whole
earth his temple, then the atonement sacrifice is that moment when
God restores to himself the body he has chosen to dwell within and
so also makes of himself an abode for his creatures. When the blood
of the people, so to speak, which is its life, now forfeited through sin,
is brought into the ambit of the *Shekhinah*, before the mercy seat, an
exchange occurs in which the life's blood of those who were perishing is made pure again, infused with the life that flows from God,
and the nuptial bond of this mutual indwelling—God in his creatures
and they in him—is repaired.

Another way of saying this is that the entire question of eucharistic sacrifice, at least for Orthodox tradition, might most plausibly be
answered in terms of the theme of *theosis*. That is to say, what occurs
in the incarnation of the Word is the consummation of that "drawing

nigh" for which all of creation is intended: its glorification in the light of God, its transformation into a vessel of the Glory of the Presence, and our transfiguration into partakers in the divine nature. As Christ is himself our *hilasmos* and *hilasterion*, our atonement and place of atonement, he accomplishes that perfect sacrifice in his person that unites us to God by emptying himself out into our nature and so filling us up with his; and the Eucharist, in Orthodox tradition, is almost always understood as the place where our offering of ourselves to God is opened up and brought to fruition within Christ's offering of himself, and it comes to pass that we dwell in him and he in us. This is, in large part, why I have chosen as the title of this essay a phrase from a part of the Byzantine anaphora that the celebrant speaks between the words of institution and the epiclesis: "Thine own of thine own, we offer unto thee, on behalf of all, and for all." God's body is what we are graciously given to offer, within which we are both offered up and made alive. Stated simply, as Christ's resurrected body is now the eternal temple where the divine glory inhabits created nature, and as it is in the bread and wine of communion that we eat his flesh and drink his blood and so have life in him, it is in the Eucharist that we enter into the miraculous exchange—the reconciling sacrifice—by which we too are being made bearers of God's glory. To unfold the claim, however, that this is an accurate characterization of the Eastern Orthodox view of the matter, I shall have to proceed by steps, not all in obviously the same direction.

In its developed form, Byzantine mystagogy tends to view the Eucharist as being a sacrifice in a threefold sense: it is at once an offering of bread and wine and so of ourselves (our substance); the one all-sufficing sacrifice made by Christ on our behalf in the economy of his earthly mission; and the abiding presence of his offered humanity upon the heavenly altar, before the throne of God, where he, as our Great High Priest, makes everlasting intercession for us. All of these sacrificial themes have a substantial, if somewhat diffuse, existence in Eastern Christian theology at least as early as the homilies of John Chrysostom, and they already constitute a profound allegorical and theological unity in the majestic eucharistic commentary of Patriarch Germanos I of Constantinople (d. 733), the *Mystic Contemplation*,[1] with its lovely interweaving of the imagery of Levitical sacrifice, Isaiah's vision in the temple, the liturgy of the heavenly court, the whole motion of Christ's *kenosis*, life, death, resurrection, and ascension, and the liturgy of the Great Church. For instance:

> The holy table corresponds to the spot in the tomb where Christ was placed. On it lies the true and heavenly bread, the mystical and unbloody sacrifice. Christ sacrifices His flesh and blood and offers it to the faithful as food for eternal life. The holy table is the throne of God, on which, borne by the Cherubim, He rested in the body.[2]

And:

> The altar corresponds to the holy tomb of Christ. On it Christ brought Himself as a sacrifice to [His] God and father through the offering of His body as a sacrificial lamb, and as high priest and Son of Man, offering and being offered as a mystical bloodless sacrifice, and appointing for the faithful reasonable worship, through which we have become sharers in eternal and immortal life...The altar is and is called the heavenly and spiritual altar, where the earthly and material priests who always assist and serve the Lord represent the spiritual, serving, and hierarchical powers of the immaterial and celestial Powers, for they also must be as a burning fire.

By the early Middle Ages, the threefold scheme has assumed a certain systematic form. The great Archbishop of Bulgaria, Theophylactos of Ochrida (ca. 1050–ca. 1108), for instance, certainly employs it in his commentary on Hebrews,[3] as does the Constantinopolitan monk Euthymios Zigabenos (d. 1118) in his commentary on the same book,[4] and both are clearly anxious to show that, even in its triplicity, there is but one atoning sacrifice in the Eucharist, present under several aspects: the already accomplished historical mission of Christ, the eternal efficacy of this mission in the presence of God, and the real availability in the present of the reconciliation it effects (in both its creaturely and divine dimensions) in the tangible—and frangible—form of Christ's body and blood. Nicholas of Methone, writing in 1157,[5] produced two brief treatments of the eucharistic sacrifice that simply presume the threefold scheme: there is one offering, made once in the past, made everlastingly in heaven, and made continually present to us in time, in the liturgy.[6] And the greatest Orthodox sacramental theologian, Nicholas Cabasilas, whose work constitutes a grand synthesis of the entire Eastern tradition on these matters, frames his account of the Eucharist's salvific efficacy, for the church as a body and for every baptized Christian, precisely in terms of this triple sacrificial economy:

> [T]he Lord was not satisfied with sending the Holy Spirit to abide with us; he has himself promised to be with us, even unto the end of the world. The Paraclete is present unseen because he has not taken a human form, but by means of the great and holy mysteries the Lord submits himself to our sight and touch and through the dread and holy mysteries, because he has taken our nature upon him and bears it eternally.
>
> Such is the power of the priesthood, such is the Priest. For after once offering himself and being made a sacrifice he did not end his priesthood, but is continually offering the sacrifice for us (*alla dienekeh toutehn leitourgei ten leitougian hemin*), by virtue of which he is our advocate before God for ever.[7]

In one sense, then, this may be said to be what Orthodox tradition understands by talk of the Eucharist as "sacrifice": our perpetual entry, through the mediation of Christ's priesthood, into that atonement—that way of return given by God first to Israel—that Christ has everlastingly accomplished for us. But, in another sense, this is to tell only half the tale.

One has not yet arrived at the heart of Byzantine eucharistic theology until one appreciates the radically ontological nature of the Eastern Christian understanding of "atonement" and of the "drawing nigh" of God in Christ that Christ's sacrifice achieves for us. As, typically, the Orthodox tradition's eucharistic discourse is determined by the logic of its Christology (and, indeed, not infrequently the reverse), its understanding of eucharistic sacrifice will remain largely unintelligible if not viewed in light of that wondrous exchange of natures, that *commercium mirabile* between the divine and the human, that occurs in Christ. It is the absolute reconciliation of God and humanity in the Person of the Incarnate Word—the divinization of human nature in its assumption by God the Son—that is, in fact, the final place of atonement, to which we gain entry in the mystery of the holy table. "Sacrifice" here means a reconciling *transitus* whose proper form is the very *communicatio idiomatum* of Christ's divinity and humanity; as Cyril of Alexandria argues, when Christ says, in John 20:17, "I am going to my Father and your Father; to my God and your God," he is describing the very essence of redemption, showing it to be so intimate an interchange of natures and preroga- tives that his Father by nature is now ours through our exaltation in him, and our God by nature is his by condescension.[8] (Of course, as scarcely needs be said, Cyril's certitude regarding the unity of Christ is always, throughout his work, secured by his belief that in the Eucharist we are experiencing nothing less than the deification of our humanity.) Christ is, so to speak, the chiasmus of the created and the divine, the tabernacle and the Glory of the Presence, and in the bread and wine of communion that everlasting reconciliation of natures, and all its transfiguring grace, is sprinkled upon his people. If Christ is himself our access to the mercy seat, our *hilasterion*, he is also the one in whom the veil between us and God's glory has been "rent in twain" (Matt 27:51; Mark 15:38; Luke 23:45), so that that glory comes forth to make its habitation immediately within our souls and bodies, and to shed its splendor upon all flesh. This is why Nicholas of Methone says that the supernatural *metabole* of the elements in the eucharistic consecration is as miraculous and incomprehensible as the incarnation, resurrection, and ascension of Christ, and has as its whole purpose and end the participation in Christ by those who receive from him eternal life and divinization (*ektheosis*);[9] and why Theophylactos, commenting on John 6:56–58, says that he who eats Christ is transformed—elementally—into Christ, and it is thus that God comes to dwell in us and we in him ("*ho trogon me,*" he under- stands Christ to be saying, "*zestai di eme anakirnomenos, hosper kai metastoicheioumenos eis eme ton zoogonein ischuonta*").[10] As Sergii Bul- gakov says, in the ascension of Christ's glorified body, "that which is of the world... already belongs to the divine life, manifesting both a perfect deification of human nature and a perfect inhumanization of the divine nature"; and, he adds, "here we find the foundation of the eucharistic dogma."[11]

Behind all such language, of course, stands that venerable patristic narrative of salvation that at one time (in the dark days of theology's intellectual and spiritual captivity to foreign gods with names like Ritschl and Harnack) was often dismissed as the "physical theory" of the atonement, a coarse mythology of "salvation" rather than a sophisticated moral narrative of justification (narrowly construed): to wit, the belief that we are saved because in the Word's *kenosis* a new and deified humanity was created, one that has now triumphed over death and the devil and ascended into the very trinitarian life of God, into which nature we are incorporated first through the very definitely corporeal mediations of the sacraments. It is that story of redemption through God's indwelling of our nature so beautifully likened by Athanasius to a king coming to dwell in a city that, as a consequence, is ennobled in its every quarter;[12] and by the same author, in more vividly material terms, as the banishment of corruption from our flesh by the Word, whose divinity saturates our nature like asbestos soaking stubble, so that fire can no longer consume it.[13] The fathers, certainly, felt no squeamishness—especially when explicitly linking this soteriology to the "medicine of immortality" that the Eucharist is for us—about describing our salvation in the most frankly physiological fashions. Gregory of Nyssa, for instance, in one of the more restrained passages in his *Catechetical Oration*, puts the matter thus:

> As, therefore, that God-bearing flesh took its substance and sustenance from this [food and drink], and as the God who made himself manifest thus mingled himself with the mortal nature of men in order that by communion with divinity the human might be made divine, through the economy of grace he disseminates himself in the faithful by means of that same flesh, which is nourished by wine and bread, blending himself with the bodies of the faithful, so that, by union with the immortal, man too may come to be a partaker in incorruptibility. These things he vouchsafes to us through the power of that blessing whereby he transforms (*metastoicheiosas*) the nature of visible things into the incorruptible.[14]

Or as John Chrysostom says, with his customary rhetorical aplomb:

> We become one body and, [as the apostle] says, members of his flesh and of his bones [Ephesians 5:30]. Let the initiated follow my words. In order that we might become such not only according to love, but in actual fact, let us be blended into that flesh. For this happens through the food he has graciously given us, wishing to reveal to us the desire he has for us; thus he has mixed himself together with us, and has kneaded his body into us... Those who long for him he has allowed not only to see him, but also to touch him, and to devour him, and to fix their teeth in his flesh, and to embrace him, and to satisfy all their desire.[15]

Indeed, as Cyril of Alexandria says,

> while we may well say of the flesh of Paul or Peter that "the flesh profiteth nothing," we must say just the opposite of the flesh... of our savior Christ, in whom dwelt all the fullness of the Godhead bodily, for it would be very odd indeed that honey should infuse its own quality into things that are naturally devoid of sweetness, and should transform the qualities (*metaskeuzein*) of those things with which it is mixed into its own, but that we should not think that the life-creating nature of God the Word should elevate into its own goodness that wherein his body dwelt.[16]

And John of Damascus's explanation of the Eucharist in *On the Orthodox Faith* is, predictably, the most systematically thorough treatment of the matter among patristic texts:

> The bread and wine are not a figure of the body and blood of Christ—God forbid!—but the actual deified body of the Lord (*to soma tou Kyriou tetheomenon*). With eyes, lips, and faces turned toward it let us receive the divine burning coal, so that the fire of the coal may be added to the desire within us to consume our sins and enlighten our hearts, and so that

by this communion of the divine fire we may be set afire and
deified (*te metousia tou Theiou puros purothomen kai
Theothomen*). Isaias saw a live coal, and this coal was not plain
wood but wood joined with fire. Thus also, the bread of communion is not plain bread, but bread joined with the Godhead.[17]

Perhaps such language is somewhat unrefined by modern standards;
but I would argue that it is still the profoundest theology, of salvation
or of sacrament; and that perhaps a failure to grasp this is sympto-
matic of a still graver failure to grasp what it means to worship an
incarnate God. It requires imagination, granted, but also some considerable breadth of theological vision to see how common bread and
wine can become for us the site where God's self-outpouring and our
exaltation occur for us, the substance of our reconciliation with God,
and the evidence of God's utter condescension for our sakes. As Gregory Palamas remarks, the union of humanity with Christ that this
sacrament accomplishes constitutes the highest expression of God's
love for us;[18] and he goes on to remark, with all the physiological liter-
alism not only of the early fathers but of Symeon the New Theologian, and with absolutely no trace of liberal Protestant pudency:

O many-sided and ineffable communion! Christ has become
our brother, for He has fellowship with us in flesh and
blood...He has bound us to Himself and united us, as the
bridegroom unites the bride to himself, through the communion of this His blood, becoming one flesh with us. He has
also become our father through divine baptism in Himself,
and He feeds us at His own breast, as a loving mother feeds
her child.[19]

In any event, this is the crux of the matter: the Eucharist is the
site where that same indissoluble bond between God and humanity
accomplished in Christ becomes our food and drink, substance and
sustenance for us, and where, as Gregory the Theologian says,
through a bloodless sacrifice, we partake of Christ, both as to his sufferings and his Godhead.[20] And in that sacrificial partaking, there is a
real exchange of substance for substance, an exhaustion of our

poverty, so to speak, to make way for the riches he pours into us. If there is any value to the ancient dispute over the use of azymes in the Eucharist (which for the most part there is not), it is the light it casts upon Eastern understandings of the connection between eucharistic theology and both Christology and soteriology; behind the Byzantine suspicion that churches that use unleavened bread are perhaps guilty of that more or less mythical heresy called "monophysitism" (and so feel free to leave unrepresented the "earthly leaven" of Christ's humanity), lies a fairly pervasive prejudice to the effect that, no less than Christ's was common flesh, so the bread of communion should be our ordinary, daily bread, our *artos epiousios*, which truly nourishes our flesh. John Meyendorff is simply conventionally Byzantine when he asserts the importance of the fact that the *erosphora* and *antidoron* consumed during and after the Divine Liturgy is true, consubstantial bread, rather than ethereal (and nutriently vapid) azymes; God has truly become our sustenance, the wine and bread that feeds our humanity, and has transfigured it into glory in his death and resurrection.[21] For Nicholas Cabasilas, food is the first fruit of our nature, and bread and wine are not only viands that we gather from the world, but uniquely human nourishments, and so in offering them we are handing over the first-fruits of our substance to God.[22] So the oblation of this our substance is assumed into his offering of our humanity, as himself the first-fruits of the human race and the first born under the law.[23] "It is he who commands us to offer bread and wine," writes Cabasilas,

> it is he who gives us in return the Living Bread, the chalice of everlasting life...He commands those to whom he would give eternal life (that is, his life-giving Body and Blood) to offer the food of our fleeting mortal life: so that we may receive life for life, eternity for temporality; so that what is grace may seem to be an exchange, so that infinite generosity may have the appearance of justice...[24]

Christ is, then, both the Way for us and the waybread that sustains us.

It is very much the same prejudice that has moved most modern Orthodox theologians to regret that the Eastern Church, in the late Middle Ages and early modern period, adopted the language of "transubstantiation" from Western theology. One cannot quite agree with John Meyendorff that this borrowing was extremely rare and in general jarring to Byzantine sensibilities.[25] Of course, we attribute it primarily to "Latinophrones" like George Gennadios (Scholarios), who, prior to the fall of Constantinople and his elevation to the patriarchate by Mechmet II, was an avid student of Western theology. His most famous text on eucharistic theology, a homily from 1453, is in fact simply a Greek translation of Latin thought: what occurs in the consecration of the elements is a *metousiosis*, wherein the substance (*ousia*) of the bread and wine is displaced by the substance of Christ's body and blood, though their accidents (*symbebekota*) are preserved.[26] But Gennadios's language is scarcely an anomaly, at least not from the perspective of later church teaching: the *Orthodox Confession* of the Metropolitan of Kiev Peter Mogila, written in 1640, uses the same terminology;[27] this document was subsequently approved by the Council of Jassy in 1642, by the patriarchs of Constantinople, Antioch, Alexandria, and Jerusalem in 1643, and by the Council of Jerusalem of 1672, at which was also adopted the *Confession* of Dositheos, Patriarch of Jerusalem, which affirms that in the consecration of the elements, the natural substance is entirely banished, so that we can partake of Christ's body and blood under the *eidei* and *typo* of bread and wine.[28] And a council held in Constantinople in 1727 declared the doctrine of *metousiosis* to be the ancient teaching of the whole Catholic Church.[29] Nevertheless, Meyendorff is essentially correct when he says that, generally speaking, "the Byzantines did not see the substance of the bread somehow changed in the Eucharistic mystery into another substance...but viewed this bread as the 'type' of the humanity: our humanity changed into the transfigured humanity of Christ."[30]

Among modern Orthodox theologians, none has been more adamant in his rejection of the language of transubstantiation than Sergii Bulgakov; for one thing, he regards it as a philosophically inane concept in an era in which the idea of intransitive "substance" has disappeared from empirical science and speculative philosophy alike, displaced by talk of quantifiable process, or dialectical determination, or linguistic contingency, or by the language of transcendental philosophy, in which context substance can mean either the purely posited but inaccessible *Ding an sich* behind any particular appearance, or the coherence of phenomenal experience achieved by the *cogito*'s transcendental unity of apperception—neither of which can bear the weight of the traditional dogma. But, more to the point, he thinks it reflects a deficient sense of the way in which the Eucharist grants us access to the deified humanity of Christ. No more than the incarnation expels the true substantial humanity of Jesus does the divine presence expel the natural substance of the eucharistic elements; just as Christ's assumed humanity, while retaining its creaturely integrity, is transformed into his glorified and heavenly body, so our bodies, and indeed the whole world, have the potential of becoming divine within their proper substances, not in spite of them.[31] Of course, whether Bulgakov has quite done justice to the theology of transubstantiation is debatable (one obvious rejoinder would be to point out that the Roman Catholic position is not that in the Eucharist the divine displaces the creaturely, but rather that the presence of the incarnate Christ, in both his divinity and humanity, is made radically available), but he definitely marks a trend. Typically, now, the touchstones to which Orthodox theologians are wont to resort in regard to the sacrament are such things as a letter traditionally ascribed to John Chrysostom from the latter half of the fifth century, which argues that when the bread of communion really becomes the body of Christ it still retains its nature as bread, just as, when the divine nature took to itself a body, two natures were made one Son;[32] or the sixth-century christological formula of Leontios of Byzantium (which will hardly strike Western ears as unfamiliar) that the supernatural does not destroy the natural, but elevates it above its "natural" capacity, educing and animating its potential so that it becomes capable of more than itself.[33]

In any event, I call attention to this matter not because I think it a particularly fruitful debate, but because, again, it demonstrates how thoroughly the Eastern view of the Eucharist is determined by its theology of incarnation and divinization, *kenosis* and exaltation; and by the certainty that we who are called to become partakers of the divine nature do so now, already, in the degree to which we are able, under the real material form of bread and wine. What we offer in the eucharistic oblation is our entire being, and what we receive is the transformation of our being in Christ, soul, mind, and body. This food is nothing less than our re-creation in Christ as sons and daughters of God, co-heirs of the kingdom, and vessels of God's glory.

One of the more peculiar aspects of the Divine Liturgy is the graduality with which it unfolds its sacrificial motion—by which I mean the numerous ways in which it adumbrates or indeed enacts a sacrifice of the gifts—well before the actual anaphora. Obvious examples are the piercing and dividing of the *prosphora* with a small spear-shaped instrument during the *prothesis* or *proscomide* (the preparation of the elements before the liturgy begins), which is accompanied by such phrases as "Sacrificed is the Lamb of God, who takes away the sin of the world, for the life of the world and its salvation"; or the extraordinary reverence of the procession of the elements into the altar during the Great Entrance, and the veneration they receive from the congregation, and the great Cherubic Hymn the choir sings, which speaks of the arrival of the "King of All, who comes invisibly upborne by the angelic hosts," and the prayers the celebrant then quietly recites over them, which speak of them as the slain body of Christ lying in the tomb, while Christ accomplishes our salvation in hell, on earth, and in heaven, making his tomb the fountain of our salvation. In truth, the "sacrifice" as such is often rather difficult to locate; it is somehow shrouded in its own ubiquity. And the history of Eastern Christian mystagogy reflects this: the tendency of Byzantine commentaries on the liturgy to expand into ever richer and more fulsome allegories, as they strain to show how the entire economy of Christ's incarnation, death, resurrection, and ascension into the heavenly place is dramaturgically represented in the celebration of the mystery, comes of a deep desire to rationalize the sheer prodigality with which the Byzantine liturgy announces the presence of Christ in the gifts and the eventuation of his sacrifice in the people's midst. Indeed, it is in large part the result of the liturgical hypertrophy of the Great Entrance—to which, for instance, the emperor Justin II in 573–574 added the Cherubic hymn, and which soon came to be accompanied, at Easter, by the hymn "Let all mortal flesh..." from the Liturgy of St. James, which seems to describe the elements as the "King of kings and Lord of lords," entering to be slain; so exuberantly profligate a display of (apparently premature) reverence simply *necessitated* the development of Byzantine theology's long tradition of the composition of ingenious mystagogical *fantasias* upon the various actions of the rite.[34] Nicholas Cabasilas feels moved to defend the congregation's veneration of the gifts at the Entrance by arguing that in fact the people are actually prostrating themselves before the priest, entreating him to remember them in his prayers in the altar;[35] and Gabriel Severus[36] feels he must isolate three distinct phases in the veneration of the bread and wine in the liturgy: they are honored first *physikos*, insofar as they are good creatures of God, then *metochikos*, when they are set apart as gifts consecrated to become Christ's body and blood, and finally *metousiastikos*, when they have been consecrated and have become worthy of full worship (*latreia*).[37] In general, however, Orthodox mystagogues, greatly to their credit, have felt no need for such apologetics.

There are two distinct tendencies in the Eastern tradition of liturgical allegory: one that elects a symbolic interpretation of the rite in conscious or unconscious preference to the radical eucharistic realism of earlier patristic theology, and another in which that realism has become so intense that it becomes positively necessary to see the whole sacrificial movement of Christ, from his *kenosis* to his session at the right hand of the Father, written—however forcibly—into the sacramental action. The two most notable representatives of the former tendency are the Pseudo-Dionysius and Maximos the Confessor, both of whom tend to subordinate sacramental *koinonia* to mystical *theoria*. The Pseudo-Dionysius sees in the eucharistic bread and wine beautiful symbols of our peaceful participation in Christ's divinity, but he also longs for the veil of symbolism to be drawn aside so that we might contemplate the intelligible reality;[38] and Maximos's *Mystagogia* never actually discusses the anaphora or the transformation of the elements, and it presents the rest of the liturgy as principally a succession of soteriological *tableaux:* our reception of the "life-giving elements," he says, *denotes* a communion and identity with Christ according to that participation through likeness (*kata methexin endechomenehn di homoitehs*) whereby man becomes God, but what we await now in faith and receive in the Spirit we will really partake of in the world to come, when we will truly see Christ translating us into himself (*metapoiountas hemas pros eauton*) and granting us those "archetypal mysteries" that are here represented by "perceptible symbols."[39] In either case, some part of the realism of Gregory of Nyssa or John Chrysostom is absent, and some small but inviolate interval appears to have been introduced between the truth of our dwelling in the temple of Christ's body and the palpable actuality of the

Eucharist's fleshly economies. Still, even these more "theoretic" approaches to the Eucharist are colored by a profound certainty that the mystery is a revelation to us of the exchange that occurs between us and Christ, and so between our humanity and his divinity, in his saving action for and in us. For the Pseudo-Dionysius, the eucharistic celebration concerns the descent of God in Christ and our total incorporation in him through continuous participation. And Maximos's allegory in every instance points toward the truth of this saving commerce, which allows us to offer ourselves in the self-oblation of Christ: the first entry of the bishop into the church and ascent into the altar, he says, is a representation of Christ's whole mission in the flesh, from his incarnation to his ascension, whereby he freed our nature from slavery to sin and death, gave us in exchange for our destructive passions his healing and life-giving passion, and entered in for us before the heavenly throne;[40] and the entry of the people into the church represents their conversion from ignorance and vice to knowledge and virtue, as they enter with Christ into God's goodness;[41] and in the sealing of the doors, and the reading of the gospel, and the mysteries that ensue, Christ leads the faithful, who have received the Spirit of adoption and have been divinized by love and made like him through participation, up to the Father.[42]

By far, however, it is the other tendency that predominates in Byzantine mystagogy: a profound sense that Christ is really present in all that we see, hear, and taste in the liturgy, so totally so that every aspect of his divine and human life is being shared with us in everything that occurs, transforming us by drawing us, at every juncture, more deeply into the saving history of the incarnation. Germanos's *Commentary* already obeys this logic, and Cabasilas is an inheritor of this tradition (though he is able to give it greater theological stability than his predecessors). It reaches its most elaborate expression in the eleventh century *Protheoria* of Nicholas of Andida, which Theodore of Andida revised in the eleventh or twelfth century;[43] in this work, images of Christ's mission are found everywhere in the liturgy: lying on the paten, the *prosphora* is the Christ-child, and the asterisk placed above it the star of Bethlehem; the *prothesis* represents the first thirty years of Jesus' life, the priest who performs the first part of the liturgy is John the Baptist, the reading of the gospel is the beginning of Christ's ministry, and so on. Nor are these aspects simply of an edifying ecclesial pageant: what one sees are not simply symbols, but manifestations of the incarnate Christ making his sacrifice present in our midst. And as, in the East, commendably, the church never actually forgot that, for the Church Fathers, it is the entirety of Christ's mission—from his sacrificial descent into our nature to his sacrificial ascent with our nature into the heavenly holy of holies—that constitutes his reconciling oblation for us,[44] even the most implausible allegorical readings of the rite have the great virtue of imparting a clear sense of the totality of Christ's action on behalf of the world. The whole course of Christ's life, as he recapitulates the human in himself and then makes it a pure offering of atonement, is his sacrifice, and the whole course of the liturgy is a progressive integration of worshipers into the journey of his life, into that wondrous exchange he brings about within the temple of his body, so that when at last the consecrated elements "scatter" him among his worshipers, his life has become theirs. As Theodore the Studite said in 754, the Eucharist is the mystery that recapitulates the entire dispensation of salvation; nor is it an image only, but the very reality of what it portrays.[45]

I am tempted to speak here of Orthodox mystagogy's "allegorical realism," by which I mean its adoption of a sacramental narrative dependent upon the *reality* of our divinizing union with God in Christ: in the Eucharist we see and are ever more drawn into the simultaneity of the incarnation's double motion, wherein (to employ a figure from a rather remote source) the journey of the Son of God into the far country is also, at the same time, the homecoming of the Son of Man; and because it is the Eucharist where we know this, we do not see this reconciliation simply as a redemptive rupture of our experience of the world, a sheer event that invades but does not inhabit our earthly time, leaving us to drift about in the ontic aftermath, but as a real presence here and now, with a real temporal axis and palpable form, a true time and place where we partake—in every sense—of the Godhead Christ has brought near. The Eucharist is that same place of atonement (*hilasterion*), then, that Christ is: the chiasmus where eternity and time are poured out into one another, where eternity empties itself and time is raised into the eternal, and where we lose ourselves in the abyss of divine beauty to find ourselves restored in the utterly humble abandon of divine love. The mystical spectacle that Byzantine commentators see in the Divine Liturgy is

like the hidden language of the Logos that Origen sees written everywhere in scripture; and the deeply rational imagination with which it
is abstracted from its "text" is no less an achievement of theological
vision than his luxuriant exegeses. The great Eastern liturgical allegories point to the same dogmatic intuitions that inform the language
of the threefold sacrificial economy discussed above: they find in the
celebration of the mystery a divine dramaturgy, unfolding for us, with
inexhaustible vividness, the single reality of Christ's sacrifice in
becoming a man, dying, rising, and ascending; the abiding presence
of his offering upon the heavenly altar and in his body, where he
accomplishes our everlasting *Yom Kippur*, so to speak; and the ever
immediate availability for us of what he accomplishes on our behalf,
the impartation of the *Shekhinah*, our transformation in him. More
simply, they display, with wonderful embroideries and brightly illuminated margins, the truth that he, our God, is now food and drink for
us, and so he dwells in us and we in him.

This brings me to my final theme: that of indwelling. After all,
Christian talk of divinization is essentially the christological radical-
ization of the language of indwelling that lies at the heart of the biblical account of God's election of Israel, and indeed of God's election of
creation, for himself, from nothingness. God fashions the world to be
the theater of his glory and intends to transfigure it, so Paul says, in
the manifestation of "the glorious liberty of the children of God"
(Rom 8:19–21). And God has dwelt in the flesh of Israel, in the midst
of the nation, though he is the boundless God: "[W]ill God indeed
dwell on the earth? Behold, the heaven and heaven of heavens cannot
contain thee; how much less this house that I have built?" (1 Kgs
8:27); and yet he *does* bring his glory to rest within the temple—"so
that the priests could not stand to minister because of the cloud: for
the glory of the Lord had filled the house of the Lord" (1 Kgs 8:11)—
just as he did within the tent of meeting's tabernacle: "And Moses was
not able to enter into the tent of the congregation, because the cloud
abode thereon, and the glory of the Lord filled the tabernacle" (Exod
40:35). It is this same glory that then tabernacles in the body of the
Mother of God: "The Holy Ghost shall come upon thee, and the
power of the Highest shall overshadow thee: therefore also that holy
thing which shall be born of thee shall be called the Son of God"
(Luke 1:35). And in Christ, whose death rends the veil of the holy of

holies, and who is himself the temple that, once torn down, is built again in three days, the inner tabernacle and the hidden glory are made manifest, as the light of the transfiguration and the light of the resurrection, which enters into us precisely because "the cup of blessing which we bless is... the communion of the blood of Christ [and] the bread which we break is... the communion of the body of Christ" (1 Cor 10:16). Thus we are heirs to the promise—which Christ himself confirms in John 10:34—adumbrated in Psalm 82:6: "Ye [are] gods, and all of you children of the most High." I recite all these pericopes because it is only within this web of associations, I want very emphatically to urge, that one can grasp the Orthodox understanding of Eucharist, and of the Eucharist as a sacrifice, and of how the mystery conducts us ever more deeply into the salvation Christ has wrought for us and the whole cosmos. When I advert to the theme of indwelling, I mean this: that all of scripture testifies to the fact that, throughout the history of God's mighty and saving acts, in creation, the election of Israel, and the calling of the nations, God has been preparing for himself a habitation; and in the incarnation, death, resurrection, and ascension of God the Son, he has brought to completion that *qurban*, that reconciling "drawing nigh" of and to the "exceeding glory," which is his plan for creation from before the foundation of the world. And as nature groans in anticipation of the day when all flesh will see that glory (Rom 8:22), and all that Christ has accomplished will be consummated for creation, and God will be all in all (1 Cor 15:28), we now enter, physically and spiritually, into that reconciling union in the Eucharist, and in the whole Christian life that it sustains. As Palamas writes,

[T]he Son of God, in his incomparable love for humanity, not only united his divine hypostasis to our nature, assuming both an animated body and rational soul so as "to appear upon the earth and live among men" (Baruch 3:38), but unites himself—O miracle of such incomparable superabundance!—even with human hypostases, mingling himself with each of the faithful through communion in his holy body, and becomes one body with us and transforms us into the temple of the whole Godhead—for in the body of Christ itself "dwelt all the fullness of the Godhead bodily" (Col. 2:9).[46]

The theme of divine indwelling, as the proper grammar for understanding the Eucharist and the way it reveals to us the *liaison* of the divine and human in Christ's eternal priesthood, everywhere pervades—and achieves its richest and most developed expression in—what, to my mind, is the finest text of sacramental theology that Christian thought, East or West, can boast: Nicholas Cabasilas's *The Life in Christ*. In this book (to which I should like briefly to surrender my prerogatives as this essay's voice) the sacraments—baptism, chrismation, and Eucharist, to be precise—are treated as moments of divine advent that reconstitute us as vessels of divine glory, even as they draw us into the shelter of Christ, who now embraces all of creation in his incarnate presence. The Lord promised, says Cabasilas, not only to be present with his saints, but, more, to make his abode in them, a union scripture portrays in terms of inhabitant and dwelling, or of vine and branch, or of a marriage, or of members and head (though, of course, none of these images is adequate to the reality).[47] To dwell in Christ is to find in him all that suffices for us, and more:

> There is nothing of which the saints are in need which He is not Himself. He gives them birth, growth, and nourishment; He is life and breath. By means of Himself he forms an eye for them and, in addition, gives them light and enables them to see Himself. He is the one who feeds and is Himself the Food; it is He who provides the Bread of life and who is Himself what He provides. He is life for those who live, the sweet odour for those who breathe, the garment for those who would be clothed. Indeed, He is the one who enables us to walk; He Himself is the way (Jn. 14:6), and in addition He is the lodging on the way and its destination.[48]

It is through the sacraments, says Cabasilas, that he thus dwells in us and we in him.[49]

This is the way we draw this life into our souls—by being initiated into the mysteries, being washed and anointed and partaking of the holy table. When we do these things, Christ comes and dwells (*ho christos epidehmoi kai enoikei*) in us, he is united to us and grows into one with us. He stifles sin in us and infuses into us his own life and merit and makes us to share in his victory.[50]

Here is where, indeed, we are given power to become children of God: just as he "united our nature to Himself through the flesh which he assumed," so he "also united each of us to His own flesh by the power of the Mysteries."[51] And of the mysteries, the Eucharist is the most perfect, because it consummates all others; while baptism and chrism, respectively, cleanse and enliven us, the holy table transforms us entirely into Christ's own state: "The clay is no longer clay when it has received the royal likeness but is already the Body of the King."[52] In this final sanctifying encounter with Christ's real presence

> [t]hat of which we partake is not something of Him, but Himself. It is not some ray and light which we receive in our souls, but the very orb of the sun. So we dwell in Him and are indwelt and become one spirit with Him. The soul and the body and all their faculties forthwith become spiritual, for our souls, our bodies and blood, are united with His.[53]

"O how great are the Mysteries!" expostulates Cabasilas; "What a thing it is for Christ's mind to be mingled with ours, our will to be blended with His, our body with His Body and our blood with His Blood!"[54] The Eucharist leads us to the summit of all goodness, the final aim of all human effort: "in it we obtain God Himself, and God is united with us in the most perfect union..."[55] And, again, the Eucharist is the site where the exchange of natures that in Christ is one life and person becomes for us a real exchange of our natural substance for his.

> He did not merely clothe Himself in a body, but He also assumed a soul, mind, and will and everything else that is human, in order to be united to the whole of our nature and completely penetrate us and resolve us into Himself by totally joining what is His to that which is ours.
>   ...So perfectly has He coalesced with that which He has taken that He imparts Himself to us by giving us what He has assumed from us. As we partake of His human Body and Blood we receive God Himself into our souls. It is thus God's Body and Blood which we receive, His soul, mind, and will, no less than those of His humanity.[56]

We are so penetrated then by Christ's presence, says Cabasilas, employing a venerable analogy common to Christology and mysticism alike, that we are like iron penetrated by fire, assuming the properties of the fire into itself; and "Christ infuses Himself into us and mingles Himself with us," says Cabasilas; "He changes and transforms us into Himself, as a small drop of water is changed by being poured into an immense sea of ointment."[57] Thus Christ liberates all who were slaves: "He makes them to share in His body, blood, spirit, and everything that is His. It is thus that He recreated us and set us free and deified us as He, the healthful, free, and true God mingled Himself with us."[58]

I should add that, for Cabasilas, this talk of divine indwelling and human deification does not concern simply the personal experience of individual Christians. As for the fathers, but with perhaps a keener emphasis, divinization for Cabasilas is an experience of the Church as a whole, and it is within the mystical body of Christ, indeed by becoming that mystical body, that Christians have access to the immediate presence of the divinized humanity made available in the bread and wine of communion. The advent of Christ in us is the work of the sanctifying grace of the Holy Spirit, which is first and foremost a pentecostal reality; it is only in the outpouring of the Spirit upon the entire church that God comes to tabernacle in the flesh of those who have been made members of his body. This is especially clear in Cabasilas's *Commentary on the Divine Liturgy*, not only in his defense of the Orthodox belief that only in the epiclesis is the consecration of the elements complete, but in his explanation of the eucharistic *zeon* (the addition of warm water to the chalice of consecrated wine, which the deacon quietly announces as "The fervency of faith, full of the Holy Spirit"): after reminding us, in good Byzantine mystagogical fashion, that in the holy bread we have seen a symbolic representation of the whole pattern of Christ's work on our behalf—the infant Christ, Christ led to his death, his crucifixion and the piercing of his side—and that we have also seen the bread genuinely transformed into the body that suffered for us, rose from the dead, ascended, and is now seated at the right hand of the Father, Cabasilas argues that it is fitting that there should in addition be a proper symbol of the later fulfillment of these great works, a representation of the ultimate effects of salvation, in order that the liturgy might be complete; hence the *zeon*: "What is the effect and the result of the sufferings and works and teaching of Christ? Considered in relation to ourselves, it is nothing other than the descent of the Holy Spirit upon the Church."[59] And it is the Spirit's descent upon the church, which is what always makes Christ present to us in the sacraments, that *is* our divinization: our being made one body in the one bread we share, and that body the body of Christ:

> For the holy mysteries are the Body and Blood of Christ, which are to the Church true food and drink. When she partakes of them, she does not transform them into the human body, as we do with ordinary food, but she is changed into them, for the higher and divine element overcomes the earthly one. When iron is placed in the fire, it becomes fire; it does not, however, give the fire the properties of iron; and just as when we see white-hot iron it seems to be fire and not metal, since all the characteristics of the iron have been destroyed by the action of the fire, so, if one could see the church of Christ, insofar as she is united to him and shares in his sacred Body, one would see nothing other than the Body of the Lord. Because of this, Paul wrote: "Ye are the body of Christ, and members in particular."[60]

I should also add that for Cabasilas the reality of the Eucharist, of course, must possess a fairly radically eschatological significance; for the end of all things will be the glorification of all of creation in Christ, when the divine indwelling will become perfect and God, in Christ, will be all in all. This is the end for which creation was shaped, for which God became a man and joined created nature to his, and for which we have been redeemed. And so the Eucharist, in its very physicality, insofar as it is both food and God's presence for us, is a proleptic foretaste of that ultimate reality when—to employ an image favored by many a modern Orthodox theologian—the world will be like the burning bush, entirely permeated with divine fire, but unconsumed. The bread we eat, says Cabasilas, is no less than the dazzlingly radiant flesh of Christ that, in coming again, will make all things to shine with its own brilliance;[61] this bread is as much as we can now bear of that final reality, but it prepares us by supplying us with gifts to take with us to the wedding feast of the kingdom: those who have eaten of it "have enjoyed the...delight of the banquet though they do not obtain it fully yet; but when Christ has been manifested they will perceive more clearly what it is they have brought with them." And this, adds Cabasilas, is "how the kingdom of heaven is within us (Luke 17:21)."[62]

I shall conclude by observing first that, in the light of these reflections, the language of the threefold economy of sacrifice from which I began my account of Orthodox eucharistic theology more fully discloses its intrinsic logic, and shows itself to be not simply a loose but evocative aggregation of motifs, pointing toward a splendid mystery, but an exceedingly lucid explication of the way in which the biblical understanding of sacrifice and atonement is summed up and recapitulated in the indissoluble unity between Christ's saving action and the celebration of the sacrament. If the sacrificial *transitus* that Christ perfects is that same reconciling approach to the divine glory that God commands of Israel, that which restores the peaceful economy of that glory's approach to and indwelling of his creatures, and if this act of atonement is oriented, as Hebrew prophecy and Christian *kerygma* proclaim, toward the eschatological reign of God's glory in the peace of all creation, then the Eucharist can have no fuller meaning. The bread and wine of communion, the body and blood of Christ: this is our surety that creation has indeed been reconciled to God, within its humblest and most material dailyness, and that God henceforth truly indwells and transfigures creation, and will transfigure it fully in himself. *Theosis*, in both its human and cosmic aspects, is the truth of Israel's *qurban*; and the Eucharist, as our *qurbana*, is our perpetual entry into that union of creation with its God that occurs forever in the unity of the God-man.

Perhaps this is the obvious conclusion of my argument; but I wish to add to it another observation. Above, when I cited a passage from Maximos the Confessor's *Mystagogia*,[63] I neglected to call attention to a fairly salient feature of its argument: that Maximos sees in the Eucharist, in the sanctifying power of our sacramental entry into Christ's body, the full trinitarian economy of salvation. In the mystery, we receive the Spirit of adoption, who unites us to Christ, who deifies us in himself and leads us up to the Father. This is of course completely right: in keeping with the dogmatically and philosophically absolutely necessary premise that the *taxis* of the economic Trinity is the *taxis* of the immanent Trinity, and that therefore the order of salvation is a revelation, quite actually, of how God is God, one must say that the Eucharist is in some essential way a trinitarian event of divine disclosure. Moreover, this is not only apposite to the theme of sacrifice, but provides us with its inmost truth and ultimate rationale. For if it is the sacramental grace accomplished by the advent of the Spirit that saves us by joining us to Christ, so that we are united by God, in God, to God, then the bread and wine we eat in the Eucharist make concrete that most extreme extent of a trinitarian outpouring and tabernacling that does nothing less than seize us up into God's triune life. This, after all, is the truth of sacrifice: that behind the mystery of Christ's offering up of himself lies the infinite truth of a God whose life is always already one of self-outpouring in another, as well as the response of love that that outpouring allows; it is because God, as God, is already thus somehow sacrificial in this biblical sense, that is, a God who goes forth from himself, and in so doing also "draws nigh"— that it is explicable that God should go forth from himself again in creating, shaping for himself a habitation in that which is not God; that he should pour forth in creatures his presence—as their glory and their sanctification—though they can add nothing to him, because he loves them from the sheer superabundance of his self-emptying love; that he should go forth to dwell in the body of Israel; and that he should go forth yet again in the sublime self-outpouring of *kenosis* for the salvation of his creatures, thus showing that no matter how far we venture from him, he has already, in his eternal life of love, ventured infinitely farther than we can ever reach. Because God is Trinity, Christ's self-oblation for us is a naturally divine act; and the divinization of creation that it brings about is the perfect revelation of the *qurban* of God's Trinitarian being; and we see this in the Eucharist. We, in some real sense, taste and are nourished by the whole mystery of our redemption, our "sacrificial" entry into the Trinity's life, and so in the drama of offering up and receiving, we gain some slight but true glimpse of the Trinity's infinite beauty.

To sum the matter up with a brevity that to this point has eluded me: in eucharistic communion, to the degree that the eyes of faith are illuminated by the wisdom that only the Spirit can impart, we see the truth of our divinization in Christ, taste the deep mystery that underlies the creation of the world, discover the hidden depths of our own nature, anticipate in our flesh the glory to which all the world has been called from eternity, and distantly, finitely experience, in the passing moment, the infinite life of God—all under the unsurpassably ordinary form of bread and wine. And so, again, the shape of Christology is the shape of sacramental sacrifice: in this radical availability of the Infinite in a condition of absolute inanition, and our transformation thereby into creatures capable of participating in the Infinite's absolute plenitude, every offering of ourselves is made possible—and every offering is made complete.

NOTES

1. The authorship of Germanos's *Historia Ekklesiastikeh kai mystikeh Theoria* was, until recently, a subject of some debate, and the text has appeared in so many variants (including the irredeemably corrupt version found in Patrologia Graeca [PG] 98: 384–453) that precise dating has often proved quite elusive; it has even been ascribed to the thirteenth-century Constantinopolitan patriarchs Germanos II and Germanos III. The traditional attribution has now, though, been sufficiently well established; see Robert F. Taft, "The Liturgy of the Great Church: An Initial Synthesis of Structure and Interpretation on the Eve of Iconoclasm," *Dumbarton Oaks Papers* 34–35 (Washington, D.C.: DO, 1980–1981). The original text has been very plausibly reconstructed by Nilo Borgia, *Il commentario liturgico di S. Germano patriarca Constantinopolitano, Studi Liturgici* 1 (Grottaferrata: 1912), and has been translated into English, with Borgia's text facing, as St. Germanus of Constantinople, *On the Divine Liturgy*, trans. Paul Meyendorff (Crestwood, N.Y.: St. Vladimir's Seminary Press, 1984).

2. Meyendorff's translation, p. 59.

3. Theophylactus of Bulgaria, *Epistolae divi Pauli ad Hebraeos expositio*, PG 125: 185–404. See especially 265Cff.

4. Euthymios's Commentaries on Paul's Epistles were published in Athens in 1887, ed. Archbishop Kalogeras. The text of his Hebrews commentary was made available to me, in scanned form, over the Internet, by P. Konstantinides, devoid (alas) of pagination.

5. Nicholas, among other things a distinguished commentator on Proclos's *Elements*, was writing in support of a council called by emperor Manuel Comnenos the previous year in Constantinople to condemn the teaching of Soterichos Panteugenos that we must say that Christ's offering was and is made only to the Father and not to the whole Trinity (lest, like the Nestorians, we erect a partition between his humanity and his divinity).

6. The two treatises were published in Leipzig in 1865, ed. Andronikos Demetrakopoulos; for their contents, however, I am trusting in part the report of Darwell Stone, *A History of the Doctrine of the Holy Eucharist*, 2 vols. (New York: Longmans, Green, and Co., 1909), who gives a much fuller account of this entire aspect of Byzantine eucharistic theology: vol. 1, pp. 143–173; and in part lectures delivered by E. Sakkos at the University of Thessaloniki in 1987.

7. Nicholas Cabasilas, *A Commentary on the Divine Liturgy*, trans. J. M. Hussey and P. A. McNulty (Crestwood, NY: St. Vladimir's Seminary Press, 1977), XXVIII, 3–4, p. 71. I take the Greek, and the paragraph numbers, from the text in Nicolas Cabasilas, *Explication de la Divine Liturgie*, trans. Sévérien Salaville; Gk. text eds. René Bomert, Jean Gouillard, and Pierre Périchon (Paris: Les Editions du Cerf, 1967), 178.

8. Cyril, *Quod Unus Sit Christus*, PG 75: 1272–1273.

9. Nicholas, *Ad eos qui haesitant, aiuntque consecratum panem et vinum non esse corpus et sanguinem domini nostri Jesu Christi*, PG 135: 509–518.

10. Theophylactus, *Enarratio in Evangelium Joannis*, PG 123: 1309–1312.

11. From "The Eucharistic Dogma," in Sergius Bulgakov, *The Holy Grail and the Eucharist*, trans. and ed. Boris Jakim (New York: Lindisfarne Books, 1997), 104.

12. Athanasius, *De Incarnatione Verbi Dei*, PG 25: 112–113.

13. Ibid., 173–176.

14. Gregory of Nyssa, *Oratio Catechetica*, XXXVII, ed. James. Herbert Srawley (Cambridge: CUP, 1956), 151–152.

15. John Chrysostom, *In Sanctum Joannem Apostolum et Evangelistam*, Homilia XLVI, PG 59: 260.

16. Cyril, *In Joannis Evangelium IV*, PG 73: 601–604.

17. The translation is that of Frederic H. Chase, Jr., in St. John of Damascus, *Writings* (Washington, D.C.: CUAP, 1958), 358–359. The Greek is taken from the text in PG 94: 1148–1149.

18. Gregory Palamas, 'ΟΜΙΛΙΑΙ, ed. S. Oikonomos (Athens: 1861), 56.6, p. 207.

19. Ibid., 56.7, pp. 207–208. 1 have borrowed the translation found in Georgios I. Mantzarides, *The Deification of Man: St Gregory Palamas and the Orthodox Tradition*, trans. Liadain Sherrard; Crestwood, N.Y.: St. Vladimir's Seminary Press, 1984), 52–53.

20. Gregory of Nazianzus, *Oratio IV.52 (Contra Julianum I)*, PG 35: 575.

21. John Meyendorff, *Byzantine Theology* (New York: Fordham, 1974), 204–205.

22. *Explication*, III, 2–4, pp. 72–74; *Commentary*, pp. 31–32.

23. *Explication*, II, 3–4, pp. 70–72; *Commentary*, p. 31.

24. *Explication*, IV, 2, p. 76; *Commentary*, pp. 32–33.

25. Meyendorff, 205.

26. Patriarch Gennadius, *De Sacramentale Corpore Jesu Christi*, PG 160: 351–373.

27. See Ernst Julius Kimmel, *Monumenta Fidei Ecclesiae Orientalis* (Jena: F. Mauke, 1850), 1: 125–126; 180–184; in the latter passage, the confession affirms that after the words of institution and the epiclesis, when the *metousiosis* occurs, only the species (*eideh*) of bread and wine remains.

28. Jean Hardouin, *Conciliorum Collectio Regia Maxima* (17), XI: 249–256. The relevant passages from the confession are translated in Stone, vol. I, 180–182. Stone provides a fuller account of this aspect of late Byzantine theology in vol. I on pp. 172–192.

29. Stone, 184–185.

30. Meyendorff, 205.

31. See "The Eucharistic Dogma," esp. pp. 137–138.

32. John Chrysostom, *Ad Caesarium monachum*, PG 52: 758.

33. Leontius of Byzantium, *Contra Nestorium et Eutychem* 11, PG 86: 1333.

34. See Hans-Joachim Schulz, *The Byzantine Liturgy*, trans. Matthew J. O'Connell (New York: Pueblo Publishing Co., 1986), 139–196.

35. *Explication*, pp. 162–164; *Commentary*, pp. 65–66.

36. Severus was made bishop of Philadelphia in 1577, but spent most of his episcopacy as bishop to the Orthodox diaspora in the Venetian states.

37. *Fides Ecclesiae Orientalis seu Gabrielis Metropolitae Philadelphiensis Opuscula*, Latin trans. and ed. Richard Simon (Paris: 1671), 3–4.

38. Dionysius the Areopagite, *Ecclesiastica Hierarchia*, III.3.1–2, PG 3: 428.

39. Maximos the Confessor, *Mystagogia* XXIV, PG 91: 704–705.

40. Ibid., VIII, PG 91: 688.

41. Ibid., IX, PG 91: 688–689.

42. Ibid., XIII, PG 91: 692.

43. Nicholas of Andida, *Brevis commentatio de divinae liturgiae symbolis ac mysteriis*, PG 140: 417–468.

44. Indeed, to cite one example at random, Patriarch Eutychius of Constantinople (c. 512–582) could call the Last Supper Christ's self-sacrifice and state that it was on rising from the dead that Christ offered himself to the Father for humanity's salvation: *Sermo de Paschate et de Sacrosancta Eucharistia*, PG 86: 2396–2397.

45. Theodore the Studite, *Antirrheticus* 1, PG 99: 340–341.

46. Gregoire Palamas, *Défense des saints hesychastes*, critical ed., Spicilegium Sacrum Lovaniense, 30–31, French trans. and ed. Jean Meyendorff (Louvain: 1959), 193.

47. Nicholas Cabasilas, *The Life in Christ*, 1, 6–8, trans. Carmino J. deCantanzaro (Crestwood, N.Y.: St. Vladimir's Seminary Press, 1998), 45–46; the Greek text and the paragraph numbers are taken from Nicolas Cabasilas, *La Vie en Christ*, 2 vols., vol. 1: French trans. and ed. Marie-Helene Congourdeau (Paris: Les Editions du Cerf, 1989), 80–82.

48. *Vie*, I, 13, vol. 1, 86–88; *Life*, 47–48.

49. *Vie*, I, 19–20, vol. 1, 94–96; *Life*, 49–50.

50. *Vie*, I, 54, vol. 1, 124; *Life*, 60.

51. *Vie*, I, 32, vol. 1, 106; *Life*, 53.

52. *Vie*, IV, 2, vol. 1, 262–264; *Life*, 113–114.

53. *Vie*, IV, 8, vol. 1, 268; *Life*, 115–116.

54. *Vie*, IV, 9, vol. 1, 270; *Life*, 116.

55. *Vie*, IV, 10, vol. 1, 270; *Life*, 116.

56. *Vie*, IV, 26, vol. 1, 286–288; *Life*, 122.

57. *Vie*, IV, 28, vol. 1, 290; *Life*, 123.

58. *Vie*, IV, 83, vol. 1, 334–336; *Life*, 140.

59. *Explication*, XXXVII, 3, pp. 226–228; *Commentary*, pp. 90–91.

60. *Explication*, XXXVIII, 2, p. 230; *Commentary*, pp. 91–92.

61. *Vie*, IV, 102, vol. 1, 350; *Life*, 146.

62. *Vie*, IV, 108–109, vol. 1, 356; *Life*, 147–148.

63. XIII; see n. 42.

A RESPONSE TO D. BENTLEY HART ON

Eucharistic Sacrifice in Orthodox Tradition

BY WILLIAM J. ABRAHAM

Let me begin with two preliminary comments. First, Professor Hart has provided us with a wonderfully rich and comprehensive account of eucharistic sacrifice in the Orthodox tradition. It is learned, rhetorically robust, full of spiritual insight and imagination, and yet clear on its central concerns and affirmations. There is a wonderful density of presentation and a marvelous engagement with and immersion in the tradition of the church.

Second, let me make a brief confession. I come from a tradition that over the years has lost not only its theological bearings but also its eucharistic and sacramental bearings. While there is much to applaud in the renewal of my tradition, we have a long way to go, not least in coming to terms with the nature of baptism and the Eucharist. It is not easy for a tradition that is seeking to relearn and reappropriate the rich theological heritage of the church to take on board at the same time a reappropriation of the classical sacramental tradition of the church. We have been, of late, so preoccupied with recovering our nerve in mission, evangelism, the study of scripture, and the exploration of serious theology that we are already stretched to the limits. Hence to enter into the world so splendidly articulated and described by Hart is a tall order. There is a real danger that in moving into that world I will stumble all over the place, knocking aside, if only unintentionally, extremely precious furniture and heirlooms.

Let me divide my remarks into three sections. First, I shall high-light those components of the paper that I think are especially power-ful, attractive, and well presented. Second, I shall identify some areas that would bear further exploration and elaboration. Finally, I shall raise a couple of questions which are pertinent to the discussion but which are not covered in the paper.

The most salient feature of Professor Hart's paper is his drawing the theme of the Eucharist or eucharistic sacrifice into a network of crucial ancillary themes.

Thus I appreciate the following:

First, I applaud the insistence that our vision of the Eucharist must be intimately related to the whole sweep of God's action in cre-ation, redemption, and restoration.

Second, I entirely agree with the insistence that our reconcilia-tion to God achieved in, with, and through the Eucharist begins first with Christology. God has entered into human existence in Christ, effecting ontologically within human nature and within human his-tory the reconciliation of the divine with the human. Hence atone-ment is not first and foremost effected or brought about in the death of Christ as an event in history; rather, it has already been brought about in the very person of Jesus Christ and in his life on earth.

Third, I welcome the insistence that the work of the Holy Spirit is integral to the effecting of the work of Christ in our lives through the sacraments in the present. To some degree this is underdeveloped in this paper, but it is beautifully captured in the significance of adding warm water to the chalice of consecrated wine. Frankly, I did not know what this meant, but it brings home in a powerful manner that there can be no Eucharist without the work of the Holy Spirit. It paves the way in a natural manner for the flourish in the last para-graph where the Eucharist is seen as a trinitarian event of divine dis-closure.

Fourth, I like the way in which the core of the eucharistic mys-tery is carefully located in the fullness of the Divine Liturgy. What-ever we want to say about, for example, the epiclesis over the bread and the wine and the changes that ensue, this cannot be divorced from the liturgy as a whole or from our experience of God in the liturgy as a whole.

Let me mention some areas that deserve further exploration and elaboration. Again, let me simply proceed by laying out a laundry list of questions.

First, how precisely are we to link the Old Testament material on atonement with the sacrifice of the Eucharist? Should we see the Eucharist as a sin offering or a peace offering or some other sort of offering? I think that there are magnificent analogies between what the bringing of, say, an animal sacrifice to God and the concomitant sacrifice of God in the incarnation in his Son mean. However, it is not as clear to me as it is to Professor Hart how we can extend this to the Eucharist. Clearly, given the plastic nature of the term "sacrifice," we can develop associations between the sacrifice of God in Christ and what goes on in the Eucharist, but there is the danger that we will think generically of a "biblical" notion of sacrifice that really ignores the particularities of the original material.

Second, I am not at all times clear as to precisely how the Eucharist is a sacrifice in a threefold sense. I wonder what exactly the three components are, how far they remain stable throughout the paper, and how far the concept of sacrifice is being overused at times. Thus, to take the first obvious case where this claim surfaces, it is not clear how far the offering of Christ in the Eucharist where he makes everlasting intercession for us is best described as a sacrifice. We can, of course, call it a sacrifice, but what does this really mean?

Third, while I applaud the effort to discern a single and coherent vision of eucharistic sacrifice down through the history of the Orthodox tradition, and I welcome the effort to bind up the wounds of the fathers in Professor Hart's interpretation of Pseudo-Dionysius and Maximos, it strikes me that the differences between the symbolic interpretation and the realist interpretation that Professor Hart prefers are more significant than he allows. Moreover, how far has there been development of complementary positions within the tradition through the years? Has there not been a genuine diversity that has been downplayed here in the interests of presenting a unified vision? In the various summaries and quotations supplied I suspect that there are more tensions than Professor Hart allows. If this is the case, how are these to be explained historically? And how are they to be integrated into a comprehensive and coherent vision?

A fourth, and related, query has to do with how we are to handle the comments made about transubstantiation. Professor Hart handles this with a delicate and light touch. He rightly mentions Bulgakov's objections to the concept, lays out this alternative, and wonders whether Bulgakov fully understood the concept. Fair enough, but the notion of substance is pivotal in the doctrine of the Trinity, so one wonders if Bulgakov's excoriation of the notion has wider ramifications that are left unexplored. Moreover, given the insistence that a whole network of Orthodox theologians and synods have endorsed the notion, it would be good to know if the term is to be taken apophatically or cataphatically. Is the term simply a way of denying by means of the *via negativa* that the Eucharist is not merely symbolic, merely a memorial, and the like? Or is it a positive effort to unpack in metaphysical categories the real presence of Christ in the bread and the wine?

A fifth and final query in this section. The deep way in which the Eucharist is linked to *theosis* and sanctification prompts this question, a question I shall put into two very different but blunt forms. What are we to make of those situations where people participate in the sacraments, including the sacrament of the Eucharist, and then head off to get drunk, destroy their neighbors, revel in sin, and the like? The same question put differently: What are we to make of those who exhibit *theosis* and sanctification within the Christian tradition but for whom the sacraments are wholly nonexistent or play a negligible role in the life of faith? The first raises the issue of the place of faith in receiving the effects of the Eucharist; the second raises the question of the necessity of sacraments in the economy of salvation.

Now for my final section, in which I want to raise two questions that are pertinent to the discussion but are not mentioned or raised in this paper.

First, delineation of the wider context of the liturgy as the setting for the Eucharist and the insistence that that wider context be kept in mind raise this question: How might we delineate the place of preaching, of reading and hearing the Word of God, as a site of divine presence and divine transformation and might this help us in thinking about the Eucharist? Consider this: in the preaching of the scriptures, there is both a human word and a divine word; there is the verbal activity of the preacher and there is the divine presence, the real presence of God, speaking to us and coming to indwell in us. This will not help us in unpacking the concept of sacrifice, but might it help us in getting through to a real presence of the risen Lord in and through the work of the creature?

Second, it strikes me that much of our work on the place of sacrifice in the Eucharist trades on tacit conceptions of language and meaning which cry out for attention. Now I realize this is like inviting you to take a walk in a very mushy and maybe even dangerous Irish bog. Much work on language in the contemporary academy obscures and confuses rather than clarifies and illuminates. However, the revolution in the understanding of language developed especially in the analytic tradition represented, say, by the later Wittgenstein and J. L. Austin, might do much to help us get a handle on the extraordinary discourse which is on display in descriptions of the Eucharist. I am fully aware that it is very easy to use various accounts of language to evacuate language about the Eucharist of its realistic resonance and content. Yet, we do need to explore with some care what kind of language is being deployed, and what kinds of claims are being explicitly or tacitly made in the rich body of material on the Eucharist. Most especially, we need to sort through the way in which metaphor, image, allegory, and the like work in this domain.

It is in no way a criticism that I raise these last two questions; on the contrary, it is a measure of the profundity and sensitivity of this paper that it drives one deep into other questions and issues.

Avery Dulles

The Eucharist as Sacrifice

The Eucharist, of course, has multiple aspects. The term "Eucharist" itself means thanksgiving. In the New Testament it is sometimes referred to as "the breaking of the bread" (Acts 2:42; cf. Luke 24:35) and the Lord's Supper (1 Cor 11:20). In Christian tradition it is often known as Holy Communion and Holy Mass. None of these terms precludes the Eucharist from being considered, under one important aspect, a sacrifice.

My intention in this paper is to consider, first, the death of Jesus as sacrifice, since this is the presupposition. Unless Jesus was sacrificed, the Eucharist could not be a sacrifice. Then I shall reflect on the Eucharist as Christ's sacrifice, and finally on the Eucharist as the church's sacrifice.

The term "sacrifice" has become controversial in our day. Modern humanism, rebelling against certain scapegoat theories of sacrifice, has dismissed the notion altogether. Many contemporary authors hold that the sacrificial language in the Bible is a relic of primitive thinking and has no place in authentic Christian faith. If this position were correct, the Eucharist certainly ought not to be considered a sacrifice. But, as we shall see, the idea of sacrifice can and should be differently understood.

The Death of Christ as Sacrifice

In the perspectives of theology, the death of Jesus cannot be dismissed as an incidental and unintended consequence of his mission.

175

The New Testament clearly and repeatedly declares that Jesus "was delivered up according to the definite plan and foreknowledge of God" (Acts 2:23, RSV). In perfect obedience to his Father's command he submits to a violent and painful death, which he would have been able to avoid (John 10:17–18). He does so to expiate the sins of the world (1 John 2:2). For his obedience he is rewarded by being raised from the dead and received into the glory of the Father (Phil 2:8–11).

Our age seems to have become almost deaf to the idea that sin, as a breach of the moral order, demands retribution. But this conviction pervades sacred scripture as a whole and is basic to Christology. God sent his Son to compensate for sins for which no human being or group of human beings could possibly have given adequate satisfaction. He was not a mere substitute for others but the divinely given representative head and first-fruits of a new and regenerate humanity.

The command of the Father is sometimes depicted as a sign that God was moved by hatred and anger. But the command is the work of God's superabundant love; he loved humankind so much that he was willing to pay the extreme price of letting his Son die for them. He did not take pleasure in the suffering and death of Jesus, which were in themselves evils, but he was pleased by the love that prompted the Son to pay so heavy a price. To signify his good pleasure he raised Jesus from the dead and crowned him with glory.[1]

Strictly speaking, the crucifixion of Jesus was not a divine punishment. Whereas punishment is imposed on one who is guilty and is strictly proportionate to the crime, Jesus was not personally guilty, he suffered freely out of love, and his satisfaction was superabundant. In all these three respects it differs from punishment. Satisfaction is, as Anselm explained, an alternative to punishment.[2]

The Father does not kill the Son, as some falsely imagine. The execution of Jesus was a heinous crime committed by evil and ignorant human beings. The responsibility rests not only on the Romans or the Jews of old but on all of us, because it was our sins that called for this act of atonement. Our redemption could not have been achieved, or appropriately achieved, without the sacrifice of the Son.

The redemptive death of Jesus, as understood in Christian doctrine, superabundantly fulfills, and in some ways corrects, the notion of sacrifice as we know it from the history of religions and from the Old Testament. It fulfills that notion because, like all sacrifice, it was an external act symbolically expressing the interior homage of the creature to God. It corrects false and inadequate notions because it does not imply that God is vengeful or that he is placated by the external ritual apart from the requisite interior dispositions. The Christian theology of sacrifice, while it does not authorize killing the innocent, maintains that unearned suffering, when accepted with patient love, can be redemptive.

The death of Jesus was foreshadowed in the Old Testament by the sacrifices of Abel, Noah, Melchizedek, Abraham, Moses, and others.[3] Many New Testament texts, including words attributed to Jesus, interpret the passion in the light of the Suffering Servant described in Isaiah, chapter 53. Jesus is also identified as the Paschal Lamb, whose blood saved the Israelites from destruction. John the Baptist points to Jesus as "the Lamb of God who takes away the sin of the world" (John 1:29). Paul tells the Corinthians that "Christ, our paschal lamb, has been sacrificed" (1 Cor 5:7, RSV). Peter's first letter speaks of Jesus as "the lamb without blemish or spot" (1 Pet 1:19, RSV). Just as the sprinkling of the blood of sacrificial victims was the gesture by which Moses sealed the Sinai Covenant (Exod 24:8), so the new and eternal covenant is established through the blood of Christ. "Without the shedding of blood," says the Letter to the Hebrews, "there is no forgiveness of sins" (Heb 9:22).

The sacrifices of the old law were by their very nature insufficient. As we read in the Letter to the Hebrews, "It is impossible that the blood of bulls and goats should take away sins" (Heb 10:4, RSV). These sacrifices derived all their salvific power from being types of the perfect offering of Christ which, as we read in the *Catechism of the Catholic Church* (*CCC*), "completes and surpasses all other sacrifices."[4]

The sacrifice of Jesus was not complete with his death, but only with the glorious resurrection and ascension by which the Father expressed his acceptance of Jesus' self-offering. The exalted Christ continues to exercise his priestly office as he intercedes for those who place their hope in him (Heb 7:25; cf. 1 John 2:1).

The Eucharist as Christ's Sacrifice

The Eucharist, as a reenactment of the paschal sacrifice of Jesus, cannot be adequately understood except in light of the Last Supper.

Just as the Eucharist looks back to the event of Calvary, so the Last Supper looks forward to it and mystically anticipates it. To understand the significance of that supper, we must recognize its close connection with the Jewish Passover. According to Luke, Jesus himself says, "I have eagerly desired to eat this Passover with you before I suffer" (Luke 22:15). If it was not itself a Passover meal, it was consciously celebrated in the context of the Passover and was linked to it by the covenant themes in the words and gestures of Jesus.[5] Some scholars have suggested that the Eucharist was instituted as a thank offering (todah), which could well have been inserted into, or appended to, a Passover meal.[6]

At the Last Supper Jesus enacts in advance the death that he is to suffer on the cross. Taking the bread and the wine, he hands them over to his disciples so that they may in truth eat his body and drink his blood, as he had promised that his followers would do when he spoke of the bread of life at Capernaum (John 6:53). Not satisfied to give a mere token of his love, he bestows his very self as food and drink. Following the emphatic realism of Jesus' teaching at Capernaum, the church adheres steadfastly to the doctrine that Jesus' flesh is "food indeed" and his blood is "drink indeed" (in 6:55, RSV). The sacrifice of Jesus, while directed to the Father, is offered for the sake of the men and women he came to save. He imparts his life to them by making himself their food and drink.

The Last Supper was intended to be perpetuated in the Eucharist as a post-resurrectional reenactment of what Jesus at the Last Supper anticipated.[7] Looking to the future, Jesus instructed the disciples, "Do this in remembrance of me" (1 Cor 11:24; cf. Luke 22:19). The term "remembrance" in the New Testament has greater depth than we might gather from the English word. Modern historical scholarship on the biblical notion of anamnesis (Hebrew zikkaron) supports the teaching of the Council of Trent that the Eucharist is not a mere recalling (nuda commemoratio, DS 1753) of what Christ did in the past. Memorial in the rich biblical sense meant a liturgical feast commemorating some foundational event in such a way that the people could participate by faith in its saving effects.[8] Participation in such liturgical acts had a significance beyond the subjective intentions of those who took part in them. Paul, for example, reasons that by partaking in the sacrificial meals of pagans, Christians would become partners with demons, who are worshiped in such rites (1 Cor 10:14–22).

The Mass, as an "unbloody" sacrifice, is not a repetition of what Christ did once and for all on Calvary, but a ritual reactualization of that once-for-all act, no less real than the anticipation of that act at the Last Supper. The sacramental sacrifice, unlike the sacrifice of the cross, is repeatable. It is not a mere imitation of the archetypal sacrifice of Jesus but that same sacrifice mysteriously renewed after the event. The Platonic metaphysics of participation, some believe, gives greater insight into this mystery than do the Aristotelian categories of formal and efficient causality.[9] Dom Odo Casel, in his classic work, *The Mystery of Christian Worship*, draws some analogies between the Pauline concept of mystery and the Platonic thought-forms that in his opinion were reflected in the Hellenistic mystery religions. The mystery of worship, he contends, is the presentation and renewal of the mystery of Christ himself and is the means whereby the Christian relives the mystery of Christ. In terms of this Platonic manner of thinking, Casel feels entitled to say:

> The Mass not only represents the death of Christ and communicates to us the effects of his sacrifice; it is an active image of the Pasch of Christ, and makes us immediate members of what once took place in and upon him. It is therefore within the power of the Mass to bring us into the same temporal dimension with the saving deeds of Christ, and to place us in their immediate presence.[10]

Casel has been criticized for overemphasizing the parallels with the Hellenistic mystery religions and for neglecting the properly biblical origins of the New Testament theology of mystery.[11] However that may be, he seems to have been essentially correct in seeing the mystery of worship as a participation in the event of Christ's sacrifice on Golgotha, as it had been previously sacramentalized at the Last Supper.

The Mass is a work of divine power that surpasses anything in the natural order. In a manner that defies human comprehension, the Holy Spirit makes it possible for Christ's redemptive act, without loss of its historical uniqueness, to be available to all ages. The humanity of Christ, personally united to the divine Word, has a unique capacity to share in the supratemporality of the divine existence. The acts of the Incarnate Word can transcend time and place in ways that the anamnetic celebrations of ancient Israel and the participatory rites of pagan Greece could not. Those who eat of the one bread and drink of the one cup are incorporated into the body of Christ, "the same yesterday, today, and forever" (Heb 13:8, NAB).

Because of its sacramental identity with the event of the cross, the Mass itself is a "true and authentic sacrifice" (*verum et proprium sacrificium*).[12] The term "sacrifice" as applied to the Eucharist is more than a metaphor. Vatican II, amplifying this doctrine of Trent, declares: "As often as the sacrifice of the Cross, by which 'Christ our Paschal lamb has been sacrificed' (1 Cor 5:7), is celebrated at the altar, the work of our redemption is carried out" (*Lumen Gentium* 3; cf. *CCC* §1364). The sacrifice is essentially the same, since the victim is the very one who was delivered up on the cross and since the offerer is the same Jesus Christ (DS 1740; cf. *CCC* §1367). But the manner of offering is somewhat different, since the principal offerer is now the risen Christ. The Eucharist thus becomes a memorial of Christ's victory over death, which was only anticipated at the Last Supper. Celebrated after Easter, the Eucharist is a festival of joy in which the Spirit of the living Christ reminds us that our true life is with the exalted Lord.

According to the Council of Trent, the Mass is not only a sacrifice of praise and thanksgiving, but a propitiatory sacrifice, a sin-offering.[13] As we have seen, the sacrifice of the cross was intended to satisfy for human sin. Jesus at the Last Supper handed over to his disciples his body "given for you" (1 Cor 11:24) and his blood "poured out for many for the forgiveness of sins" (Matt 26:28). Since the Mass actualizes the same sacrifice as the Last Supper did, it too has propitiatory or expiatory value. It adds nothing to the value of Christ's own sacrifice, but makes it present in particular worshiping and praying communities. Fulfilling the prophecy of Malachi, the pure offering made in every time and place makes God's name great among the nations (Mal 1:11).

Unlike a mere sacrifice of praise and thanksgiving, the Eucharist atones for sins and draws down blessings upon those for whom it is offered, according to their various dispositions. It serves to move sinners to repentance, to remit the guilt of sins, and to heal the disorder brought about by sin.[14] The multitude for whom the Eucharist is offered includes not only those physically present and those who are specially remembered at the liturgy, but all men and women, living and dead, who stand in need of Christ's redemptive grace.

Pius XII in his 1947 encyclical on the liturgy distinguished four ends or purposes of the Sacrifice of the Mass: praise, thanksgiving, propitiation, and impetration.[15] As we seek to enter into the offering, it is important to be aware that the Eucharist is a sacrifice of praise and thanksgiving, as the term "Eucharist" itself implies. At the Last Supper Jesus blessed the bread and gave thanks (Matt 26:26–27). In the Mass, the prayer of praise and thanksgiving at the Preface provides the context within which the church enters into Christ's self-giving and makes it her own.

Although the sacrificial character of the Mass has often been denied in Protestant theology, the ecumenical dialogues of the twentieth century have established significant convergences and, in some cases, agreements on this issue. The Anglican-Orthodox Theological Consultation of 1988 registered a consensus between the two communions that the memorial of the Eucharist "does not merely 'remind' us of the sacrifice of Christ; it makes this sacrifice truly present."[16]

Even if many Protestants are still hesitant to speak of the Eucharist itself as a sacrifice, increasing numbers agree that it is an efficacious sign of Christ's own sacrifice, of which it is a visible memorial. The Faith and Order Commission in its Lima Paper of 1982 reported a broad ecumenical consensus to this effect: "The Eucharist is a memorial of the crucified and risen Christ, i.e., the living and effective sign of his sacrifice, accomplished once and for all on the cross and still operative on behalf of all humankind. The biblical idea of memorial as applied to the Eucharist refers to this present efficacy of God's work when it is celebrated by God's people in a liturgy."[17] A little later the Lima Paper states: "The Eucharist is the sacrament of the unique sacrifice of Christ, who ever lives to make intercession for us."[18] That conclusion differs hardly, if at all, from the Catholic position that the Eucharist is a "sacramental sacrifice." The response to the Lima Paper by the Holy See stated: "The connection established between the sacrifice of the cross and the Eucharist corresponds to the Roman

Catholic understanding. The sacrifice of the Eucharist is one in which the sacrifice of the cross is represented to the end that its saving power be applied here and now for the salvation of the world."[19]

The Eucharist as the Church's Sacrifice

At this point we reach the issue on which the interconfessional divergence is probably sharpest. Protestants commonly prefer to say that Christ alone offers the sacrifice and that the church's role is to receive the fruits of that offering, including the sublime gift of the Eucharist. The Catholic Church, here as at other points, takes a more positive view of human cooperation in the work of redemption. Since human beings are active as well as receptive, their activity needs to be healed and sanctified by Christ and the Holy Spirit. The church rejoices that Christ enabled his beloved spouse the church to have "a visible sacrifice (as human nature demands)."[20] Exalted in heaven, Christ acts as head of his mystical body, the church, and in so doing makes use of that body in a subordinate, or instrumental, capacity.

The eucharistic prayers in the Roman Missal reflect the sense that the church herself, in union with her divine Lord, is privileged to offer the sacrifice. At the Offertory, for example, the priest addresses the people: "Brothers, pray that my sacrifice and yours may be acceptable to God the Father almighty." In the first Eucharistic Prayer, the priest asks God to bless the gifts "which we offer you for your Holy Catholic Church." The words "we offer" (*offerimus*) resound like a refrain throughout the approved eucharistic prayers. The Mass may therefore be seen not only as the sacrifice of Christ but also as the church's liturgical presentation of his sacrifice. In offering Christ, the church offers herself in union with him to the Father.

The manner of offering is indeed different. The ritual sacrifice is made under the species of bread and wine, which symbolize the separation of the body and blood of Christ and therefore his death. But the double consecration also suggests the union of Christ's body and blood at the resurrection. In the risen Christ the separation is overcome, so that the whole Christ is present in every fragment of the Host and in every drop of the Precious Blood.

Some have contended that the bread and wine are sacrificed by the transubstantiation whereby they are converted into the body and blood of Christ or that the consecrated elements are sacrificed by being consumed. Catholics who accept the doctrine of transubstantiation can certainly agree that the bread and wine cease to exist as such after the consecration, and thus are in a certain sense "sacrificed." But the sacrifice of the Mass does not consist either in the transmutation of the bread and wine or in the consumption of the consecrated elements. What counts in God's eyes is the sacrifice of Christ on the cross, which, as was said above, is present in the Eucharist. There is no need to look beyond the cross for some additional sacrifice.

The Eucharist is not a purely private act but an offering of the church as such. It must therefore be conducted by someone qualified to speak and act publicly for the church itself. The ministerial priest, as Christ's sacramentally ordained representative, brings about the sacrifice by speaking the words of consecration in the very person of Christ the head (*in persona Christi capitis*). This is not a matter of play-acting but of ecclesial and sacramental deputation.

The Catholic Church interprets the words of Jesus, "Do this in commemoration of me" (1 Cor 11:24; Luke 22:19), spoken to the Twelve at the Last Supper, as a command that implicitly empowers the apostles and their successors to bring about the sacrifice and to make Christ really present on the altar (DS 1752). The ministerial priest does not act by his own power but by the power of Christ working through him when, in obedience to Christ, he does what is commanded. As St. John Chrysostom expressed it, the priest "lends his tongue and gives his hand" to Christ.[21]

The official action of the ordained minister, however, is not separable from the offering of the whole church, including the congregation that is gathered at the celebration. The faithful offer the sacrifice together with the priest, not as the priest does by consecrating the elements, but by consenting to Christ's own will to be offered as a victim. All, therefore, are invited and urged to participate in a more than passive way. They are not to be spectators but active participants according to their role in the church.

The congregation, while it does not bring about the eucharistic sacrifice, may be seen as perpetuating in time and space the role of Mary and the other holy disciples who were gathered at the foot of the cross. The holy women did not accomplish the redemptive sacrifice of Christ, but they humbly and trustingly accepted God's will that it should take place. They did so not without pain, for at that moment the prophecy of Simeon that a sword would pierce Mary's heart was supremely fulfilled. At the church's Eucharist the pain and sorrow of our earthly existence are taken up into the self-offering of Christ, transformed by union with his afflictions, and suffused with the healing power of his victory.

The objective memorial of the sacramental mystery is given to us in order that we may appropriate it in faith, which renders the mystery active in and for us. The priest celebrant and the entire congregation are called to surrender themselves to the Father's will and to let the Spirit of Christ remold their lives in the likeness of the crucified and risen Lord.[22] In the words of Vatican II, "All are invited and led to offer themselves, their works, and all creation together with Christ" (*Presbyterorum Ordinis* 5; cf. *Sacrosanctum Concilium* 11). This offering, if made with a sincere heart, leads to greater holiness of life and closer conformity to the divine Master.

By baptism we are already initiated into the new life of grace, being reborn in the likeness of the risen Savior. But this initiation calls for completion through identification with the glorified Victim who is offered and received in the Eucharist. By the worthy reception of Holy Communion we welcome Christ into our hearts and become progressively transformed into his image. The more suitably we are disposed to enter into the sacrifice of the incarnate Son, the more perfectly will we put on the mind and heart of Christ. The offering of the sacrifice gives glory to God to the extent that it results in personal sanctification. Our own lives, like his, become a pleasing sacrifice.

Since the Eucharist is by nature a sacrificial banquet, the reception of Holy Communion is no mere appendix. It pertains to the integrity of the sacrifice itself.[23] In instructing his disciples to eat and drink, Jesus signified his will that the consecrated elements should be consumed. At least the priest must receive in order for the sacrifice to be complete.[24] But it is recommended that the faithful, if suitably prepared, receive Holy Communion and do so from the same sacrifice as that from which the priest has received.[25] In this way they participate more fully and actively in the liturgy.

Conclusion

The Catholic position on the Eucharist as sacrifice, which I have sought to summarize in this presentation, combines strong biblical realism with ecclesial personalism. It insists on the intrinsic connections among the sacrifice of Christ on the cross, the sacrificial meal of the Last Supper, the liturgical sacrifice of the church, and the personal sacrifice of those who participate. The church and its members are privileged not only to receive the fruits of Christ's redemptive sacrifice but also to take part, according to their respective offices and vocations, in the supreme act of Christ's own priestly ministry. God has singularly blessed the church by inviting it to offer and partake of that sacrifice which eminently deserves to be called a "clean oblation" (Mal 1:11), perfectly pleasing to God. Had he not done so, our human longing to offer God a gift truly worthy of himself would remain perpetually unfulfilled.

In the liturgy itself, the Eucharist is hailed as the "mystery of faith." This designation may be understood both objectively and subjectively. Objectively, the doctrine of the Eucharist stands at the point of intersection of the principal articles of the Christian faith. It is inseparably bound up with the mysteries of the Blessed Trinity, the Incarnation, the Redemption, the forgiveness of sin, the life of grace, and the hope of final glory. As a manifestation of what the church is called to be, it builds up the church here on earth as a sign of the living Christ.[26] As a prelude to the heavenly liturgy, it quickens the church's hope for the age to come.[27] The sacrifice, therefore, is as a memorial of the passion, an offering of the church today, and a foretaste of the New Jerusalem.

Subjectively, participation in the Eucharist demands and at the same time fosters an attitude of faith. By definition faith is a sacrifice of our own autonomous reason and a trustful submission to the word of God. Faith alone assures us that the Eucharist is a true sacrifice in which Christ himself is present. By that same faith we allow the sacrifice of Christ to set the pattern of our lives. Surrendering our habitual self-centeredness, we let ourselves be taken up into the paschal mystery so that the great drama of sacred history, culminating in Christ's sacrifice, may find expression here and now. As he gave himself for the redemption of the human family, we are moved to live, and if necessary to die, for others. Looking forward beyond earthly time, we hasten to the sanctuary in which we, together with all the saints, will offer unceasing adoration to the Almighty and to the Lamb who was slain (Rev 21:22). What will heaven be if not a Eucharist in which faith is fulfilled vision, the symbols yield to the truth they contain, and the shadows of time give way to the radiance of eternity?

NOTES

1. I have dealt with these questions at greater length in "The Death of Jesus as Sacrifice," *Josephinum Journal of Theology* 3 (Summer/Fall 1996): 4–17.

2. Anselm, *Cur Deus homo*, Book I, chap. 12; in *St. Anselm: Basic Writings*, ed. S. N. Deane (La Salle, Ill.: Open Court, 1974), 203–206.

3. 1 Cf. *Enchiridion Symbolorum*, ed. H. Denzinger and A. Schönmetzer, 36th expanded ed. (Freiburg: Herder 1976), 1742. From now on referred to as DS.

4. *Catechism of the Catholic Church*, 2d ed. (Vatican City: Libreria Editrice Vaticana, 2000), §§613–614.

5. The conclusions of recent scholarship on the relationship between the Last Supper and the Passover are lucidly summarized in Jerome Kodell, *The Eucharist in the New Testament* (Wilmington, Del.: Michael Glazier, 1988), 53–57.

6. Hartmut Gese, *Essays on Biblical Theology* (Minneapolis: Augsburg, 1981), 117–140; Joseph Ratzinger, *The Feast of Faith: Approaches to a Theology of the Liturgy* (San Francisco: Ignatius Press, 1986), 51–60.

7. John Paul II, *Letter to Priests for Holy Thursday*, 1987: John Paul II, *Letters to My Brother Priests, 1979–1999*, 3rd ed. (Princeton: Scepter Publishers, 2000), 129–139, at 130.

8. Edward J. Kilmartin, *The Eucharist in the West: History and Theology* (Collegeville, Minn.: Liturgical Press, 1998), 367.

9. On this point, see Hans Urs von Balthasar, "The Mass: A Sacrifice of the Church?" in *Explorations in Theology*, III, *Creator Spirit* (San Francisco: Ignatius Press, 1993), 185–243, esp. 194–202.

10. Odo Casel, *The Mystery of Christian Worship and Other Writings* (Westminster, Md.: Newman, 1962), 101.

11. Louis Bouyer makes this criticism in *Eucharist: Theology and Spirituality of the Eucharistic Prayer* (Notre Dame, Ind.: University of Notre Dame Press, 1968), 16–17.

12. DS 1751

13. DS 1753

14. DS 1753.

15. Pius XII, encyclical *Mediator Dei* (New York: America Press, 1948), §§71–74.

16. Anglican-Orthodox Theological Consultation in the United States, "Agreed Statement on the Eucharist," §10, in *Growing Consensus: Church Dialogues in the United States, 1962–1991, Ecumenical Documents* V, ed. Joseph A. Burgess and Jeffrey Gros (New York: Paulist Press, 1995), 343–347, at 345.

17. *Baptism, Eucharist and Ministry*. (Faith and Order Paper No. 111; Geneva: World Council of Churches, 1982), "Eucharist" §5, p. 10.

18. Ibid., §8, p. 11.

19. "Baptism, Eucharist, and Ministry: An Appraisal," *Origins* 17 (November 19, 1987): 401–416, at 409.

20. DS 1740.

21. St. John Chrysostom, *In Joann. Hom.*, 86:4, quoted by Pius XII, *Mediator Dei*, §69. The text may be found in Migne, Patrologia Graeca 59: 472 and in *Nicene and Post-Nicene Fathers*, 14: 326.

22. Bouyer, *Eucharist*, 470–471.

23. Pius XII, *Mediator Dei*, §115.

24. Ibid., §112.

25. Vatican II, *Sacrosanctum Concilium*, Constitution on the Sacred Liturgy, 55.

26. *Sacrosanctum Concilium* 41.

27. *Sacrosanctum Concilium* 8.

A RESPONSE TO CARDINAL AVERY DULLES ON

The Eucharist as Sacrifice

BY PETER CASARELLA

I find myself in fundamental agreement with virtually everything in Fr. Dulles's presentation. Rather than offering a critique, my response will underscore the importance of some of his points and then raise some additional points that are intended to complement his presentation.

With respect to Jesus' sacrificial offering on the cross, I agree with Fr. Dulles that there is a tendency in modern Catholic thinking to saddle the christological language of sacrifice with the charge of "scapegoating."[1] Not infrequently, St. Anselm of Canterbury is himself "scapegoated" for having linked the reason for the incarnation to the reparation of the cosmic breach initiated by the offense of Adam's sin against God's honor. While it is beyond question that Anselm's rhetoric (e.g., "*aut poena aut satisfactio*") echoes the Teutonic feudal law of the Middle Ages, Anselm's application of this legalism is aesthetic and intended to be "attractive because of the utility and beauty of the argument (*pulchritudo rationis*)."[2] Thus, Anselm not only contrasts satisfaction with punishment, as noted by Fr. Dulles, but points to a theory of atonement at odds with the caricature that contemporary theology has imposed upon him.

Building upon and going beyond Anselm, one can say that God's glory is a non-juridical and aesthetic reality expressed through (rather than in spite of) the evident ugliness of the cross. This insight into the saving beauty of the cross seems to me essential to contemporary theol-

ogy and faith today. It needs to be recovered along with St. Thomas's
corrective notion that the incarnation manifests not only God's honor
but also (by virtue of his hypostatic union of divinity and humanity) the
greatness of God's love (*magnitudo caritatis*).[3] Likewise, the idea in the
Letter to the Hebrews that "[w]ithout shedding of blood there is no
forgiveness of sins" (9:22) is indispensable once it is recognized that
Hebrews emphasizes the newness of Christ's self-offering in relation to
the sacrificial offerings of the Old Covenant (3:3, 9:1–5).[4]

All of this is meant to confirm what Fr. Dulles says in the first
part of his presentation. The only point that I would add to Fr.
Dulles's presentation concerns the underdeveloped anthropology of
sacrifice. This is not the proper place even to lay out the essential elements of such an anthropology. Here it will have to suffice to hint at a
path that may be worth pursuing. Anselm's presentation of the incarnation's redemptive logic fails to respond to the existential questions
of a contemporary believer regarding the meaning of Christ's sacrifice. Given that a significant number of recent theologians (e.g., Karl
Rahner and D. Sölle) found reason to fault the idea that Christ dies a
representative death ("*Stellvertretung*") because personal freedom is
and must remain the self-actualization of the creaturely subject in his
or her entirety, it seems paramount to reconstruct an alternative.
These theologians problematize the representative character of the
death of Jesus Christ in such a way as to render innocuous the words
"for the sake of our salvation" in the Nicene-Constantinopolitan
creed.[5] In fact, Christ's death for our sake is an act of unfathomable
love that uniquely explains why Christians both imitate and follow
Christ. Consequently, I would like to propose as an alternative to the
Rahnerian thesis an understanding of the human person in terms of
donated freedom, more precisely, "according to the measure of
Christ's own self-gift."[6]

In the second part of his paper, Fr. Dulles elaborates the very
notion of sacramentality as it applies to Christ's sacrifice in the Mass. I
concur with his conclusions regarding the perpetuation of the sacrifice
on Calvary as well as the need to promote ecumenical consensus without abandoning a Catholic interpretation of sacramental sacrifice.[7] In
the Mass a sacrifice coincides with a meal so that the memorial of this
sacrifice is not a bare repetition but the actual re-membering of the
diverse, memorializing community.[8]

My response to this section consists in a brief comment on the following assertion. Fr. Dulles states:

> The humanity of Christ, personally united to the divine Word, has a unique capacity to share in the supratemporality of the divine existence. The acts of the Incarnate Word can transcend time and place in ways that the anamnetic celebrations of ancient Israel and the participatory rites of pagan Greece could not. Those who eat of the one bread and drink of the one cup are incorporated into the body of Christ, "the same yesterday, today, and forever" (Heb 13:8).

In other words, the eucharistic union of humanity and divinity in the Word introduces a new language of time. The Hebrew Passover and Greek mystery cults prepare for a view of time measured by the liturgical invitation to partake of Christ's body. Mere repetition of a past act as well as a speculative flight into a timeless eternity pale in comparison to Christianity's new approach to time.[9] In sum, the liturgy transfigures rather than concludes being in time.[10] In the Eucharist, time and eternity cannot be defined by the absence of the other. Eucharistic temporality resists a simple opposition of time and eternity and likewise rejects a cutting down of the eternal Word to more humanly manageable installments. According to the draft position paper circulated prior to this conference, "eucharistic memorial is a transformation deeper than subjective remembrances into the events of Jesus' life, death and resurrection." To this I would add that eucharistic time continually confronts the sting of death, just as Christ does when he descends into death's realm on Holy Saturday.

Moreover, eucharistic time allows for surprise of sorts. The time of the Eucharist is founded on the unexpected fulfillment of a prophecy whereby the key to understanding history appeared suddenly in the form of a marginal Jew. Liturgical surprise also arises from the sometimes counter-intuitive certainty that heavenly choirs attend every Mass in each and every Catholic parish throughout the globe (and not only there). The eucharistic transcendence of *chronos* irrupts from within the quotidian and points to its eschatological transfiguration.

With regard to the Eucharist as the church's sacrifice, Fr. Dulles highlights the words "we offer" (*offerimus*) in the church's eucharistic prayers. This action defines the stance of the church as receptive rather than imitative. I agree that there is no need to look beyond the cross to some other sacrifice, and I also agree that the action of the ordained minister is "essentially" different from the activity performed by those whose mission is defined solely by their common baptismal priesthood (i.e., the laity). The crucifixion scene in John, centered on the fulfillment of the prophecy that Mary's heart would be pierced, is theologically very significant.[11] This last insight could be deepened, perhaps, by considering the degree to which the Marian stance is indicative of the act of faith itself.[12] The Marian stance is perhaps implicit in Fr. Dulles's statement that a eucharistic piety forces us to surrender our habitual self-centeredness. Marian receptivity thus conceived is a meaningful figure of the entire church.[13] Consequently, there is an opening to talk about spousal mystery simultaneously as an ecclesiological datum and as a starting point for theological anthropology. Pope John Paul II's theological reflections on the nuptial meaning of the body are for this purpose instructive,[14] for he makes an explicit connection between nuptiality and anthropology, albeit in the context of marriage.[15] Bringing together the moral and sacramental dimensions of the nuptial mystery with the anthropological dimensions of the liturgy would be fascinating, but this task involves a further (yet hopefully still compatible) line of inquiry, which, strictly speaking, moves beyond the confines of what Fr. Dulles or anyone else should have been expected to treat in a lecture on the Eucharist as sacrifice.

NOTES

1. René Girard emphasizes this theme, and his theories are frequently cited for this purpose. In Girard's later work, however, he makes the decisive move of highlighting Christ's death as that which liberates us from a pattern of scapegoating. Cf. René Girard, *Job: The Victim of His People* (Stanford: Stanford University Press, 1987), 154–168, especially 157: "Christ is the God of the victims primarily because he shares their lot until the end." See also the material in René Girard, *Des choses cachées depuis la fondation du monde* (Paris: Grasset, 1978), 163–304.

2. Anselm of Canterbury, *Cur Deus homo*, I, 1 in *Why God Became Man and The Virginal Conception and Original Sin*, trans. Joseph M. Colleran (Albany, N.Y.: Magi, 1969), 64. On Anselm and Teutonic law, one may consult Gisbert Greshake, "Redemption and Freedom," *Theology Digest* 25 (1977): 61–65.

3. *Summa Theologiae*, III, q. 48, art. 2. Cf. Roch Kereszty, O.Cist., *Jesus Christ: Fundamentals of Christology* (New York: Alba House, 1991), 222.

4. Not all scripture scholars agree on the eucharistic implications of this letter. For discussion, see Roch Kereszty, O.Cist., "The Eucharist in the Letter to the Hebrews," *Communio* 26 (Spring 1999): 154–167.

5. Cf. Hans Urs von Balthasar, *Theodramatik* III, *Die Handlung* (Einsiedeln: Johannes, 1980), 153–162.

6. Cf. Peter Casarella, "*Analogia donationis*: Hans Urs von Balthasar on the Eucharist," *Philosophy and Theology* 11, no. 1 (1998): 147–177.

7. See also my essay in this volume "Eucharist: Presence of a Gift."

8. On "re-membering," see the essay by Rabbi David Stern in this volume.

9. By mere repetition, I am referring to the idea that two millennia of history separate us from the cross of Calvary and therefore we can only replay in our minds what truly happened then. By speculative flight I am referring to a notion of eternity as *nunc stans*, a never-fading present moment. Martin Heidegger critiques this notion without exploring the possibilities for an alternative interpretation in its traditional context. See Martin Heidegger, *Being and Time*, trans. John Macquarrie and Edward Robinson (New York: Harper and Row, 1962), 499 (H. 427), n. xiii.

10. Cf. Catherine Pickstock, *After Writing: On the Liturgical Consummation of Philosophy* (Oxford: Blackwell, 1998), 220–223.

11. John 19:25–30.

12. Cf. Hans Urs von Balthasar, *The Glory of the Lord: A Theological Aesthetics* (San Francisco: Ignatius Press, 1982), 362–365.

13. Cf. Vatican II, *Lumen Gentium*, Dogmatic Constitution on the Church, 58, and the *Catechism of the Catholic Church*, §§964 and 967.

14. John Paul II, *The Theology of the Body: Human Love in the Divine Plan* (Boston: Daughters of St. Paul, 1997), 60–63, 475–476.

15. This is not to say that the pope is unaware of the liturgical implications of this anthropology. See *The Theology of the Body*, 342–344, 480–481: "The 'sincere gift' contained in the sacrifice of the cross gives definitive prominence to the spousal meaning of God's love … The Eucharist makes present and realizes anew in a sacramental manner the redemptive act of Christ, who 'creates' the Church, his body. All this contained in *The Letter to the Ephesians*. The perennial 'unity of two' that exists between man and woman from the very 'beginning' is introduced into this 'great mystery' of Christ and of the Church."

A RESPONSE TO CARDINAL AVERY DULLES ON

The Eucharist as Sacrifice

BY DURWOOD FOSTER

It is a privilege to respond to Fr. Dulles's instructive paper. With faithful erudition and irenic ecumenical spirit, he, whom we appreciate as a stellar systematician within his tradition, gives an overview of the Catholic understanding of the Eucharist as sacrifice. He views the Catholic perspective as joining "biblical realism" with "ecclesial personalism" and spells out four cardinal elements of (1) the sacrifice of Christ on the cross, (2) the sacrificial meal of the Last Supper, (3) the liturgical sacrifice of the church, and (4) the personal sacrifice of participants. Throughout Fr. Dulles's presentation I gained illumination and also have numerous questions. We responders were cautioned to work with the paper and not expound our own positions, but it cannot hurt for me, a Protestant, to affirm gladly the biblical intentionality evinced by Fr. Dulles and also his emphasis on the personal participation of believers. I salute as well his endorsement of the theme of Christ's sacrificial death on the cross (not to be disjoined of course from the resurrection), and his eucharistic thematization that corresponds well with what many Protestants name the "real presence"—the unique and efficacious presence—of Christ at the communion table. Here the main stream of Protestantism, I like to believe, along with Catholicism and Orthodoxy, receives the continuous instantiation of the historic Christ's salvific act and being, which is indeed the nourishment by which we live and hope.

A Protestant sensibility could quibble or rejoice probably in every paragraph at something or other, but it seems obvious that the salient tensions with traditions indebted to the Reformation arise, as Fr. Dulles recognizes, in regard to his third and fourth elements: that is, the liturgical sacrifice of the church, and the personal sacrifice of participants. For we hardly need reminding that almost all the Reformation confessional documents contain something like Number XX of the Methodist Articles of Religion:

> The offering of Christ, once made, is that perfect redemption, propitiation, and satisfaction for all the sins of the whole world, both original and actual; and there is none other satisfaction for sin but that alone. Wherefore the sacrifice of masses, in the which it is commonly said that the priest doth offer Christ for the quick and the dead, to have remission of pain or guilt, is a blasphemous fable and dangerous deceit.[1]

That asseveration pertains to Element 3 in Father Dulles's presentation. But he notes also, as pertains to Element 4, that Catholicism (in his words) "takes a more positive view of human cooperation in the work of redemption" than did the Reformation. I shall return to both these matters, but first there are some ancillary concerns to mention.

The first of these centers in the term "sacrifice." I feel the need, as I'm sure others of our potential audience would, for a probing discussion of this key term. It has long been recognized in comparative phenomenology that sacrifice is one of religion's most primordial and central features. Venerable names like Durkheim, Tylor, and Frazer come to mind. Yet even today the meaning of sacrifice remains in many respects unresolved, as illustrated in the ongoing discussion of the ideas of Rene Girard of Stanford University. Recent meetings of the Society of Biblical Literature and the American Academy of Religion have been energized, in part, by Girard's work and its use by theologians like Robert Hamerton-Kelly and Ted Peters. Clearly Fr. Dulles could not have attempted to compass this sprawling inquiry in his systematic overview for our conference. He tersely says that "like all sacrifice," that of Jesus "was an external act symbolically expressing the interior homage of the creature to God." This seems too broad to be a definition, as it would hardly demarcate sacrifice from worship in general;

and in positing "the creature" as agent it seems (inadvertently but puz-zlingly) to preclude, both Godward and humanward, the participation as well as offering of the Divine in Christ. Constraints of time do not permit pursuing these paticular issues. My interest is simply that we all affirm in principle that our Christian dogmatic or systematic conceptu-ality cannot thrive in a self-contained semantics. An effort should be made to explain our terms in relation to what we know of their prove-nance in the wider world. The value of the Jewish context has been shown in this conference by the input of Rabbi David Stern, and some-day, in a parley of this sort, I hope we may include those who trace the comparative history of religious ideas.

Second, there is the historiographical problem. How do the bibli-cal reports concerning the Eucharist (and in principle concerning all Christian doctrine and practice) relate to the ongoing current work of historical research? I have endorsed the biblical intentionality of Fr. Dulles's paper. But it was in fact, I thought, a specific aim (among others) of this conference to ponder how biblical intentionality should be affected by contemporary results of scholarly inquiry. In a paper just received from Professor William Farmer, he asserts, "We live at a time when the Catholic Church in the United States has no viable alternative but to deal openly and honestly with Robert Funk and the Jesus Seminar." Professor Farmer then deals with Funk and the Seminar quite trenchantly. One could add to those he names a numerous company of other scholars here and abroad, including Gerd Luedemann of Göttingin University, Burton Mack, and Elisa-beth Schüssler-Fiorenza, just to scratch the surface. Again, I don't pretend to know how Fr. Dulles could have addressed such scholars and also given us the rounded systematic treatment he did. I am glad he did what he did. But I feel we must be aware of the unsettling situ-ation, not to say renewed crisis, in which all of our biblical generaliza-tions find themselves today historiographically. It cannot suffice to say to such scholars as those named that something "pervades sacred scripture as a whole" or that "the New Testament clearly and repeat-edly declares" this or that. Yes, the biblical canon may, but the histori-ography of Christian origins delves today into the more primitive building blocks of the tradition and allegedly discovers, in such (partly hypothetical) sources as "Q" and the Gospel of Thomas, evi-dence that some of the earliest Jesus traditions show no inkling of the sacrificial atonement or the Eucharist as we know it. Many of the educated public, and many theological students, are deeply confused by this. What can systematic theology say to them? I simply pose the question, lest we forget.

In addition to the semantic and the historiographical problems there is a third kind of issue which in a sense subsumes these but is, in the propagation of our faith, more sweeping and more decisive. This could be called the hermeneutic or the apologetic issue, or perhaps, in Catholic parlance, the issue of fundamental theology. It is what such recent theological giants as Paul Tillich and Karl Rahner addressed with notable insistence. How can we make the Christian witness intelligible to informed and honest persons of the modern world? Without specialists who would call themselves apologists (or whatever), in our conference it would be systematic theology in whose lap this task would mainly fall. Thus, when Fr. Dulles assures us that "the church adheres steadfastly to the doctrine that Jesus' flesh is 'food indeed' and his blood is 'drink indeed,'" might we not expect here some explication as to whether the assertion is intended literally or figuratively, and in either case how it might be understood? Johannine exegesis surely does not suggest that all the sayings the Fourth Gospel puts in the mouth of Jesus (such as that about the vine and the branches) can be understood literally. On the other hand, historical theology shows, as in Professor Bingham's paper, that venerable forerunners in our faith, such as Justin Martyr, Irenaeus, and Martin Luther, did understand such expressions literally. But we live not in the second or the sixteenth century, but in a world where, for an awful lot of people, for all kinds of reasons, it has seemed to become both impossible and unnecessary to believe that the words of consecration literally transmute bread and wine into a supernatural corporeality that potentiates physically the eventual resurrection of our dying bodies. One has here a theological tiger by the tail, and I am glad it is not my assignment to cage the tiger. Again, I would only point out that there is at this juncture, in the expectation of many, a task of interpretation—called by Bultmann "demythologization" and better called by Tillich "deliteralization"—a task that seems, I have to say, inadequately addressed in all of the conference papers, including the systematic thematization of Fr. Dulles where one might have hoped to get the most enlightenment on the matter.

Let me come back to the two matters earlier identified as salient points of tension with historic Protestantism: the Eucharist as the church's sacrifice, and the personal enactment of sacrifice by participants in the Eucharist.

On the first point Fr. Dulles appears to me to vacillate. He stresses that "what counts in God's eyes is the sacrifice of Christ on the cross, which...is present in the Eucharist. There is no need to look beyond the cross for some additional sacrifice." Well and good, Luther, Calvin, and Wesley could say. Let's embrace and be done with controversy. But is it not precisely an "additional sacrifice" which Catholic praxis and doctrine, as clearly cited by Fr. Dulles, do wish to propound as the third element or phase of the Mass? Read the second full paragraph on p. 182. It is patently clear that the church offers the sacrifice to God. The separate and distinct character of this sacrifice is blurred, at the end of the paragraph, by the statement that it is the church's "liturgical presentation" of Christ's own original sacrifice. If it were only that, what need would there be to differentiate the second from the third element of the Eucharist? I would entreat Fr. Dulles to elucidate this further. As for the biblical grounding of this third element—the church's sacrifice—can we really regard the dominical words "Do this in commemoration of me" (1 Cor 11:24) as implicitly empowering the apostles to bring about the sacrifice in question? Ironically, I always thought *that* passage favored the Zwinglian idea that the Eucharist is a memorial. Exegetically, I confess I am stuck with the conviction of John Wesley, adopted from the Anglican Articles, that, as far as the biblical witness regarding the Eucharist is concerned, the "offering of Christ once made is the perfect satisfaction for the sins of the whole world, and there is none other satisfaction for sin but that alone."

Nevertheless, I am myself far from content with the historic Protestant position at this point, as are many other Protestants today. If we consider the biblical witness as a whole, and our ongoing experience as Christians, there is patently the imperative stated by St. Paul in Romans 12:1: that we present our bodies a "living sacrifice" to God, which is our reasonable service. This brings us to the fourth element of Fr. Dulles's articulation of the Eucharist, the personal sacrifice of participating individuals. Protestantism, I believe, has been impoverished at this point by Luther's obsession with "faith alone," parallelled by Calvin's with predestination. The Catholic tradition is more biblical and more right-headed to take, as Fr. Dulles puts it, "a more positive view of human cooperation in the work of redemption." Why then should this not be reflected and involved in the meaning and action of the Eucharist, the axis of our Christian worship? It has actually been Protestantism which tended to insist on full communal participation in the eucharistic celebration. If the radical priority and uniqueness of *Christ's* sacrifice can be clearly upheld, perhaps one could say that Protestantism till now has had a better praxis of individual participation in communion with him, and Catholicism a better theory; while the main point would be that each might hopefully learn from the other.

However, if human cooperation in redemption has a place in the liturgical Eucharist, it has all the more so an imperative claim upon the whole of our lives. Thus the eucharistic enactment and impulse should carry forth from formal worship as the *ethical obedience* of the faithful in all their secular involvements. I think Fr. Dulles would agree with this, being careful both in eucharistic liturgy and in our secular discipleship to emphasize the normative priority of Christ, and therewith the sufficiency of his justifying grace, along with the enabling summons of his sanctifying love.

Problems in the conceptualization of Christ's sacrifice which I would have addressed, had time allowed, include the relation of the Father and the Son, along with that of the crucified and risen Lord, and that of the humanity and divinity of Jesus' person at successive phases of the eucharistic reality. These can wait. I appreciate Fr. Dulles's sense of mystery in such connections, as well as his sense of their wholeness and integrity. What a vast and exciting agenda we have in the Christian theological enterprise. And how gratifying it is to be in interdisciplinary and ecumenical dialogue about these challenging and inspiring issues! Thank you.

NOTE

1. *The Book of Discipline of the United Methodist Church* (Nashville, Tenn.: Methodist Publishing House, 1992), Section 67, p. 63.

Eucharist: Presence of a Gift[1]

by Peter Casarella

Jesus is God's trinitarian self-expression. When we encounter the person of Jesus Christ in his myriad expressions (in the Eucharist, in scripture, in the faces of the poor), we come face to face with an icon of the invisible Father's beauty and power. Jesus is a truly visible expression of God, but not in the sense of opening a random window to an amorphous eternity. Jesus expresses the inexhaustible reality of God's being in a specific way, i.e., with a definite yet infinitely transcendent form.[2] Jesus' forgiveness of sins, the transformative wisdom of his parables, his radical compassion for the poor, marginalized, dispossessed, and infirm, his utterance "Do this in memory of me," his washing of the feet of his disciples—these words and actions, *inter multa alia*, express the unfathomable scope of God's desire that everyone come to know the truth.[3] There is little, if anything, about Jesus' human expressivity that fails to translate into our language some aspect of the trinitarian being of God.

The mystery of salvation par excellence is the fact that the death and resurrection of the one man Jesus Christ takes place for the sake of all women and men and ultimately for the transfiguration of the entire cosmos.[4] The life, death, and resurrection of this particular man, Jesus the Christ, are the self-expression of God's triune identity. We do not come to know the triune mystery of God except through the paschal mystery of our Lord.[5] The concrete implications of taking the paschal Trinity as one's starting point are manifold. In this essay I will draw out only some consequences of adopting this starting point

for our understanding of the mystery of the Eucharist.[6] I will deal
with the question of real presence as well as the much debated relation between the ordained priesthood and the priesthood of all the
baptized. This essay is not an attempt to define each of these points in
a comprehensive fashion. The aim here is of a different sort, namely,
to provide a point of entry to the eucharistic mystery that will promote both faith and reflection.

The need for a new starting point appears increasingly relevant.
Let me cite just two highly publicized examples. In 1994 the *New York
Times* reported the result of a poll that said that a majority of
Catholics when queried about the eucharistic mystery favored "symbolic reminder" over real, physical presence.[7] If one relied upon these
data and subsequent reports in the media about it, it seems that few
respondents paused to consider the questionable premise upon which
these polling data were assembled, namely, that one must choose
between a symbolic manifestation (that could nonetheless be real) and
a crude physical presence. Thus many, especially of the younger generation, quite reasonably favored symbolism over physical presence.[8]
Similarly, a Vatican instruction from 1997 urged that a sharp distinction be maintained between ordained and common priesthood.[9] This
document met with a mixed reception in the United States and elsewhere, and church officials were left trying to explain a basic element
of the church's eucharistic practice without much confidence that
even well-informed lay Catholics had an adequate theology of the
priesthood.[10] Without trying to sweep under the rug the diverse
issues created by these highly public controversies, the conviction
that undergirds this paper is that neither the basic needs of the faithful nor long-disputed questions such as real presence and the nature
of the ordained priesthood can be properly addressed without a trinitarian starting point.

Eucharistia: Jesus and Trinitarian Communion

Sometimes we get stuck in conceiving the activity of the Eucharist in one-sidedly human terms. We can avoid this problem by considering the origins of the term. Our word "Eucharist" comes from
the Greek, and the Greek term *eucharistia* means "thanksgiving." In

the Mass the principal form of thanksgiving, around which all other praise circulates, is the praise given by the Son to the Father. Hans Urs von Balthasar explains how the Son is pure *eucharistia*, the perfect expression of praise to the Father:

> The Son thanks the Father (*eucharistein, eulogein*) for having permitted the Son to be so disposed that the highest revelation of divine love (its glorification) and the becoming healed of men and women resulted simultaneously.[11]

In other words, if we consider Christ's self-gift as the ultimate form of thanksgiving, then we need to see the whole passion of our Lord as a gradual unveiling of the Father's infinite love for the world.[12] When Christ's body is nailed to the cross, when his spirit is exhausted with the words "My God, my God, why have you abandoned me?" when the water and blood are sacramentally poured out of his side—all of these highly meaningful activities symbolize the self-giving love that comes from the Father.[13] Throughout the passion, Jesus seems to be more of a passive recipient of externally inflicted suffering, injustice, and abasement than an active agent of praise, yet even these expressions of abandonment are activities of praise. All of these activities portray the man Jesus as receptive to the divine will of the Father. Through them we see the Son uttering praise to the Father as much through the language of his body as in speech. The entire meaning of the passion is directed to the alignment of a truly human self-determination with the Father's plan of salvation: "Let not my will be done, but thine."[14]

This reflection shows that the Son of God himself is not only the highest Eucharist but precisely by appearing as such is the most expressive form known to man of God's communion of love. The priesthood of Christ is another way of expressing Christ's communion with us. His priesthood is no merely institutional reality; it is one of the most spiritually profound senses in which his eucharistic gift can be expressed. The Letter to the Hebrews describes Christ's priesthood as a gift of the paschal Trinity. Although this epistle is sometimes dismissed for its absorption of the world-view of Greek philosophy, it is actually an engaging meditation on the newness of Christ's priesthood. The priesthood of Christ is described as "worthy of more glory than Moses."[15] The renewal of the covenant already proclaimed by the prophet Jeremiah has been uniquely fulfilled through Christ's self-offering.[16]

The first covenant also had its laws governing worship, and its sanctuary, a sanctuary on this earth...But now Christ has come, as the high priest of all the blessings which were to come...He brings a new covenant, as the mediator, only so that the people who were called to an eternal inheritance may actually receive what was promised.[17]

Christ's eternal priesthood expresses newness through the single act of his self-offering on the cross. All of the sacrifices of the Old Testament are completed in this one act. But the shedding of blood on the cross is also a symbol of divine love, for it is precisely this offering that now mediates salvation universally. When the author of Hebrews states that "he brings a new covenant as a mediator, only so that the people who were called to an eternal inheritance may actually receive what was promised," the paschal mystery symbolizes God's embrace of all of humanity. This is no mere reprise of ancient philosophical speculation. On the contrary, it is the very same "blood of the new covenant" to which Christ called his disciples in the Last Supper and in which we partake in the Mass.[18]

The Sacrifice He Offers: The Presence of a Gift

Through his self-gift Christ offers us communion with the Father. What does this actually mean? What is termed by the Second Vatican Council the "conscious, active participation" of the faithful in the liturgy is still binding.[19] We are actively involved with Christ's *eucharistia* no less by acknowledging the priority of the divine gift. In fact, the spiritual participation of the priestly people is enhanced rather than diminished by recognizing the priority of the sacrifice that Christ offers to the gifts that we offer. The *Catechism of the Catholic Church* captures this sense of participation nicely:

> Before so great a sacrament, the faithful can only echo humbly and with ardent faith the words of the Centurion: ..."Lord, I am not worthy that you should enter under my roof, but only say the word and my soul will be healed" (cf.

Matt 8:8)...And in the Divine Liturgy of Saint John Chrysostom the faithful pray in the same spirit: "O Son of God, bring me into communion today with your mystical supper. I shall not tell your enemies the secret, nor kiss you with Judas' kiss. But like the good thief I cry, "Jesus, remember me when you come into your kingdom."[20]

We accept what God offers. As the faithful (including the presider) make their own the words based upon a Roman centurion's plea to have his boy healed, the self-offering of the entire communal body can be incorporated into the divine gift. As with the boy's healing, "the one who meets us in this text is Jesus, risen from the dead and radiant with the light of the Sonship that, in the depths of his being, was his from all eternity."[21] Significantly, Christ's communion with us in no way cancels out our communion with him. On the contrary, Christ's own eucharistic activity is what makes possible our act of thanksgiving in the Eucharist. Christ's praise to the Father lends us the freedom to offer ourselves to God.[22]

In the Mass the sacrifices that we offer and Christ's unique sacrifice are simultaneously present. Even though the relationship between the sacrifice that Christ offers and that made by the community may not be reversed, it is also important not to let the reality of God's presence overshadow the human initiative.[23] This raises the question of how properly to understand the relationship between what God gives us and what we give him.[24] A number of points suggest themselves. First, there is an interaction between our giving thanks back to the Father and the giving of thanks by the Son. This interaction shows that the love of God whereby we are offered salvation is never very far away. By entering into the human form of Jesus, God committed himself, as it were, always to seek companionship with men and women. The so-called "agape" meals of the earliest Christian communities were, among other things, ways of reinforcing God's companionship with his people in the light of the startling news of his resurrection from the dead. The typology of the holy banquet that appears from the time of the Old Testament figures the new form of Christ's sharing in a meal with his disciples.[25] The fact and manner of Christ's sharing in the meal "with publicans and sinners" are taken in the gospels as realizations of a messianic banquet.[26]

Some might object that nowadays it is more compelling to emphasize that the Mass is a meal in which people of many different walks of life are called to participate. The choice, however, between meal and sacrifice is based upon a false dichotomy.[27] According to the Second Vatican Council, the institution of the Eucharist perpetuates the sacrifice of the Mass throughout the centuries but is also a paschal banquet in which Christ is consumed, the mind is filled with grace, and pledge of future glory is given to us.[28] The imperative to include everyone in the meal is enhanced rather than undermined if we conceive of Christ's sacrifice as a real symbol of an all-embracing and incomprehensible love.

Beyond the companionship of the meal and the offering of love expressed through the sacrifice, there is also a spousal relation between Christ and the church. The believing church stands as a bride of Christ in accepting the bridegroom's offer of love.[29] Joy and a real desire to celebrate a feast accompany the presence of the bridegroom, as is illustrated in the following exchange between Jesus and his disciples:

> One day when John's disciples and the Pharisees were fasting, some people came and said to him, "Why is it that John's disciples and the disciples of the Pharisees fast, but your disciples do not?" Jesus replied, "Surely the bridegroom's attendants would never think of fasting while the bridegroom is still with them? As long as they have the bridegroom with them, they could not think of fasting.[30]

The spontaneous receptivity of the believing community is thus a response to the covenant that Christ has made with the church. By sealing Christ's marriage to the church in the Eucharist, these two entities are not melded together. An opposition between God and humanity still remains. Moreover, there is also the danger, as in any loving relationship, that one of the parties will smother the other with love. The nuptial bond between what we offer and what he offers is not like this. Coercion and the loss of individual self-determination are exactly the opposite of genuinely spousal love. On the contrary, we are free to accept or reject the offer of salvation represented by Christ. When the baptized participate in the Eucharist, they are truly entering into a mystery of God's presence as other. They are drawn to the attractiveness and the glory of the Lord and can rejoice just as a smitten lover can return joyfully to the arms of her beloved. This language of love is what we encounter in the Canticle of Canticles:

> On my bed, at night, I sought him whom my heart loves ... The watchmen came upon me on their rounds in the City: "Have you seen him whom my heart loves?" Scarcely had I passed them that I found him whom my heart loves. I held him fast, nor would I let him go till I had brought him into my mother's house, into the room of her who conceived me.[31]

It is no wonder that this same canticle also contains an invitation to participate in the celebration of a nuptial banquet.[32]

In sum, there is an analogy of giving whereby what God gives to us in the person of the Son is the very condition for our giving thanks back to the Father. A parallel can be drawn to the exchange that takes place with the apostle Peter. This exchange occurs during Jesus' washing of the disciples' feet before the Last Supper in John's gospel.[33] Jesus bends down to serve his apostles. The Lord's assumption of the posture of a slave catches Peter off guard. Peter's confusion and initial refusal to have his feet washed is met with the response: "If I do not wash you, you have no part of me" (RSV). Here Jesus is beckoning Peter, a unique representative of the entire church, to share a part of him. Peter can participate in Christ because he is being cleansed by the one who alone will shed blood and water for the sake of humanity. Peter is drawn into the Lord's offer of love, a fact that becomes evident in his response, "Lord, not my feet only but also my hands and my head."[34] Precisely in his bewilderment, Peter evinces an uncomprehending acceptance of what will later come to pass in the Lord's passion. Peter has gained a faint glimpse of the paschal mystery of salvation that has not yet been fully explained. Having his feet washed is a prefiguration of the cleansing that Jesus will offer to the entire world through his death and resurrection. In the washing of the feet, as in the Mass itself, we come to understand God's self-offering love as simultaneously near and distant.

Real Presence

Many Catholics today seem confused about the question of real presence. According to the poll conducted by the *New York Times* mentioned above, one must choose between an affirmation of the "physical presence" of Christ in the Eucharist or the view that bread and wine are merely "symbolic reminders" of Christ's presence. This false dichotomy does not represent an uncommon view. The level of understanding of real presence among the faithful appears so weak that few Catholics today are actually capable of thinking beyond widely promulgated distortions. The issue is often not dissent but improper catechesis or even a total absence of a language and lived context within which to approach these sacred mysteries. To that end, the following reflections are intended to aid those faithful who are seeking understanding without in any way attempting to resolve what is assuredly the thorniest problem in the history of Christian thought.

Christ is truly present in the bread and wine of the Eucharist. What does this mean? In the Mass his presence is in no way dependent upon whether or not we remember his initial sacrifice or make a symbolic connection with his Calvary. Such a view is far too subjective and has rightly been considered outside the bounds of the normative faith in the history of the Catholic Church.[35] On the other hand, the Eucharist is clearly a memorial meal filled with many symbolic actions and rites. The real presence of Christ is enhanced rather than diminished if we acknowledge that the assembled believers themselves represent a form of eucharistic communion. Christ is also present in that the members of the assembled community offer themselves to him in the memorial meal. The community partakes of and imitates from a distance Christ's own giving of praise to the Father. Much more could be said about the specific relations between the God of Jesus Christ and the assembly, but the point here is that there are multiple symbolic aspects to real presence. These symbols are not abstractions; they draw the faithful into the living presence of Christ at the heart of the mystery. Such an acknowledgment of the efficacy of the symbol is far superior to an affirmation of a crude physical presence. In this latter view, the awe-inspiring truth signified in the bread and wine stands wholly apart from the active participation of the believing community.

The real presence of Christ is therefore neither wholly subjective nor abstract and distant. Both of these determinations are negations. How can we state in positive terms the church's teaching on real presence? The *Catechism of the Catholic Church* follows a long tradition of Western theological speculation and authoritative church doctrine in stating that real presence is a substantial presence: "This presence is called 'real'...because it is presence in the fullest sense: that is to say, it is a substantial presence by which Christ, God and man, makes himself wholly and entirely present."[36] In this context the word "substantial" has a specific, technical meaning and should not be taken as a simple reaffirmation of the fact that Christ is really, truly among us in the bread and wine. In other words, the meaning of "substantial presence" cannot be explained by turning a declarative sentence into an exclamation, namely, "This presence is called real!" Substantial presence is, rather, real, spiritual presence.

Without elaborating the fascinating historical unfolding of the doctrine of substantial presence, I will simply underscore two points that bear on the pastoral implications of this teaching. First, substantial presence signifies that in the Eucharist a real transformation takes place. The transformation is not a this-worldly one, as if the priest had access to a special ecclesiastical chemistry. The transformation partakes even now of the messianic banquet that is still to come. Real presence is of "his glorified body and blood, which share in the eternity of the celestial Eucharist."[37] With the eyes of faith we encounter the bread as Christ's body and the wine as Christ's blood in the fullest, most spiritual sense of their reality. St. Ambrose, to whom the church owes one of its earliest articulations of this teaching, emphasized that the natural state of the bread and wine does not remain the same by virtue of God's activity in the conversion:

> Be convinced that this is not what nature has formed, but what the blessing has consecrated. The power of the blessing prevails over that of nature, because by the blessing nature itself is changed.[38]

The truth of the conversion is therefore not dependent on the quality of the believer's faith. Moreover, the transformation of the elements into the body and blood of Christ is also not dependent upon the quality of the priest's faith.

Second, the definition from the *Catechism* explains the real transformation in terms of Christ's presence "wholly" and "entirely." Thus, in the Eucharist we encounter the totality of a person. An analogy to concrete experience may help. Consider the case of someone introduced to you as the person who is responsible for your ultimate well-being. For the sake of argument, assume that this premise is not only plausible but one that you are willing to accept. After assenting to this premise, you are then informed that the aforementioned person has said he cannot afford to give you as much time as you feel that you need to experience ultimate well-being. The analogy is somewhat crude, but the point should be clear. Christ gives himself totally in the eucharistic encounter, just as he gave himself totally at Calvary. In the Eucharist there are no limits to the way in which Christ makes himself available to us. He is present as a gift, a total self-offering.[39]

What is a gift? This simple query actually raises an interesting theoretical question, namely, whether one can speak of the substantial reality of a gift. Many gifts are not really gifts at all.[40] Kenneth Schmitz distinguishes between presents that are given out of social convention and genuine gifts.[41] For example, a token given in obligatory circumstances, for one's own advantage, or only to impress is really more of a transaction than a gift. Gifts given out of compulsion or with an expectation of reward lack substance. Strictly speaking, a gift is never owed, and only certain gifts are given as an expression of what one can really give of oneself.

The lives of saints and martyrs are good examples of total self-giving. The little way of St. Thérèse of Lisieux, for example, was an exercise in total self-giving to the Lord lived out in the idiom of everyday experience.[42] For a gift to have substance, it must be freely given and given as an expression of the very person of the giver. The personal quality of the gift is not a sentiment attached to a concrete thing that is given. The personal nature of the genuine gift is evident in both the thing given and in the act of giving. In the eucharistic exchange, for example, the concrete objects brought to the altar as the offertory gifts are not the real gifts; they symbolize the gifts of self that we make to the Lord.

What makes the eucharistic gift real and substantial? Once again, we must begin with a reflection on the nature of the gift. What Christ actually gives us in the eucharistic gift is a love so abundant and total that it defies human understanding. Christ pours his love out for the sake of the entire world, but without faith we cannot point our finger at the visible form of this love. The absoluteness of the gift introduces a certain paradox into our thinking. How can we say that Christ is really and substantially present in the Eucharist if the content of his gift was already expended on the cross? To sharpen the point even further, if we conceive of the Eucharist as a total gift of self, i.e., as a self-emptying love, do we thereby undermine real, substantial presence?

One way to respond to these questions is to reflect on the idea that in the Eucharist the gift of love is given.[43] A careful analysis of this one statement is highly elucidating. The statement "the gift of love is given" must first be broken down into its component parts, for it includes both the affirmation of a substantial presence and the symbolic manifestation of an act rendered for the sake of another. In order to emphasize the real transformation that takes place in the Eucharist, we need to underline the substantiality of a thing that nonetheless transcends our understanding. In grammatical terms, we need to emphasize the copula: "the gift of love is given." The copula in this sentence indicates that Christ truly gives himself to us with "a pledge of the glory to come."[44]

Three things need to be said from the outset about the substance of the love that is given in such a statement. First, Christ gives himself as a person and not as an object. Persons are not present in the same ways as objects. If a biologist or social anthropologist provided an empirical description of the person standing in front of me, you still would not know whether that person was my father, my son, my best friend, or my sworn enemy. When Christ gives himself to us with a pledge of the glory to come, it is the "who" of his presence and not the "what" that interests us. What is at stake is not so much the difference between objective and subjective relations, for the phenomena of being a son, parent, friend, and enemy still involve objective realities. What is at stake is the distinctiveness of a relation in which we encounter personal love. In the eucharistic encounter we not only know Christ, but he knows us exactly as we are. The distinction between the givenness of persons and the givenness of things

should not be too exaggerated. Even Christ, the firstborn of all creation and the one sent from the Father, also participates in a certain
sense in the cosmic givenness of things.

Second, Christ gives himself as a divine person. We are dealing
here with the Christ of negative theology.[45] As the Incarnate Word,
Jesus gives more than human love. The paradox of the eucharistic
encounter is that we receive love that is fully human and fully divine.
In the words of Dionysius the Areopagite, Jesus' love for humanity
"has the force of a negation pointing toward transcendence."[46]
Dionysius insists that Jesus was humanly born but far superior to
man:

> It was not by virtue of being God that he did divine things,
> not by virtue of being a man that he did what was human, but
> rather, by the fact of being God-made-man he accomplished
> something new in our midst—the activity of the God-man.[47]

Christ's love is distant and transcends all understanding. Christ's
power to transform human hearts, however, remains quite near. His
hiddenness is not exhausted by being revealed but remains a mystery
that beckons us further into the reality of God. In Christ something
radically new and totally other has appeared in our midst. What is
this something? It is a gift from God that has taken on human flesh.
The substance of this gift is divine charity, and this charity is
expressed through Christ's sacramental body.[48]

Third, the substance of a gift is given in the recipient. The interior reception of the gift does not mean that the gift ceases to be a
factual reality in the world. The mode of reception signifies, rather,
that the recipient of the gift does not create this substance. The recipient is transformed by the gift. When I give someone a gift, I am not
actually doing something to that person. Once removed from the
realm of transaction and exchange, an incalculable freedom accompanies the giving of a gift. The recipient is nonetheless an indirect
object of my giving. The recipient embodies a form of receptivity that
is quite different from a merely passive condition. When a messenger
delivers a message, the reception of the communication is quite passive, even though the subsequent reaction to the message can be self-
involving. (This passivity, incidentally, explains why people are so

readily disposed to employ wholly impersonal means to receive mes-
sages, e.g., faxes, voicemail, e-mail, and "instant messengers.") Receptivity to the substance of the gift, by contrast, entails a personal
stance, for the gift has the potential to change who we are as persons.
We are the indirect objects of God's gloriously transformative love.[49]
The communication of the substance of the gift thus highlights the
"dative" character of our existence.[50] St. Paul underscored the radically dative character of his own missionary existence when he wrote:
"I have been crucified with Christ, and I live now not with my own
life but with the life of Christ who lives in me."[51]

So far we have examined the substance of the gift expressed in the
copula "is." We have ascertained that the substance of the love given is
personal, divine (and therefore incomprehensible), and received into
our own lives. Beyond substance, however, the statement in question
also affirms an act. In order to emphasize the personal and free act
whereby Christ offers himself for our sake, we could underline the
past participle of the statement: "the gift of love is given." We are
speaking now of a form of givenness that is the result of an event. We
are speaking of what is called in French "*donation*" but has only a loose
English equivalent ("gifting") since "donation" in English generally
refers to a check in the mail or some other "charitable" transaction.[52]

What kind of act is signified when a gift is given? Our concern is
not to specify one activity (e.g., sacrificing) and distinguish it from
another (e.g., celebrating a meal). Our concern rather is to speak to
the phenomenon of donation (gifting) itself. Jean-Luc Marion has
argued that all existing phenomena appear as given.[53] He states:
"Everything that appears has come unto us as given."[54] What happens
happens as given, and the givenness of the donation is an essential
characteristic of the event.[55] According to Marion, this is true of all
that happens and is by no means particular to religious experiences.
In this view, one acknowledges that events happen and appear as
given to me, but the event character of the happening is not taken to
be hidden behind a veil of appearances. The radical suspicion of all
appearances that accompanies the modern scientific consciousness is
bracketed to disclose the given appearance qua appearance.[56]

Givenness is not limited to factual truth, and herein lies the crucial significance of the event character of the donation. "To take
something as a given" can imply that the donation is of no more con-

sequence than adding another datum to our collection of experience. Clearly, this view strips the donation altogether of the character of an event, and reduces the eucharistic event to a psychological experience. David Power, for example, has articulated the sense in which the eucharistic gift could be seen as a paschal event:

> The gift/giving of God through Word and Spirit is continually manifested in the sacramental self-giving of Christ through the memorial of his death and in the gift of the Spirit which works from within to allow the Church to take this memorial into the actuality of Christian community.[57]

The eucharistic gift enters into the web of our collective, fragmented experience of joy and sorrow as a dynamic and life-giving reality. For Power the donation in the sacramental gift is intrinsically self-giving and self-emptying. The substance of the gift is transferred in a Hegelian fashion to the Spirit that enlivens the Christian community. For Power the paschal event is also a "language event."[58] The sacrament, as "the event of God's Word in the Spirit," has to be interpreted in terms of the discontinuities and disruptions of linguistic events (and the ethical practices that accompany such events) "without having to look for some causative force outside language usage itself."[59] Power's hermeneutic of the eucharistic event is intertextual. Thus, there is no path beyond the interplay of written texts and their oral performance to a reality outside of these inscriptions; nothing appears outside of the text. Jean-Luc Marion, by contrast, localizes the event of the eucharistic gift *hors texte* ("outside of the text").[60]

To claim, as we have been doing, that the event of the Eucharist is one with the event-like givenness of all things is to attempt to render intelligible the incomprehensible activity of giving in the sacrament. In some sense, we are attempting an impossible task, yet the mode of inquiry can be taken at least one step further. Just how intelligible is the act of donation? In natural phenomena, every given begets the question of a giver, but the eucharistic donation comes from a transcendent, "supernatural" source. How, if at all, can the donor/giver of the eucharistic gift be known? It may be that the knowability of the donor is inversely related to the measure of freedom given in the gift. Marion attempts to bracket the question of the donor in order to bring into relief the phenomality of the donation.[61] Marion is not saying that the God who gives himself in the Eucharist is abolished by the bracketing of the donor. On the contrary, he himself underscores the complementarity of a traditional metaphysical approach in which the presence of God or some other transcendent source is taken as a starting point and the phenomenological approach in which God's absence is postulated. The purpose of such bracketing is to bring to light the dynamics of the gift as such.[62] I think that this bracketing is quite necessary and even enhances our recognition of the reality and necessity of the gift. First, the phenomenological bracketing of the donor focuses our attention on the immanence of God's gift. As Dionysius stated above, it is God's love for humanity that has appeared in our midst. The method of immanence as employed by Marion highlights the coming into our midst of a wholly other gift. Second, Marion's phenomenology safeguards the gratuity of the gift by distinguishing the phenomenon of donation from economies of exchange.[63] By examining the presence of an unknowable gift in its immanent structure and activity, we do not make the mistake of extrapolating from a worldly system of gift-giving to a fully transcendent donor of the gift. Through the method of immanence, the activity of a transcendent donor remains free in the fullest sense.

The bracketing of the donor can be conceived by a number of analogies. These include receiving an anonymous inheritance or a loan from an unknown lender. There are many other forms of giving in which the donor expects nothing in return. According to Marion, the artist gives pleasure to others by performing his activity without regard to compensation and even without regard to the donation itself. The scriptural injunction to give alms in secret ("your left hand must not know what your right hand is doing")[64] is cited as another example of a donation in which the donor is left intentionally unknown. Marion's point is that these specific examples actually elucidate a general feature of the gift, namely, that in an act of pure giving the donor recedes into the background. In the case of the anonymous inheritance, for example, the donor's death initiates both his condition of anonymity and the giving of the gift. "The donor is not (he is missing, disappears, remains unknown, anonymous) inasmuch as he gives [himself]."[65]

The bracketing of the donor highlights a central feature of the phenomenon of donation. When one brackets the donor, the recipient of the donation is not left with just some thing, i.e., a gift. Nonetheless, one cannot say that the recipient knows any particular thing about the donor, since this information has been erased. Indebtedness is taken by Marion as a general feature of the phenomenon of the gift. The debtor, for example, is indebted to someone even if he has no knowledge of the identity of the lender. Marion therefore concludes that the recipient of the gift recognizes the donor in the donation.[66] The event of the gift thus discloses a donor in his very absence. The recognition, however, is not of something apart from the donation itself. In other words, the method of immanence has yielded no knowledge about a transcendent donor, since such a presence has been methodologically suppressed. Yet in that very suppression we see the intimations of what could be called a phenomenology of absolute charity. The person who receives the gift receives a gift of self from an anonymous donor, and this act of self-giving is recognized as such.

What is the significance of the phenomenological analysis for a theology of the eucharistic gift? Theologically, the question of the unknowable donor parallels the one posed above about the Christ of negative theology. To assign the gift of love given for the sake of the world to "God" as a known objective referent can be to miss the enormity of the claim. Faith does not recognize "God" as one object among others. The one known according to the trinitarian confession of faith as the God of Jesus Christ is not just a variant on a generic theme in the history of religions.[67] The God revealed in the person of Jesus Christ is not a thing but a person, whose appearance in our very midst nonetheless defies human understanding. To return to the assertion "the gift of love is given," we can now state that a specific appearance of giving is disclosed when the love given in the eucharistic donation is understood in properly trinitarian terms. The bread of life who gave himself for the sake of the world nourishes us through the sacrifice that he offers. Through his self-offering, we are made the recipients of an offer of eternal life. His cruciform appearance is not accidental to his offering appearance. The cross of Christ is the very form in which the offer is made to us.

The formal, grammatical analysis of the affirmation "the gift of love is given" shows that substantial presence and the event of giving a gift come into play as intrinsically related. The giving of the gift may transcend our understanding, but the acknowledgment of the incomprehensibility of love shed for the sake of humanity does not evacuate the gift of its content. It would be highly misleading to see these two results (presence, the giving of a gift) as separate or even separable. The point is in fact the opposite. In the Eucharist, substantial change is identical with free self-offering.

Some Presences of Christ in the Celebration of the Mass

There are many real presences of Christ in the donation of the Eucharist, but God offers us just one gift, his only Son. The disclosure of multiple presences of Christ is an ancient teaching of the church that was reaffirmed by the Second Vatican Council and by *Mysterium Fidei* of Paul VI and is even mentioned in the *Catechism of the Catholic Church*.[68] What follows in this last section presupposes this teaching about manifold presences and even presupposes what these documents say about the preeminence of Christ's presence in the eucharistic species. The focus of these remarks, however, is on two other real presences.

In the celebration of the Mass, the priest stands *in persona Christi* and therefore represents Christ the high priest in a unique way. By virtue of Christ's commandment "Where two or three are gathered in my name, I shall be there with them,"[69] the community of believers also discloses a distinct manifestation of the body of Christ. Those in the gathered assembly bring with them a share in Christ's priesthood by virtue of their baptismal priesthood. I will offer a few "lay" reflections on the difference and relation between these two presences of Christ and his priesthood as they make their appearance in the Mass.

The ordained priest partakes in a unique fashion in the sacrifice of the Mass. According to the *Catechism*, "[t]he presentation of the offerings at the altar takes up the gesture of Melchizedek and commits the Creator's gifts into the hands of Christ who, in his sacrifice, brings to perfection all human attempts to offer sacrifices."[70] There are many reasons why this activity of the ordained priest in the Mass is unique. The 1997 Vatican instruction on this topic makes these points. When the ordained priest stands "in the person of Christ," he is vested with a sacred power originally entrusted to the twelve apostles that is expressed through his Christ-like activity as Head and shepherd.[71] The priest's unique representation of Christ is no merely symbolic gesture but rather "a frightening mandate" that is meant to measure the priest's entire activity as priest.[72] As a servant of Christ and the church, the priest authoritatively proclaims the word of God, administers the sacraments, and directs the faithful pastorally. All of these duties pertain uniquely to the ordained priest. All of these duties are to be administered by the ordained priest without the least hint of clericalism, for the same 1997 instruction makes it unequivocally clear that the ordained priest is to carry out this sacred power without any illusions of being holier than the laity. The laity and the ordained priest are both called to holiness and to share in the one priesthood of Christ. As a layman, I do not feel that my own response to this universal vocation to sanctity is hindered by the unique and essentially different role of the ordained priest in the Mass.

How does the laity partake of Christ's priesthood during the Mass? Let us begin once again with the *Catechism:*

> Christ, high priest and unique mediator, has made of the Church "a kingdom, priests for his God and Father" (Rev. 1:6). The whole community of believers is, as such, priestly. The faithful exercise their baptismal priesthood through their participation, each according to his own vocation, in Christ's mission as priest, prophet and king.[73]

In other words, Christ's priesthood, the new form of sacrificial love that he introduces out of obedience to the Father, is indivisible. As already stated, no one is given just a part of the person. Christ encounters each one of us in the totality of his personhood. Lay people and clergy alike are called to partake wholly of Christ's priesthood.

In my opinion, the baptismal priesthood of the laity is best understood in terms of "a kneeling theology." This stance is only indirectly related to the physical act of kneeling during the Mass, for it entails no less of an openness to the world itself. When we offer thanksgiving to the Father and when we offer ourselves as sinners to the Father's mercy, lay people embody this stance. This idea is strongly supported by the Second Vatican Council. According to *Lumen Gentium*, the baptismal priesthood applies not only to the offering of sacrifices made by the lay faithful during the sacrifice of the Mass but to the whole of their lives:

> For their work, prayers and apostolic endeavors, their ordinary married life and family life, their daily labor, their mental and physical relaxation, if carried out in the Spirit, and even the hardships of life if patiently borne—all of these become spiritual sacrifices acceptable to God through Jesus Christ (cf. 1 Pet 2:5). During the celebration of the Eucharist these sacrifices are most lovingly offered to the Father along with the Lord's body. Thus as worshipers whose every deed is holy, the lay faithful consecrate the world itself to God.[74]

Whereas the ordained priest consecrates the Eucharist in the Mass and serves as Christ's servant in all of his other priestly activities as well, the lay person participates in Christ's priesthood through the no less important task of consecrating the world itself to God. The act of consecration performed by the laity is not less spiritual than the priest's consecration in the Mass. What makes the laity's patient labors of everyday life into spiritual sacrifices acceptable to God (and therefore one with kneeling) is a concerted attachment to prayer, a prayer offered up for the sake of the entire world. There are therefore two complementary activities of consecration. These two modes of participating in Christ's priesthood do not compete with one another.[75]

How does the ordained or ministerial priesthood differ from the common priesthood of the baptized? The Vatican Council's Constitution on the Church, *Lumen Gentium*, emphasizes that the difference is neither merely functional nor the basis for "a ranking" of one's closeness to Christ the high priest:

> Though they differ essentially and not only in degree, the common priesthood of the faithful and the ministerial or hierarchical priesthood are nonetheless ordered one to another;

each in its own proper way shares in the one priesthood of
Christ. The ministerial priest, by the sacred power that he has,
forms and rules the priestly people; in the person of Christ he
effects the eucharistic sacrifice and offers it to God in the
name of all the people. The faithful indeed, by virtue of their
royal priesthood, participate in the offering of the Eucharist.
They exercise that priesthood, too, by the reception of the
sacraments, prayer and thanksgiving, the witness of a holy life,
abnegation and active charity.[76]

Again, both priesthoods partake of the unique priestly sacrifice of
Christ during the Mass. There is not just one way in which to participate in Christ's priesthood. There are two. By the same token, the
differences between these two paths to the self-offering of Christ are
real in the fullest ontological sense of the term. Their difference is
not just functional. The ministerial priest alone stands "in the person
of Christ," "effects the eucharistic sacrifice[,] and offers it to God in
the name of all the people." His unique ability to perform these rituals has nothing to do with his ability to perform, gather the community, or speak in a way that leads people to genuine conversion. He is
really different whether or not he measures up to whatever standards
of "performance" that he himself, the laity, his fellow priests, or the
bishop may set for him. Although there is a real difference between
the two priesthoods, this difference nonetheless leaves no room for
someone to claim that he emulates Christ's priesthood more perfectly
by virtue of his state of life.

An interesting paradox arises in the consideration of this ontological difference. Does the priest also kneel in his heart? On this question the official documents of the church are silent; however, there is
nothing about the church's recommendation that we emphasize the
real distinction between the two priesthoods that precludes the idea
that the priest, in his simultaneous role as layman, is also kneeling in
his heart. I use the phrase "in his heart" to signify the fact that there
is—in fact, there must be—nothing about the visible appearance of
the priest in the celebration of the Mass that indicates an attitude of
kneeling as I have defined the term. In fact, the two senses of presence may even be related inversely. The more the priest performs
outwardly to show a common participation with the faithful, e.g.,

establishing eye contact with the people during the words "Take this, all of you, and eat it," the less is he able to appear focused on the unique sense in which he as ordained priest represents Christ the high priest.[77] If, on the contrary, the priest acts so as to appear that he is offering himself to Christ in the celebration of the Mass, the more likely he is kneeling in his heart. Suitably, the priest partakes of the royal priesthood of the laity by being more rather than less of an ordained priest. Ironically, an ontological ordering of the distinct senses of priesthood is the surest safeguard against elitism.

Conclusion

In this essay I have considered some elements of a trinitarian eucharistic theology. One could rightly object that the trinitarian vantage point is still too abstract for many people. Inasmuch as I have drawn upon the debates of contemporary theology, it must be acknowledged that many of the difficulties that people face in their lives are not solved by introducing these concepts. On the other hand, the real test of a Christian theology, in my opinion, is its ability to present believers with an account of the Eucharist as a profound mystery of faith, that is, as a substantial gift from God. If a theologian fails in this regard, then other serious problems will inevitably follow. Sincere believers today are very vulnerable to distortions of the central mysteries of faith. Many people of good will do not even know where to turn to find answers to vital questions. The reflections in this essay are hardly definitive. They are meant only to spur further reflection and hopefully some prayer as well. More than anything else, these words are intended to nurture a hope for a future eucharistic theology that nourishes both the hearts and minds of the faithful.

NOTES

1. Earlier versions of this text were presented at the 2000 Eucharistic Congress of the Archdiocese of Washington and the St. Thomas Aquinas Center at Purdue University. I would like to thank these sponsors and especially those participants whose questions provoked me to refine the text.

2. St. Bonaventure speaks of four faces to wisdom's beauty in *Collationes in Hex-aemeron*, II: uniform wisdom (the rules of the divine law), manifold wisdom (the mysteries of divine scriptures), omniform wisdom (in the traces of God's hand in creation), and formless wisdom (*forma nulliformis*) or mystical theology. St. Bonaventure makes it clear that the negation in the formless fourth face of wisdom does not destroy the preceding faces (ibid., II, 28). St. Bonaventure, *Collations on the Six Days*, trans. José de Vinck (Paterson, N.J.: St. Anthony Guild Press, 1970), 21–40.

3. 1 Tim 2:4. Biblical citations are from the *New Revised Standard Version* unless otherwise indicated.

4. Cf. Peter Casarella, "Waiting for a Cosmic Christ in an Uncreated World," *Communio* (2001), forthcoming.

5. For a brief overview of this development in recent theology, one may consult Anne Hunt, *The Trinity and the Paschal Mystery: A Development in Recent Catholic Theology* (Collegeville, Minn.: Liturgical Press, 1997). More to the point, however, are *La Trinità e il pensare: figure, percorsi, prospettive*, ed. Piero Coda and Andreas Tapken (Rome: Città Nuova, 1997), and *Abitando la Trinità: Per un rinnovamento dell'ontologia*, ed. Piero Coda and L'ubomír Žák (Rome: Città Nuova, 1998).

6. The topic of Trinity and Eucharist is quite vast and has been treated amply in many recent studies. See, for example, Edward J. Kilmartin, *The Eucharist in the West: History and Theology*, ed. Robert Daly (Collegeville, Minn.: Liturgical Press, 1998); David N. Power, "Roman Catholic Theologies of Eucharistic Communion," *Theological Studies* 57 (1996): 587–610; and the several essays in the issue of *Communio* 27 (Summer 2000) dedicated to this theme.

7. *New York Times*, June 1, 1994, B8.

8. See my own letter to the editor on this point: *New York Times*, June 18, 1994, A20, and the discussion of the same in Msgr. Kevin Irwin, "Models of the Eucharist," *Origins* 31 (May 31, 2001), 34–35.

9. "On Certain Questions Regarding the Collaboration of the Non-Ordained Faithful in the Sacred Ministry of the Priest," August 13, 1997.

10. Gabriel Meyer, "Line Between Clergy and Laity Remains Blurred," *National Catholic Register* (April 5–11, 1998), 1, 7.

11. Hans Urs von Balthasar, *Theologie der Drei Tagen* (Einsiedeln: Johannes Verlag, 1990), 95; English translation: *Mysterium Paschale: The Mystery of Easter* (Edinburgh: T&T Clark, 1990), 99. See also Power, "Roman Catholic Theologies of Eucharistic Communion," 590.

12. Cf. Peter Casarella, "*Analogia donationis*: Hans Urs von Balthasar on the Eucharist," *Philosophy and Theology* 11, no. 1 (1998), 156–159, and Nicola Reali, *La ragione e la forma, Il sacramento nella teologia di H.U. von Balthasar* (Rome: Pontificia Università Lateranense, 1999), 71–155.

13. The cry of Jesus abandoned has been interpreted this way since at least Pope

Leo the Great. For contemporary articulations, see Pope John Paul II, *Novo Millenio Ineunte* (apostolic letter of Jan. 6, 2001), par. 26, and Chiara Lubich, *The Cry of Jesus Crucified and Forsaken* (Hyde Park, N.Y.: New City Press, 2001).

14. Luke 22:42. Cf. Matt 26:39; John 5:30; 12:27.

15. Heb 3:3.

16. Heb 8:6–13. Cf. Jer 31:31–34.

17. Heb 9:1, 11, 15.

18. Luke 22:19–20. Cf. the *Catechism of the Catholic Church* (*CCC*) (New York: Image, 1995), §1365.

19. See Vatican Council II, *Sacrosanctum Concilium* 14, in which "full, conscious, and active participation" is said to be "demanded by the liturgy" and that "to which the Christian people, 'a chosen race, a royal priesthood, a holy nation, a redeemed people' (*1 Pet* 2:9, 4–5) have a right and obligation by reason of their baptism." In other words, participation according to the text of the Council signifies as much a vertical relationship initiated by God as a horizontal relation of the individual to the worshiping community.

20. *CCC* §1386.

21. Francis Martin, "St. Matthew's Spiritual Understanding of the Healing of the Centurion Boy," *Communio* 25 (Spring 1998): 176.

22. Reali, 125–132.

23. What follows is based upon Casarella, "*Analogia donationis*," 156–159.

24. Cf. Hans Urs von Balthasar, "The Mass: A Sacrifice of the Church?" in *Explorations in Theology III. Creator Spirit* (San Francisco: Ignatius Press, 1993), 185–243.

25. Louis Bouyer, *The Bible and the Liturgy* (Notre Dame, Ind.: University of Notre Dame Press, 1956), 155.

26. Ibid., 155–160. Cf. Irwin, 41–42.

27. Cf. ibid., 40; Kilmartin, 199; and Hans Urs von Balthasar, *Theologie der Drei Tagen*, 93–95 (Eng. trans.: *Mysterium Paschale*, 97–99).

28. *Sacrosanctum Concilium* 47. See also Casarella, "*Analogia donationis*," 166, and *CCC* §1382.

29. In what follows, I treat the spousal relation from the perspective of the lay faithful. In the case of the ordained priest who stands *in persona Christi* in the Mass, the relationships are reversed. See, for example, Congregation for the Clergy, *Directory for the Life and Ministry of Priests*, §13: "[Priests]...must be faithful to the Bride and almost like living icons of Christ the Spouse render fruitful the multi-form donation of Christ to his Church" (Vatican City: Libreria Editrice Vaticana, 1994), 15.

30. Mark 2:18–19 (Jerusalem Bible).

31. Cant 3:1, 3–4 (Jerusalem Bible).

32. Cant 5:1: "Eat, friends, and drink,/drink deep, my dearest friends" (Jerusalem Bible). Cf. Bouyer, 203ff.

33. John 13:1–20. See Casarella, *"Analogia donationis,"* 158.

34. John 13:9.

35. See, for example, Denzinger-Schönmetzer (DS) 1501 (Council of Rome, 1079), 1504 (profession of faith prescribed to the Waldensians, 1208), 1513, 1526, 1531 (Council of Trent, 1551); *Sacrosanctum Concilium* 7 (Vatican Council II, 1963); and DS 1578–1579 (Paul VI, *Mysterium Fidei,* 1965). This is not to deny that a certain tension between symbolic and real presence is a long-standing feature of the Western theological tradition since at least the condemnation of Berengar of Tours in the eleventh century. For discussion, see, for example, Louis-Marie Chauvet, *Symbol and Sacrament: A Sacramental Reinterpretation of Christian Existence* (Collegeville, Minn.: Liturgical Press, 1995), 291–297.

36. *CCC* §1374, citing Paul VI, *Mysterium Fidei* §39. Cf. Council of Trent (1551): DS 1651. For discussion, see Joseph Ratzinger, *Il problema della transustanzione e del significato dell'Eucaristia* (Rome: Paoline, 1969), 39–58. This material is taken from an article originally published by the same author in *Tübinger Theologische Quartalschrift* 2 (1967), 129–158.

37. Robert Sokolowski, "The Eucharist and Transubstantiation," *Communio: International Catholic Review* 24 (Winter 1997): 870.

38. St. Ambrose, *De myst.* 9, 50 (Patrologia Latina 16, 405ff.), as cited in *CCC* §1375.

39. The language of "gift" is also used in Committee on Doctrine of the National Conference of Catholic Bishops, "The Real Presence of Jesus Christ in the Sacrament of the Eucharist: Basic Questions and Answers" (Washington, D.C.: United States Catholic Conference, 2001). The conclusion to this statement reads: "With this *gift* of Christ's presence in our midst, the Church is truly blessed...In the Eucharist the Church both receives the *gift* of Jesus Christ and *gives* grateful thanks to God for such a blessing...[T]hrough this *gift* of himself in the celebration of the Eucharist under the appearances of bread and wine Christ *gives* us the *gift* of eternal life" (italics added).

40. See Kenneth Schmitz, *The Gift: Creation* (Milwaukee: Marquette University Press, 1982).

41. Ibid., 45–46. Schmitz freely admits that there are manifold instances in which the distinction between the present and the gift is not so clear. "Postmodern" thinkers who follow Jacques Derrida are very suspicious of this distinction, for in their view no exchange of gifts can be abstracted from an economy of credits and debts. This is at least how Derrida differentiates himself from the position of Jean-Luc Marion in *God, the Gift, and Postmodernism,* ed. John D. Caputo and Michael J. Scanlon (Bloomington,

Ind.: Indiana University Press, 1999), 59ff. The position that I am taking in this essay is that some distinction between gifting and economies of exchange is necessary for a theology of the Eucharist, even though individual human experience and social structures are saturated with mixed phenomena.

42. See Peter Casarella, "Sisters in Doing the Truth: Dorothy Day and St. Thérèse of Lisieux," *Communio: International Catholic Review* 24 (Fall 1997): 468–498.

43. This reflection was inspired by the interpretation of Edmund Husserl's notion of *Gegebenheit* in Jean-Luc Marion, *Étant donné. Essai d'une phenomenologie de la donation* (Paris: Presses Universitaires de France, 1997), especially 78–102. See also idem, *Dieu sans l'être* (Paris: Presses Universitaires de Paris, 1991), 225–258. Given that the category of the "gift" has now become a staple of postmodern thought, a number of proposals have appeared that use similar language. On the general question of the gift, see *God, the Gift, and Postmodernism,* ed. John D. Caputo and Michael J. Scanlon (Bloomington, Ind.: Indiana University Press, 1999). For an application of the postmodern category of the gift to the Eucharist, which differs in important ways from this essay, see David N. Power, *Sacrament: The Language of God's Giving* (New York: The Crossroad Publishing Company, 1999), 274–310. In this book Power treats Marion's theory of the icon as a Balthasarian prelude to a more authentically "post[-]modern" rejection of ontotheology. In this essay I am treating a different aspect of Marion's contribution to theology and not under the rubric of "post[-]modern" thought. Like Power, however, I too maintain that "the analogy of the gift needs to be complemented by the [properly Thomistic] analogy of being" (281).

44. Cf. *CCC* §§1402–1405.

45. Cf. Peter Casarella, *"His Name Is Jesus*: Negative Theology and Christology in Two Writings of Nicholas of Cusa from 1440," in *Nicholas of Cusa on Christ and the Church,* ed. Gerald Christianson and Thomas M. Izbicki (Leiden: E.J. Brill, 1996), 281–307.

46. *Letter 4,* 1072B. Pseudo-Dionysius, *The Complete Works,* trans. Colm Luibheid (New York: Paulist Press, 1987), 264–265.

47. Ibid., 1072C, p. 265.

48. Cf. Marion, *Dieu sans l'être,* 252.

49. See *Sermon 9* (*Quasi stella matutina*) of Meister Eckhart's German sermons, in which Eckhart compares the human soul to an adverb that modifies God as verb. *Meister Eckhart: Teacher and Preacher,* ed. Bernard McGinn (New York: Paulist Press, 1986), 260.

50. I first encountered this term through the work of Thomas Prufer. Cf. idem, *Recapitulations: Essays in Philosophy* (Washington, D.C.: The Catholic University of America Press, 1993).

51. Gal 2:20.

52. Power, *Sacrament*, 311, n. 2.

53. *God, the Gift, and Postmodernism*, 56–57.

54. Ibid., 57.

55. Not all givens, however, are gifts in the same sense or even at all. To give someone a cold is not a welcome or even an intentional *donation*. Marion's point is that phenomena as such cannot be divorced from their being given. *Given* that I have a cold, for example, I may try to educe who infected me. In this case, the given cannot be separated from a possibly known giver. Below we consider the phenomenon of a gift with an unknowable giver.

56. Cf. Robert Sokolowski, *Eucharistic Presence: A Study in the Theology of Disclosure* (Washington, D.C.: The Catholic University of America Press, 1994), 5–12.

57. Power, *Sacrament*, 85.

58. Ibid., 74–76.

59. Ibid., 76, 75.

60. *Dieu sans l'être*, 12.

61. *Étant donné*, 136–147, for this and what follows. Marion maintains that the gift (*don*) as such would disappear without the bracketing of the donor (136). Note that Marion also explores the bracketing of the gift and the recipient, but for our purposes it suffices to present just one bracketing.

62. Ibid., 143, n. 2.

63. Among "post-modern" thinkers, this is one of the most disputed features of Marion's philosophy. On this point, he may be following an insight of St. Thomas Aquinas. Cf. *Summa Theologiae*, Ia, q. 38, art. 2, c.

64. Matt 6:3.

65. *Étant donné*, 141.

66. In French, the opposition between the absence of knowledge (*connaissance*) and the recognition of an absent presence (*reconnaissance*) is clearer. "*Reconnaisance*" in French also can mean gratitude.

67. See Walter Kasper, *The God of Jesus Christ* (New York: The Crossroad Publishing Company, 1984).

68. *Sacrosanctum Concilium* 7, *Mysterium Fidei* (1965) §39, *CCC* §1373, and "The Real Presence of Jesus Christ in the Sacrament of the Eucharist," §13. For discussion, see David N. Power, *The Eucharistic Mystery: Revitalizing the Tradition* (New York: The Crossroad Publishing Company, 1992), and Michael Witczak, "The Manifold Presence of Christ in the Liturgy," *Theological Studies* 59 (December 1998): 680–702.

69. Matt 18:20.

70. *CCC* §1350. Cf. §1544.

71 For this and what follows, see "On Certain Questions Regarding the Collaboration of the Non-Ordained Faithful in the Sacred Ministry of the Priest," 29–35.

72. Joseph Cardinal Ratzinger, *A New Song for the Lord* (New York: Crossroad, 1996), 176.

73. *CCC* §1546.

74. *Lumen Gentium* 34. See also *Christifideles Laici* 14.

75. Cf. "On Certain Questions Regarding the Collaboration of the Non-Ordained Faithful," 26.

76. *Lumen Gentium* 10.

77. Cf. Sokolowski, *Eucharistic Presence*, 87.

The Eucharist
and the Mystery of the Trinity

by Avery Dulles

The conference in which we are now participating, as an ecumenical consideration of the Eucharist, fits admirably into Pope John Paul II's program for the current year. In 1984 he designated the year 2000 as a Great Jubilee in which the celebration would aim at giving glory to the Trinity. He particularly wished to emphasize the Eucharist, since it is the means by which Christ, who is the only way to the Father, perpetuates his living and saving presence. He also expressed the hope that, besides being trinitarian and eucharistic, the Sacred Jubilee would be inclusive: it should have an ecumenical and universal character. The Eucharist should be a bond of union, not a bone of contention, among Christians who worship the same triune God.

I have been asked to speak on the subject of the Eucharist and the Trinity. I do so as a Roman Catholic, relying on the approved liturgical texts of the Catholic Church. It will be for others to say to what extent they, from their respective traditions, can resonate with what I say. The Eastern liturgies of St. Basil and St. John Chrysostom, and non-Roman Western liturgies such as those of Taizé and Lima, could provide ecumenical reinforcement of many of the points I hope to make.

Until recently I had never thought much about the Eucharist except as a sacrament in which Christ perpetuates his sacrifice and makes himself our food and drink. But in preparing this lecture, I

226

have gained a deeper realization of the relationship of the other two divine persons to this sacrament. Recognizing the Eucharist as a trinitarian event, Bishop Peter Henrici has recently written:

> In the celebration of the Eucharist, we are drawn through prayer in a privileged way into the mystery of the Trinitarian God. The event that occurs in this celebration happens, so to say, in the midst of the divine life unfolding between Father, Son, and Spirit—so much so that we must say that the Eucharist is the proper access to this Trinitarian life and that there can be no access to the Eucharist other than by way of the Trinity. To be sure, we were baptized in the name of the triune God, and we received the gift of the Spirit in a special way in the sacrament of Confirmation. Yet, these two sacraments are essentially sacraments of access to the Eucharist— and they play this role precisely insofar as they initiate us, not only into the communion of believers, but, at the same time, into communion with the Trinitarian God.[1]

To clear the way for the discussion we may note at the outset that eucharistic worship in the Christian liturgy is directed exclusively to the divine persons. The Mass begins "in the name of the Father, and of the Son, and of the Holy Spirit." It concludes: "May almighty God bless you, the Father, the Son, and the Holy Spirit." Although saints are commemorated in the Eucharistic Prayer and the sanctoral cycle, the prayers of these texts are addressed not to them but only to God. Liturgical prayers are typically directed to the Father, through the Son, and in the Holy Spirit. This threefold structure will provide me with an outline for my text.

To the Father

Theologically speaking, the Father is the source and font of all that exists and the goal toward which all creation is ordered. The whole plan of creation and redemption originates with God the Father and points back to him, so that in the end all things, including the Son himself, may be subjected to the Father as universal Lord (cf.

1 Cor 15:28). This perspective permeates the eucharistic liturgy as we find it in the Offertory, the Preface, and the Eucharistic Prayer itself.

The Offertory begins with the blessing of the gifts. The priest, in the name of the community, first invokes the Father as the blessed Lord and God of all creation, through whose goodness we have the bread and wine to offer. He then asks God to be pleased with the sacrifice, which we offer with humble and contrite hearts. The priest asks the people to pray with him that his sacrifice and theirs be acceptable to God the Father almighty. They respond by praying that the Father will accept the sacrifice to the praise and glory of his name.

The Preface, which follows the Offertory, is a hymn of thanksgiving directed likewise to God the Father. The celebrant introduces it with the words: "Let us give thanks to the Lord our God." The people respond: "It is truly meet and just." The priest then continues: "It is truly meet and just, right and availing unto salvation that we should always and everywhere give thanks to you, Lord, holy Father, all-powerful and eternal God." (The translation printed in the Missals does not do justice to the Latin, which I have tried to follow more closely in my quotations.) At the end of the Preface the people join in the Sanctus, extolling the Lord God of hosts (*Dominus Deus Sabaoth*) in the words attributed to the angels in Isaiah 6:3.

The Eucharistic Prayer proper, which may also be called the "*anaphora*," is a long supplication addressed to God the Father. It begins, in the Roman canon: "Therefore, O Lord, we humbly beseech and ask you, most merciful Father, through Jesus Christ your Son, that you will accept and bless these gifts, these holy sacrifices which we offer..." In the course of the prayer, mention is made of the action of Jesus at the Last Supper. Turning to the Father, the priest recalls how Jesus on that occasion looked up to heaven, "gave thanks to you, his all-powerful Father," blessed the food and wine, and gave them to the disciples.

"Eucharist," as we know, is a Greek word meaning thanksgiving. After the sacrifice of thanksgiving offered by Jesus to the Father has been reenacted, the anaphora fittingly ends with the doxology: "All honor and glory is yours, almighty Father, for ever and ever." This doxology leads directly into the Lord's Prayer, which of course is addressed to the Father alone.

The repeated reference to the Father in the eucharistic texts is of some importance. It means, for one thing, that the Eucharist does not revolve simply about Christ the Redeemer. Even more fundamentally, it acknowledges God as the Creator of the whole world and thanks him for all the gifts of creation and redemption. As a sacrifice of praise, the Eucharist is offered in the name of all creation. As we read in the third Eucharistic Prayer, "All creation rightly gives you praise. All life, all holiness comes from you..." The liturgy thus tends to impart a sense of God's transcendence as source and goal of the whole universe. It reminds us of our total dependence upon the Father as creatures and of the church's identity as a people gathered by the Father. It arouses our awareness of being destined to him as the final goal of all that has been made. He is the ground of all being and the crown of all salvation.

One particular benefit of the recognition given to the Father is to elicit thanksgiving, which is always directed to him as the ultimate source of all good things. We are all too inclined to take creation for granted; we need to be reminded that the light and nourishment we daily receive, and indeed our life itself, are freely bestowed upon us by a loving Creator, to whom we render thanks for all the benefits of nature and grace. In the Gloria we thank and praise God not only for his gifts but also for being what he is: "We give thanks to you for your great glory." If we failed to attend to this dimension of praise and gratitude, we would find it hard to see why the Mass is called *Eucharistia*, thanksgiving.

Jesus on many occasions throughout his life offered thanks to the Father. He did so in particular before meals, as we can see from the account of the feeding of the multitudes at Capernaum and the Last Supper itself. When we come to celebrate the Lord's Supper, we are invited to share in the Lord's own attitudes of thanksgiving toward the Father from whom every perfect gift descends. The entire life of the church should be, in the words of Alexander Schmemann, "one continuous burst of praise, blessing and thanksgiving."[2]

Still another benefit of this emphasis on the Father is that it sharpens our understanding of the sacrificial dimension, since sacrifice in the Christian understanding is always offered to God the Father. Because the Eucharist is an external act that symbolically expresses the interior homage of the creature to God, it fulfills the definition of sacrifice. Most of us today have very little appreciation of sacrifice, perhaps because we think so rarely and superficially about our dependence on the Father and the ways in which we have offended him. The Eucharist is a sacrifice of praise, thanksgiving, and propitiation. We shall further examine this sacrificial aspect as we consider the Son, who offers the sacrifice.

Through the Son

The relationship of the Eucharist to the Son is so obvious that it scarcely needs to be explained. But further reflection on the liturgy can always enrich our understanding. The Eucharist is a privileged point from which to understand the mission of the Son since, as Hans Urs von Balthasar has said, "only the Eucharist completes the Incarnation...in the Eucharist of his surrendered Son, God concludes his new and eternal covenant with mankind, committing himself to it utterly and with no reservation."[3]

In the Eucharist, as in the incarnation, the Father gives the Son to us for our salvation. The very one who was conceived by the Holy Spirit and born of the Virgin Mary becomes present again upon the altar, under alien forms. The paten and the chalice now cradle the very person of Christ, who comes into our midst, body and blood, soul and divinity.

In his earthly life, the Son generously entered into his role as the Father's supreme gift to the world and completed the gift by obediently offering himself up as a victim for sin. At the Last Supper he anticipated his own death on Calvary and gave himself with his own hands to the disciples whom he loved. He commanded them, "Do this in remembrance of me" (Luke 22:19; 1 Cor 11:24–25).

In the anaphora the narrative of the Last Supper is retold, reproducing the words and deeds of Jesus. At an important point it takes the form of direct discourse: "This is my body...This is my blood of the New Covenant" (Mark 14:22, 24). These words, spoken by the celebrant in the person of Christ, are believed to effect the sacrifice of the Mass and bring about the real presence of Christ on the altar.[4]

As we know from Vatican II and many other authoritative documents, Christ's presence in the eucharistic liturgy is manifold. He is present in the celebrant, who speaks and acts in the very person of Christ (*in persona Christi capitis*), in such a way that the priest does only what Christ is doing through him. Christ is present in the proclaimed word, whereby he addresses the congregation; he is present in the congregation itself, as it sings and prays; he is present in the sacramental action and, most of all, in the consecrated elements.[5] The real presence under the forms of bread and wine is held to be "substantial," because the elements in their deepest reality actually become Jesus himself, and are to be adored as he is adored. This presence of Jesus in the sacrament is sometimes called "sacramental" or "mystical" because the Eucharist mysteriously actualizes in space and time the presence of Christ, who continues to reign in glory at the right hand of the Father.

The Eucharist is rightly called a "memorial" of the passion and death of Christ. Since Jesus was a divine person, his salvific action was capable of participating in his eternity and thus of becoming present to all times (*Catechism of the Catholic Church* [*CCC*] §1085). "As often as the sacrifice of the cross...is celebrated on the altar, the work of our redemption is carried out" (*Lumen Gentium* 3). The sacrifice of the Mass is therefore one and the same as that of the cross. The priest and the victim are the same as at Calvary, but the manner of offering, as the Council of Trent declared, is different. The sacramental sacrifice is offered in an unbloody manner and takes place through the ministry of an ordained priest (DS 1743; *CCC* §1366).

When the church offers the sacrifice, it commemorates not only the death of Jesus but also his resurrection and ascension, whereby the Father accepted his offering. The Christ who comes to our altar today is not simply the one who lived in Galilee two millennia ago; he is the Christ who now lives and reigns in heaven. The Host is not simply a token of the past, it is a living though veiled presence of the Lord as he exists today.

Under still another aspect, the Eucharist is a pledge of his future coming in glory. In the Embolism after the Lord's Prayer, the priest alludes to the text from Paul's Letter to Titus: "awaiting our blessed hope, the appearing in glory of our great God and Savior Christ Jesus" (Titus 2:13, RSV).

The orientation of the Eucharist toward the final coming of Christ, while often overlooked in the past, was brought to light by

Vatican II, in a memorable paragraph of its Constitution on the
Sacred Liturgy:

> In the earthly liturgy, by way of foretaste, we share in the
> heavenly liturgy which is celebrated in the holy city of
> Jerusalem, the goal toward which we journey as pilgrims,
> where Christ is sitting at the right hand of God as the minis-
> ter of the sanctuary and of the true tabernacle (cf. Rev 21:2;
> Col 3:1; Heb 8:2); we sing the hymn of the Lord's glory with
> all the troops of the heavenly army; venerating the memory
> of the saints, we hope for some part and fellowship with
> them; we eagerly await the Savior, our Lord Jesus Christ,
> until he, our life, appears and until we too appear with him in
> glory (cf. Phil 3:20; Col 3:4). (*Sacrosanctum Concilium* 8)

The Christology of the Eucharist therefore unfolds in three
tenses—past, present, and future. In the first acclamation after the
consecration in the English text of the Mass, the congregation proclaims: "Christ has died, Christ is risen, Christ will come in glory."
The Eucharist is a memorial of Christ's passion, an experience of his
present grace, and a foretaste of final coming in glory.[6]

The Council of Trent insisted against certain Protestant groups
that the Mass is not a merely subjective occurrence in the minds of
believers. The real presence of Christ in the sacrifice is brought about
by the power of God's word and does not depend on the faith and
devotion of the people who witness it. Sometimes one has the impres-
sion that Catholics may have learned the lesson of objectivity all too
well. They seem to see the Eucharist simply as an object out there,
which produces its effect in an automatic way, regardless of our
involvement or noninvolvement. An authentic eucharistic spirituality
can serve to correct this deviation. For our assistance at the Eucharist
to be fruitful, we must consciously participate by acts of faith and
love. The Lord exhorts us to open our minds and hearts to him as he
stands at the door and knocks (cf. Rev 3:20).

The personal presence of Christ in the Eucharist culminates in
Holy Communion. The Communion rite follows immediately after
the Our Father and the Embolism attached to it. At this point, a
notable shift occurs. The prayers, instead of being directed to the

Father, as heretofore, are now addressed to the Son: first the Prayer for Peace, next the *Agnus Dei*, then the priest's private prayer to be spared from damnation and freed from sin by Christ's holy body and blood, and finally, the "Lord, I am not worthy..." recited by the whole congregation.

The Communion is an essential element in the Mass as a sacrificial banquet. Quite apart from the words accompanying it, the action itself clearly focuses on Christ, who gives himself as food and drink, according to his promise in the discourse at Capernaum (John, chapter 6) and his declaration at the Last Supper. The primary gift we receive, therefore, is Jesus himself, but the Father and the Holy Spirit are also received by way of concomitance, insofar as they cannot be absent where the Son is present. In worthily eating and drinking, those who communicate enter into intimate union with Christ the Head, and are thus drawn more deeply into the life of his Mystical Body, the church.

Our relationship to Christ in the Eucharist, like our relationship to the Father, has major implications for the interior life. As the most personal of all God's gifts to us, the gift of the Son in the Eucharist intensifies our loving reliance on the Father and our gratitude toward him. As we offer the sacrifice of Christ we are drawn into his own attitude of loving service and surrender. While the whole assembly offers him as the immaculate Victim, it also offers itself as his Mystical Body, with the hope of being more perfectly conformed to the divine Head. Through Holy Communion we have the privilege of entering into deeper companionship with Jesus who promised, "He who eats my flesh and drinks my blood abides in me, and I in him" (John 6:56, RSV). By partaking in the one bread and the one cup we are, in addition, integrated more fully into the community of the faithful, who constitute Christ's body on earth. We receive new motivation to imitate Christ's selfless gift of himself to others.

In the Holy Spirit

Jesus did not mention the Holy Spirit in the words of institution, but the Letter to the Hebrews, interpreting his sacrifice, says that "Christ... through the eternal Spirit offered himself without blemish to God" (Heb 9:14). The offering of the Son on the cross was, so to speak, carried to the Father by the Holy Spirit.[7]

When the church celebrates the Eucharist, likewise, the Holy Spirit is engaged in the action performed on the altar and in the minds and hearts of the faithful. The Father acts through the Son as offerer and through the Holy Spirit as sanctifier. The sacrifice rises to the Father, as it did on Calvary, through the mediation of the Spirit. Explaining the role of the Holy Spirit, the *Catechism of the Catholic Church* quotes from the Eastern Father, St. John Damascene:

> You ask how the bread becomes the Body of Christ, and the wine...the Blood of Christ. I shall tell you: the Holy Spirit comes upon them and accomplishes what surpasses every word and thought...Let it be enough for you to understand that it is by the Holy Spirit, just as it was of the Holy Virgin and by the Holy Spirit that the Lord, through and in himself, took flesh.[8]

This teaching regarding the role of the Holy Spirit is not an exclusively Eastern doctrine. In the Missal of St. Pius V, the Roman liturgy contained the following Secret Prayer for the Octave of Pentecost: "Lord, may this divine fire, which through the descent of the Holy Spirit inflamed the hearts of the disciples of your Son Jesus Christ, consume these sacrifices that are offered in your presence." The action of the priest extending his hands over the offerings at the moment of the consecration signifies the coming of the Holy Spirit.

Besides being active in the transformation of the elements, the Spirit is at work in the congregation. According to Edward Kilmartin, the Holy Spirit is both the ontological principle for the operative presence of Christ in the liturgy and the subjective principle of worship. "Only in the Spirit," he writes, "can the truth of Christ be taught and heard, [and only in him can] the Church pray and accomplish the liturgical-sacramental celebrations."[9] Since he is the Spirit of holiness, his grace is needed to bring about the conversion of heart and adherence to the Father's will that are needed for worshipers to enter fruitfully into the mystery they celebrate.[10]

At this point we encounter the problem of the epiclesis, or invocation of the Holy Spirit. This prayer has figured prominently in most Eastern liturgies, but was absent from the Roman canon in general use before Vatican II. Until recently the epiclesis was a major theme of polemics between East and West. Some Oriental theologians ascribed the consecration and the real presence of Christ to the invocation of the Holy Spirit upon the elements, and therefore regarded Western eucharistic liturgies as severely deficient, if not invalid. The Holy See, in a series of documents dealing primarily with the Armenians, insisted that no epiclesis was necessary because the priest's recitation of Jesus' words of institution effected the consecration.[11] The Western church did not, however, deny that the Holy Spirit was active in the consecration.

The problem has been greatly mitigated, if not overcome, by the addition of the epiclesis in the three new eucharistic prayers approved by Paul VI in 1967. The second Eucharistic Prayer, before the consecration, inserts the prayer to the Father, "Sanctify these gifts, we beseech you, by pouring forth your Holy Spirit." The third Eucharistic Prayer beseeches the Father to sanctify the gifts by the power of the Holy Spirit. The fourth Eucharistic Prayer, which is based on the ancient liturgy of Saint Basil, speaks of how the Father sent the Holy Spirit as his first gift to those who believe, and remains active to complete God's saving work in the world. Then it goes on to implore the Father to sanctify the eucharistic elements by the same Spirit, so that they may become the body and blood of Christ.

In each of the three new eucharistic prayers there is, in addition to the epiclesis preceding the consecration, a second epiclesis following the consecration, asking that the sacrament be made fruitful through the action of the Holy Spirit. In all three of these eucharistic prayers, the Father is asked to send the Spirit upon the faithful so as to unify the church throughout the world and make it one body and one spirit.

Although one cannot say that all theological differences on the subject of the epiclesis between East and West have been resolved, the difficulties may today be regarded as pastoral and theological rather than dogmatic, and may consequently be judged not to be by themselves church-dividing. The Catholic-Orthodox Joint International Commission, in a statement issued in 1982 on Church and the Eucharist, was able to conclude: "The Spirit transforms the sacred gifts into the body and blood of Christ (*metabole*) in order to bring about the growth of the body which is the Church. In this sense, the entire celebration is an epiclesis, which becomes more explicit at certain moments. The Church is continually in a state of epiclesis."[12]

A little later the same statement declared: "The epiclesis is not merely an invocation for the sacramental transforming of the bread and the cup. It is also a prayer for the full effect of the communion of all in the mystery revealed by the Son."[13]

With regard to the ritual differences between Byzantium and Rome, the great Orthodox liturgist Alexander Schmemann felt entitled to write, some years before Vatican II: "Almost all the Byzantine arguments against the Latin rites have long since become unimportant, and only the genuinely dogmatic deviations of Rome have remained."[14] Yves Congar, after quoting this statement in a chapter on the epiclesis, expresses his own opinion that the major difference between East and West today is undoubtedly the doctrine of the procession of the Holy Spirit rather than any doctrine directly related to the Eucharist.[15]

The Holy Spirit is above all else a principle of unity. Within the Godhead, the Spirit expresses and seals the loving union between the Father and the Son. In the church, likewise, the Holy Spirit is one person gathering many persons into communion, causing them to live "in the unity of the Holy Spirit." Alluding to the vivifying presence of the Spirit, Saint Augustine was able to hail the Eucharist: "O mystery of piety! O sign of unity! O bond of charity!"[16]

Our communion in the church on earth is still imperfect, but it is an authentic foretaste of the enduring peace and joy of the blessed in heaven. The Spirit is the eschatological gift that leads us through the Son into the blessed presence of the Father.[17] That final blessedness for which we hope is the work of the Trinity as a whole.

Conclusion

At the beginning of this paper I quoted a statement of Bishop Peter Henrici to the effect that the Eucharist is the proper road of access to the Trinity. Our explorations have, I believe, confirmed that thesis in many ways. In this sacrament we encounter the Father in the very act of sending his Son and breathing forth the Holy Spirit to carry on the work of our redemption. Here the Son still visibly on earth continues to praise and serve the eternal Father, offering him the supreme sacrifice of his own life. Here, too, the Holy Spirit is at work sanctifying the gifts on the altar and strengthening, consoling, reconciling, and divinizing those who worthily partake of the sacred victim. In offering the Eucharist and in receiving Holy Communion we progressively put on the mind and heart of the incarnate Son, allowing him to transform us into his likeness, so that, empowered by his Spirit, we may dedicate our lives to the service and glory of the Father. No other action performed on earth can draw us so intimately into the very depths of God's trinitarian life.

It would be excessive to expect the liturgy to yield a complete or systematic theology of the Trinity. A few liturgical texts point in that direction, but they are somewhat atypical, since they evidently bear the stamp of the dogmatic teaching of ecumenical councils. The Nicene-Constantipolitan Creed, which has been inserted into the Mass for Sundays and Solemnities, can claim a rightful place in the ritual because it is based on a baptismal creed. It has a liturgical matrix, even though it has been modified with a view to imparting certain dogmatic truths. Highly theological, likewise, is the Preface for the Feast of the Holy Trinity, which calls upon us to acknowledge "three persons equal in majesty, undivided in splendor, yet one Lord, one God." This preface, in the Latin original, speaks of the true and eternal Godhead, the distinctive properties of the persons, the unity of the divine essence, and the equal majesty of the three persons. These trinitarian texts, cast as they are in the form of prayer, preserve a devotional style, but because of their theological content, they depart from the customary tenor of liturgy.

A full doctrinal consideration of the Trinity would have to take us far beyond the Eucharist or any ritual action. Abstract theological discourse, which has its own importance for the church, normally takes its cue not from the liturgy alone but also from other sources, including scripture, speculative thought, and magisterial teaching. My paper has a relatively modest aim. Eschewing the complexities of dogma and theology, it contents itself with reflection on the eucharistic liturgy. That liturgy provides unparalleled opportunities for salvific encounter with the three divine persons and a privileged point of entry into trinitarian doctrine.

NOTES

1. Peter Henrici, "Trinity and Eucharist," *Communio* 27 (Summer 2000): 211–216, at 213.

2. Alexander Schmemann, *The Eucharist: Sacrament of the Kingdom* (Crestwood, N.Y.: St. Vladimir's Seminary Press, 1988), 176.

3. Hans Urs von Balthasar, *Theo-Drama: Theological Dramatic Theory*, vol. 4, *The Action* (San Francisco: Ignatius Press, 1994), 348–349.

4. Such was the teaching of the Council of Florence (1439) in the Decree for the Armenians (Denzinger-Schönmetzer [DS] 1321), reiterating a letter of Benedict XII to the Armenians in 1341 (DS 1017) and of Clement VI to the Catholicos of the Armenians in 1351 (*Dictionnaire de Théologie Catholique* [DTC], 5:199). The same teaching was repeated by the Council of Trent (Decree on the Eucharist, DS 1640), by Benedict XIII in an instruction to the Melchite Patriarch of Antioch in 1729 (*DTC* 5:200), by Benedict XIV in a brief of 1741 (*Collectio lacensis* 2:197), by Pius VII in a brief of 1822 (DS 1822), by Pius X in a letter to the apostolic delegates of the East in 1910 (DS 3556), and by the Holy Office in a declaration of May 23, 1957 (*Acta Apostolicae Sedis* 49 [1957]: 370).

5. Pius XII, *Mediator Dei* 20 (New York: America Press, 1948), p. 20; *Sacrosanctum Concilium* 7; *CCC* §1087.

6. As we read in the Antiphon for the Magnificat on the Feast of Corpus Christi, "*O sacrum convivium, in quo Christus sumitur; recolitur memoria passionis eius, mens impletur gratia, et futurae gloriae nobis pignus datur.*" This antiphon is commonly attributed to Thomas Aquinas. It certainly corresponds to his theology as found in the *Summa Theologiae*, Part III, q. 79.

7. This point is well made in the official catechetical text of the Theological Historical Commission for the Great Jubilee, *The Eucharist, Gift of Divine Life* (New York: Crossroad, 1999), 62.

8. Saint John Damascene, *De fide orthodoxa* 4, 13 (Patrologia Graeca [PG] 94: 1145A), quoted in *CCC* §1106.

9. Edward J. Kilmartin, *Christian Liturgy*, Vol. I, *Systematic Theology* (Kansas City, Mo.: Sheed & Ward, 1988), 321.

10. *CCC* §§1098 and 1102.

11. See note 4 above.

12. Joint International Commission, "The Mystery of the Church and of the Eucharist in the Light of the Mystery of the Holy Trinity," 1982, in *The Quest for Unity: Orthodox and Catholics in Dialogue*, ed. John Borelli and John H. Erickson (Crestwood, N.Y.: St. Vladimir's Seminary Press and Washington, D.C.: United States Catholic Conference, 1996), 53–64, at 55.

13. Ibid., 56.

14. Alexander Schmemann, *The Historical Road of Eastern Orthodoxy* (New York: Holt, Rinehart and Winston, 1963), 248. He mentions in particular the use of unleavened bread, fasting on Saturday, and the singing of Alleluia on Easter. Schmemann's book was first published in Russian in 1954.

15. Yves Congar, *I Believe in the Holy Spirit*, vol. 3 (New York: Seabury, 1983), 244.

16. Augustine, *Tract. in Evang. Joan.*, 26, no. 13 (NPNF 7:172). St. Thomas likewise regards the Eucharist as the "sacrament of ecclesiastical unity" *(Summa Theol.*, Part III, q. 73, arts. 2 and 3) and as the "sacrament of unity and peace" (q. 83, art. 4), but he does not, to my knowledge, explicitly link this unitive efficacy to the Holy Spirit.

17. *CCC* §1050, quoting St. Cyril of Jerusalem, *Catech. illum.* 18:29 (PG 33: 1049).

The Eucharist of the Church
and the One Self-Offering of Christ

by Roch Kereszty

In its original form, this essay served as a position paper for the conference, attempting to focus its various papers on the theme the title above indicates. Inevitably, the individual papers and responses have reached beyond this pre-defined scope and accumulated a wealth of insights regarding all aspects of the mystery of the Eucharist. At the end, then, it seems appropriate that, enriched by the individual conferences, responses, and discussions, we would re-focus on the original theme and attempt a synthesis from a Catholic perspective that should, by its very nature, be also ecumenical.

Theme and Method

The inexhaustible riches of the mystery of the Eucharist invite an equally rich variety of approaches. This essay, however, intends to investigate the mystery of the Eucharist from one perspective only, that of the relationship between the Eucharist celebrated in the ongoing life of the church and the one historical self-offering of Christ. We chose this theme because its better understanding could eliminate some of the painful doctrinal conflicts of the past and promote—to a small degree at least—a renewal of eucharistic theology and praxis in and outside the Roman Catholic Church.

The method of this essay is situated within the range of possible Roman Catholic theological methods. Following the majority patristic view, we consider the scriptures of the Old and New Testaments as containing, by God's providential care, the fullness of God's revelation in Christ, a fullness that constantly needs the church's interpretive function. The same Spirit that inspired the scriptures guides its interpretation in the church to which he entrusted the scriptures. Through its liturgy and magisterium, and in a different way through its theologians, the church continues to bring to light all the implications of the mystery of Christ who is fully present to her in the Eucharist.[1] This ecclesial view of the scriptures liberates us to see the very same mystery of the Eucharist prepared in the Old Testament, witnessed to in the writings of the New Covenant, celebrated in the liturgy of the church, commented upon by theologians, and defended against errors by the magisterium throughout history.

In spite of a tortuous path of partial understandings and dangerous misunderstandings, the truth of the eucharistic mystery has been preserved throughout the ages, and has been expressed in various thought forms and philosophical terms. As the church struggles to safeguard and articulate the mystery of the Eucharist, it has transformed the philosophical notions of different ages. In our own times we must take up the same struggle. However, to find the best approach to expressing the mystery in our own culture, we must first search for its different expressions in past cultures. In this way we may hope to integrate past insights with new ones, keeping all the while within the perimeters of the one faith of the church.

Since our method is unambiguously Roman Catholic, for this very reason it must also be ecumenical. We believe that, in different ways and to a varying extent, the Spirit of Christ has been at work in our Christian brothers and sisters who are separated from full communion with the Roman Catholic Church. For some of them, the Eucharist has remained important or is becoming increasingly so; thus, we must also learn from them.

Knowing from revelation that God's saving grace is offered to all fallen human beings of all times, we can detect the working of that grace even in some of the rituals outside the Jewish-Christian matrix. Thus, an integral treatise on the Eucharist requires that it be situated within the universal context of the history of religions.

While our method is theological even in the biblical part—and therefore more comprehensive than the historical-critical method—it must integrate the solid gains obtained by the latter.[2] Thus, this paper and the conference as a whole take into account the historical-critical essays at two previous conferences, the Cambridge Conference on the Eucharist[3] and the Baylor Conference about the influence of Isaiah 53 on Christian origins,[4] as well as the first part of the article "Eucharist" of the International Bible Commentary.[5]

Regarding the history of the Eucharist we draw especially on the works of J. Betz[6] and E. Kilmartin.[7] The systematic part presupposes also the knowledge of the works of O. Casel[8] and G. Söhngen.[9]

Biblical Witness

The Last Supper of Jesus appears in all four gospels not as an isolated narrative[10] but as the climax of Jesus' public ministry; it is prepared for by what Jesus did and preached beforehand. At the same time, the Last Supper accounts—in different ways and contexts— define also the meaning of the imminent crucifixion and resurrection.

The banquet of the Father to which the sinners, the poor, and the lame, in fact all those who acknowledge their need for God's mercy, are invited is a central theme in the parables of the kingdom. The multiplication of loaves stories (two in Matthew and Mark, one in Luke and in John) underline the centrality of the banquet in Jesus' preaching. All four evangelists—to varying degrees—present them as anticipations of the Eucharist: Jesus is the host of the meal, he feeds the crowd by multiplying the loaves; his gestures anticipate the Last Supper: He took the loaves, gave thanks, and gave them to his disciples (Matt 14:19; 15:36; Mark 6:41, 8:6; Luke 9:16; John 6:11).

The Last Supper accomplishes what the parables of the banquet and the multiplication(s) of the loaves have only prepared for: Here Jesus is not simply the host of a joyous messianic banquet; he is also the food and drink that he serves to his disciples. This last meal before entering his kingdom already anticipates the entering of Jesus and his disciples into that kingdom. The Last Supper, however, indicates also that the kingdom cannot come in a smooth, peaceful way; it will suffer violence. Because of our sins, because of the growing opposition to Jesus' good news of God's forgiving love, it will come through Jesus' violent death.

The food Jesus offers is not simply his bodily self, but his body which is to be given up for us in death; the drink he bids his disciples to drink is not merely his blood, but his blood that is to be poured out in death for the multitude unto the remission of sins. In this way, the Last Supper defines the sacrificial meaning of Jesus' violent death. He freely gives up now for sinful humankind his life that tomorrow will be taken away from him by violence. In fact, he offers himself not only freely but also in thanksgiving to his Father as the ultimate expression of his love for him. In the Synoptic Eucharist accounts, Jesus' last solemn act of thanksgiving, prepared by the thanksgiving prayers at the feeding(s) of the multitude, envelops the words and gestures that express atonement.[11] Thanksgiving and atonement are so closely linked in the Matthean text as to suggest that the atonement is the result of the gift of his self to God in thanksgiving.[12] It is not some impersonal, magic quality in Jesus' poured out blood that obtains forgiveness, but what he expresses in his freely accepted death, his love for the Father and for us, the love that manifests itself in praise and thanksgiving at the Last Supper.

It is by being an atonement sacrifice that the Last Supper is also a covenant sacrifice: it fulfills the Mosaic Covenant (Matt–Mark) by inaugurating the New Covenant (1 Cor–Luke) that obtains the forgiveness of sins (Matt 26:28) and a new interiority of God within the hearts of his people (Jer 31:31–34; Ezek 36:25–27).

While being its fulfillment, the free self-offering of Jesus to God in the form of becoming a gift for us radically transcends the Old Testament notion of object sacrifice. Although the idea that the sacrificial objects (animals and first-fruits of the land) are only symbols of the free gift of the self is present already in the ancient tradition of Abraham's sacrifice, the voluntary gift of a human self in death as a sin offering for obtaining forgiveness is expressed only in the Hebrew text of Isaiah 53 about the Suffering Servant. A critical study of the eucharistic texts of the New Testament has resulted in the highly probable conclusion that Jesus interpreted his prophetic sign action at the Last Supper in the light of the Suffering Servant prophecies. By applying to himself the role of the Servant,[13] Jesus fulfilled (both by contrasting and transcending) the Old Testament institution of animal sin offerings in his own free self-offering for our sins.

Yet, not even the Servant texts suffice to explicate the novelty of Jesus' acts at the Last Supper. Nothing seems comprehensible unless we accept Jesus' implied divine dignity. According to the Hebrew understanding, all blood, as the seat and symbol of life (Lev 17:11), belongs to God alone. If a mere human being commanded people to drink his own blood, even symbolically, he would commit the most hideous crime of abusing God's exclusive possession of all lives.[14] Only if Jesus is acting in the awareness of his divine dignity may he give us a share in his own blood, in his own divine-human life. Who else but God can give us his own blood, the symbol of his own life, to drink? Thus, if Jesus is not to act as the usurper of God's right, he must be acting as God's Son in the full transcendent sense of the word. In this context the awesome majesty of the eucharistic sacrifice begins to dawn upon us. By giving us his own blood to drink in the sign of wine, the Son bestows upon us God's own life.[15] Moreover, we now understand why Jesus' blood speaks more eloquently than that of Abel: it does not cry out for vengeance but intercedes for us in the sight of God until the end of history. Thus, the sacrifice of the Son is incomparably more effective than any human sacrifice could be; it has obtained the forgiveness of our sins and given us the New Covenant whereby God's Spirit dwells in us so that we may share in God's own life.

What Jesus does proleptically at the Last Supper he brings to completion on the cross: he entrusts his life into the hands of the Father for our sake, the expression of a love greater than which no one has. In the resurrection-exaltation-ascension the Father responds to the gift of his Son by raising him from the dead and enthroning him on his right hand in the glory the Son has had from the beginning of the world. Yet the glorified Son retains his priesthood forever, and Christians of all times have access to his sprinkled blood in the heavenly Jerusalem (Heb 12:24). In 1 Corinthians 11:24–25 and in Luke 22:19, Jesus explicitly hands over to the twelve apostles, the patriarchs of the eschatological Israel, the task of "doing this in memory of me." Through the risen Lord's appearances to the disciples at the breaking of the bread, it becomes clear that this command includes not only the essential gestures of the Last Supper, but the celebration of the paschal mystery in its integrity; in other words, the church is to celebrate, under the signs of bread and wine, that definitive self-giving of the

Son to the Father which he has begun in the Last Supper, consummated on the cross, and eternalized in the resurrection.

In Israel the memorial celebration of God's mighty deeds, in particular, that of the Passover (Exod 12:26), is not a mere psychological recalling of past events. The celebrants of the Passover meal are believed to participate truly in the saving event of the Exodus. By sharing in the Passover lamb, they ratify again and again the covenant for themselves. The celebration of the Eucharist, however, is to be done "in memory of me" in the personal memory of Jesus himself. Thus, as the *Shekinah* (the mysterious cloud of God's presence) covers the celebrants of the Passover meal, so does the personal presence of the risen Christ encompass the community that celebrates the Eucharist. His presence, however, is a sacrificial presence, since the Eucharist is the celebration of the New Covenant. Therefore, the personal presence radiates from his sacrificed (and glorified) body and blood by which the New Covenant has been concluded. How could we celebrate the New Covenant without the sharing of the covenant blood?[16]

The church of the New Testament does not make explicit how the paschal sacrifice of Christ and the eucharistic sacrifice of the church are related. It takes for granted a close link if not a certain kind of identity. We are redeemed by the once-and-for-all sacrifice of Jesus and yet Christians have an altar from which the unconverted Jews may not eat and Christians may not participate in pagan sacrifices (Heb 10:10; 13:10; 1 Cor 10:19–22).[17] The letters of Paul explain that all those who partake (worthily) of the Eucharist are built up into the one Body of Christ by participation in his dying and rising to a new life. The elucidation of this relationship between the sacrifice of Christ and that of the church will be attempted in different ways throughout history and it still remains a task for us today.

As soon as the apostolic communities began to celebrate the Eucharist, they had to separate its essential elements from a Passover meal, which was the probable setting of Jesus' Last Supper. I leave the question open as to whether or not the Last Supper was an actual or anticipated Passover meal; nor can I exclude a recent hypothesis according to which the setting of the institution of the Eucharist was a unique form of *todah* sacrifice in which Jesus dedicated his life to God in praise and thanksgiving, anticipating his glorious resurrection. The fact, however, that the apostolic church saw in Jesus' last meal and passion-resurrection the fulfillment of the Jewish Passover is solidly documented. Regardless how it began, the church could not celebrate the daily or weekly Eucharist in the time-bound context of the Jewish Pasch. The research of H. Gese and C. Giraudo point to a highly probable genesis of the form of the early Eucharist in the *todah* meal sacrifice that did not have to be celebrated in the temple but could take place in private homes.[18]

Re-examining the conclusions of form criticism, Denis Farkasfalvy's careful analysis in this book provides considerable evidence for the eucharistic provenance of most New Testament texts. Not only the passion and resurrection narratives and the multiplication of loaves stories, but all gospel pericopes about Jesus' words and deeds were recounted and shaped within a eucharistic celebration. The letters of the apostles were also meant to be read at such worship services. The visions of the Book of Revelation take place on the day of the Lord in the context of the heavenly liturgy.[19] If Farkasfalvy's thesis is true, we have ample biblical foundation for the fathers' belief that the eucharistic sacrifice makes present not only Christ's death and resurrection, but his entire mystery, including his incarnation and mighty deeds on earth and his eternal liturgy in heaven.

Historical Developments

In the liturgies of both East and West the eucharistic prayers (*anaphoras*) retain the form of thanksgiving sacrifice into which the atoning aspect is integrated. The latter is expressed mainly in the words of institution. It is in the form of thanksgiving that the church, in communion with all the angels and saints, appropriates the sacrifice of Christ through the epiclesis and the recitation of Jesus' words of institution. In the perspective of the liturgy, just as in the Letter to the Hebrews, Jesus' sacrifice begins with the incarnation, is effectively anticipated at the Last Supper, and is completed on the cross and in the resurrection-ascension. While taking for granted a very close link (in some texts a certain kind of identity) between the historical sacrifice of Christ and the Eucharist of the church, the liturgy does not clarify the nature of the relationship.

In the history of the church this relationship has been explained in roughly three alternate ways:

1. Christ is the ultimate subject of each eucharistic sacrifice of the church. However, he does not offer himself again and again, but the church participates in the one and the same, once-and-for-all act of Jesus' self-offering.

2. The subject of each eucharistic sacrifice is not Christ but the church which offers Christ again and again in every Mass.

3. While reference to the historical sacrifice of Christ remains, Christ posits a new sacrificial act (e.g., humbling himself to become present among us in the appearance of bread and wine) or endures a new sacrificial act (such as a symbolic separation of his body and blood) again and again in every new eucharistic sacrifice.

In the East the Antiochene theology of the fourth century, in particular, St. John Chrysostom, and in the West Augustine and Thomas Aquinas (and their close followers) seem to move in the direction of the first alternative. For Chrysostom the notion of *anamnesis* provides the key to understanding the relationship of the one sacrifice of Christ and the many offerings of the Eucharist. Similar to the biblical notion of remembrance, the *anamnesis* for Chrysostom's school is not a mere subjective act of remembering but an act of participating in "that very sacrifice that has then been offered, the sacrifice that is inexhaustible (*analoton*)."[20] Augustine also implies a certain identity between the sacrifice of Christ and that of the church: the Eucharist is the daily sacrament (*sacramentum quotidianum*) of the Lord's sacrifice and the church "learns to offer herself through it."[21] St. Thomas likewise teaches that the eucharistic celebration is rightly called the sacrament of the sacrifice of Christ (*immolatio Christi*) not only because it represents his passion, but also because it brings about the effects of Christ's passion in the celebrating community.[22]

However, while the liturgical and patristic notion of sacrifice includes the whole life of Christ as well as his return to the Father through death, resurrection, and ascension, in scholastic theology the notion of sacrifice tended to be restricted to the death of Jesus.

In the late medieval period and in the times before the Protestant Reform, different variations of the second alternative prevailed. The real presence of Christ in the Mass was separated from the Mass's sacrificial character. Every Mass was considered a sacrifice because the church offers Christ again and again and therefore the fruits of the Mass are limited according to the devotion of the celebrant and the participants.[23]

Even without the more radical distortions of the sacrificial character of the Mass (as held by some theologians at the time of Luther),[24] the above theory makes Luther's protest quite justifiable: if the Mass is a sacrifice insofar as the church offers Christ again and again for the forgiveness of sins, how can one simultaneously maintain that the self-offering of Christ on the cross has been the once-and-for-all perfect sacrifice that has atoned for all sins?

The Council of Trent did not endorse those sacrificial theories of the Mass which Luther impugned; on the contrary, it declared that the Mass is the same sacrifice as the sacrifice of the cross (since Christ is both the offerer and the victim in both cases) and only the manner of offering is different.[25]

However, Trent left many crucial issues unanswered and thus could not fully respond to the Protestant protest: (1) It did not explain how the Mass can be a real sacrifice without detracting from the perfection of the one historical sacrifice of Christ. (2) It did not affirm that the act of the self-offering of Christ in every Mass is the same act (*numerice idem*) as his historical act of self-offering. (3) It did not clarify what the propitiatory character of the Mass is and how propitiation is related to the Mass as sacrifice of praise and thanksgiving.[26]

The post-Tridentine theories regarding the relationship between the historical sacrifice of Christ and the Eucharist fall in various ways into the third category. They try to safeguard the sacrificial character of the Mass by either affirming that in each Mass something happens to Christ (such as a symbolic separation of his body and blood or a "mystical immolation" which, of course, excludes actual death and suffering), or in each Mass Christ performs a new internal act of self-offering to God by accepting the humiliation of coming among us in the appearances of bread and wine.

The problem with such theories is manifold. (1) None of them recovers the comprehensive patristic notion of sacrifice which includes the whole mystery of Christ beginning with the incarnation and cul-minating in his ascension and heavenly intercession. The sacrificial moment is narrowly identified with his death. (2) The aspect of thanksgiving and praise in the eucharistic sacrifice is neglected, let alone integrated with its propitiatory aspect. (3) Since the sacrificial character of the Mass derives from what happens to Christ or from what Christ does anew in each Mass, the perfect sufficiency of the sac-rifice of the cross is indeed jeopardized and, therefore, the Protestant protest is not without a foundation.

Only in the biblical and patristic renewal of the twentieth century did Catholic theologians and the magisterium rediscover the thanks-giving and praise dimension of the Eucharist; only then did they re-apply and deepen the Thomistic notion of sacramental sacrifice. In each and every Mass not only are the offerer and the victim the same Christ who offered himself on the cross, but the one and the same act of His self-offering is participated in by the church. Thus understood, the Mass does not add a new sacrifice of Christ to his perfect histori-cal self-offering. The additional newness of each and every Mass con-sists in a church community's sacramental and existential participation in Christ's perfect once-and-for-all sacrifice.[27]

Systematic Considerations

The biblical and historical surveys brought to light that fidelity to revelation requires both the affirmation that Christ has redeemed us once and for all by his historical sacrifice as well as the acknowledg-ment that Christ has given over this sacrifice to his church in the Eucharist as the church's very own. In the history of theology the most appropriate way to reconcile both truths proved to be an appli-cation of the specifically Christian philosophical-theological doctrine of participation. In the Eucharist the church participates in the one sacrifice of Christ so perfectly that not only are the offerer and the victim identical with that of the historical sacrifice, but even the many liturgical acts of offering participate in the one, once-and-for-all act of Christ's self-offering.

The biblical-historical survey has also shown that the sacrifice of Christ is not to be restricted to the Last Supper and to the crucifixion but includes Jesus' entire life which culminates in the Last Supper and on the cross; through his resurrection and ascension, then, Christ's sacrifice becomes eternal.[28]

Moreover, the New Testament reveals that it is through his love expressed in thanksgiving and praise that Christ atoned for our sins. Likewise, it is through a prayer of thanksgiving (the eucharistic anaphora) that the church appropriates the sacrifice of Christ and unites herself with it.

In what follows we attempt to make the above data more intelligible.

1. Our participation in the sacrifice of Christ through the Eucharist is possible only because his actions and sufferings were not simply the actions and sufferings of a mere human being, but the theandric actions of God the Son made man. Thus, while in the Eucharist the risen Christ becomes present, his earthly life and passion—insofar as they cause our redemption—also reach and transform us through the Holy Spirit.[29]

If being present to someone in time results from a causal relationship, then in the Eucharist we have a unique case of it. The whole saving history of Jesus becomes present to us insofar as it effects in us a participation in his history, particularly in his death and resurrection. Thus Christ's *transitus* brings about in the Eucharist our *transitus*. The more we share in his death and resurrection, the more we are united with the glorified Christ and thus enter his eternal kingdom which is Christ with his angels and saints.

The mystery of this participation can be better articulated if we compare "liturgical time" with the "time of secular celebrations." For instance, when we celebrate our birthday, we recall the first remembered events of our lives and these memories affect us in the present celebration. However, it is not the past events themselves that affect us here and now, but their present memory which typically is quite different from the events themselves. In the eucharistic memorial, however, it is not only the subjective remembrance of Jesus' life, suffering, death, and resurrection that affect us, but the events themselves transform our very being on a level incomparably deeper than what psychological remembrance can attain.[30]

2. That Christ himself is personally present in the Eucharist (as gift to the Father insofar as he becomes food and drink for us) has been expressed in different ways through the history of eucharistic theology. In today's culture, the best analogy—one that shows both similarities and profound differences—seems to be the symbolically expressed human gift of the self between human beings.

If we want to express our gift of self through a sign (such as a mother cooking the best meal for her returning children, the food she serves signifying in some way her gift of self), our gift retains its material reality and remains distinct from our self. However, if the God-man, Jesus Christ, wants to give himself fully and definitively to us through a physical sign (by adjusting his way of acting to our physical nature), he should be able to do it in reality (ontologically). The gift (the bread and wine) cannot just remain a psychological reminder; it must become identical with his very self. Otherwise, Christ's will to give himself to us as food and drink would remain on the level of mere human desire.[31]

3. In this context, the often-misrepresented doctrine of transubstantiation[32] obtains a significance that has been largely forgotten. The doctrine affirms that the substance of the bread and wine (understood in a non-technical sense as that which makes the bread, bread and the wine, wine) are changed into the body and blood of Christ (that is, into his sacrificed and glorified humanity) while their appearances (in today's language, their phenomenological reality) remain unchanged. If Christ's body and blood were present "with, in, and under the bread and wine" but without change in the elements according to the classic Lutheran formulation, it would eliminate the analogy between the transformation of our offerings into Christ as sacrificial gift and that of our bodily selves into the likeness of Christ.[33] Alternately, it could suggest that Christ is merely given to us as the promise of salvation but does not sanctify our very being in order to become an offering to the Father and a gift to others in union with him.[34] The later Lutheran doctrine of "impanation" may also imply that God has excluded the material universe from becoming the effective sign of Christ's gift of self to the Father and from becoming the effective sign of Christ as food and drink for us.

Once, however, we affirm transubstantiation, we affirm thereby
that in the Eucharist we desire to be transformed into Christ and
anticipate the highest eschatological perfection of the material universe.[35] In the Eucharist, material creation perfected by human work
reaches its ultimate goal, a goal that infinitely transcends the potential
of matter and yet fulfills rather than destroys it: a part of nature that
through the civilizing work of humankind became bread and wine is
transformed by the Holy Spirit into "the bread of life" and into "the
cup of eternal salvation." They become food and drink that communicate Christ himself to us, the Christ who, by being a gift for us, is
the most perfect gift to his Father.

4. If the form of the sacrifice of Christ to the Father is his becoming
food and drink for us, we perceive the intrinsic connection between
the communitarian and theocentric dimensions of the Eucharist.
Christ offers himself to the Father by distributing himself to us. So, if
we celebrate the Eucharist with the right disposition, we must imitate
what we celebrate: we are to worship the Father in praise, thanksgiving, and atoning love as we support and nourish our brothers and sisters not only by our actions but by our very existence.

Ecumenical Implications

A mutual rapprochement between Protestants and Catholics in
our understanding of the Eucharist has already been achieved.[36] On
the Catholic side, the biblical renewal in the twentieth century and in
particular the teachings of Vatican II[37] promoted a biblically inspired
theology of the Eucharist that was more appreciated by Protestant
theologians than the abstract treatises of neo-scholasticism. Catholic
theology rediscovered also the importance of the Liturgy of the Word
that has always been central to Protestant worship: through his proclaimed word, Christ himself teaches us on the road of this life so that
we may recognize his personal, eschatological presence "in the breaking of the bread" (cf. Luke 24:13–35). On the other side, many
Protestant theologians are beginning to see the continuity between
biblical faith, the faith of the church fathers, and the magisterial documents of the Roman Catholic Church. Such a mutual rapproche-

ment has already led to some significant break-through agreements in formulating what is common in our understanding of the Eucharist. Besides the documents produced by several joint commissions consisting of Catholic and Protestant theologians of different denominations, the most important ecumenical document was published by the Faith and Order Commission of the World Council of Churches: *Baptism, Eucharist and Ministry*.[38] Some form of real presence of Christ in the eucharistic celebration has been commonly expressed in the joint text: "the eucharistic meal is the sacrament of the body and blood of Christ, the sacrament of his real presence" (#13). It has also been accepted that the "eucharist is the memorial of the crucified and risen Christ, i.e., the living and effective sign of his sacrifice, accomplished once and for all on the cross and still operative on behalf of all humankind" (#5). The Faith and Order document also states clearly the transformative role of the Eucharist in Christian life: "Christ empowers us to live with him, to suffer with him and to pray through him as justified sinners" (#9). "In Christ we offer ourselves as a living and holy sacrifice in our daily lives" (#10). The eschatological dimension of the Eucharist is also expressed in the document: "the eucharist is...the foretaste of (Christ's) Parousia and of the final kingdom" (#6).

However, disagreements on various points between the Catholic faith and this expressed consensus still exist, as it appears both from the *Baptism, Eucharist and Ministry* document and from the official response of the Doctrinal Congregation. Moreover, even the achieved consensus in the eucharistic theology of the document is still far from being accepted and practiced by many Protestant churches. Here I would like to point out how the essays and discussions of our conference may inspire some further convergence.

1. The formulation of the real presence of Christ in the *Baptism, Eucharist and Ministry* document tries to accommodate the beliefs of all Christian denominations. They all believe that Christ is really present at the celebration, but not all denominations link this presence essentially to the eucharistic bread and wine. Roman Catholic theologians can contribute to a further convergence by explaining that we do not consider the presence of Christ in the eucharistic signs as a magic presence: a diminutive Christ squeezed into the host and into the wine, Christ "the prisoner of the tabernacle." The presence

in the eucharistic signs is not only not opposed to Christ's personal presence but is its radiating center. Christ in his risen but truly human reality cannot be present in the same way in the individual believer as in the material signs. We cannot worship the believers, even though Christ may be present in them through the Holy Spirit. We may not even worship the pregnant Mother of God, although she carried Christ in her womb. The material signs of bread and wine, however, are able "to surrender" in the eucharistic celebration their substantial reality to expressing Christ's personal presence.[39]

2. The Catholic and Orthodox doctrine that the bread and wine are ontologically transformed during the eucharistic celebration into the body and blood of Christ while retaining their empirical properties of bread and wine could be expressed in such a way as to acknowledge the valid concerns of Lutheran eucharistic theology. On the one hand Jesus declares: "This is my body," "This is my blood of the covenant," thus identifying what he holds in his hands with his body and blood. On the other hand, Christ also calls his (eucharistic) flesh the bread of life. In a similar way of speech, the liturgy also identifies the consecrated bread and wine with the body and blood of the Lord but, at the same time, calls the consecrated elements "the bread of life" and "the cup of eternal salvation." In other words, the church's teaching on ontological transformation (transubstantiation) presupposes that Jesus becomes really present but under the real sign of bread and wine. Bread and wine, then, are not annihilated (analogously to the human person who offers himself to God through Christ) but rather reach their ultimate, God-intended perfection in becoming the effective signs of Christ's presence in the eucharistic consecration. Therefore, Catholics should be more careful in defining the meaning of the word "appearance" in eucharistic theology. God does not intend to deceive us by false appearances: the empirical qualities of bread and wine are real and they must remain in order to express Christ as true food and true drink for the believers who still live in the world of sense experience. In this way we could do justice to a legitimate Protestant objection while, at the same time, articulating better the Catholic dogma of transubstantiation in such a way that it might appear as an organic development of scripture and patristic doctrine rather than the outdated creation of what Luther called the "Aristotelian church."

3. Once the ontological transformation of the elements is accepted, the permanent presence of Christ in the Eucharist naturally follows. This permanent presence (as long as the signs of bread and wine remain) assures that Christ's eucharistic presence is prior to, and does not depend on, the faith of the celebrating community. Thus, the priority of God's sovereign grace over human "works," a central concern of the Protestant Reform, receives an unexpected confirmation in a deeper understanding of Christ's abiding presence in the Holy Eucharist.

4. Concerning the issue of the propitiatory character of the Eucharist, we can find a common basis with Protestant Christians if we reflect together on the biblical truth that the risen Christ is also the crucified one. According to John, the risen Christ displays his wounds and according to the Book of Revelation the victorious Lamb stands "in the midst of the throne in the state of being slain" (John 20:20, 27; Rev 5:6; 13:8). This symbolic language shows that the risen Christ remains forever our propitiatory sacrifice even though he can no longer suffer or die.

Moreover, Protestants do accept that the Lord's Supper is *Eucharistia*, the church's sacrifice of thanksgiving, praise, and self-giving in love, but the average Protestant theologian (not the *Baptism, Eucharist and Ministry* document) is reluctant to call the Eucharist a sacrifice of atonement or propitiation for sins. In the Protestant understanding it contradicts the efficacy of the once-and-for-all sacrifice of Christ on the cross. Here two considerations may be helpful:

(a) Is it not the love of Christ by which he glorifies and thanks the Father that has made his death truly the source of forgiveness? It was not some magic in the death itself, it was the love that animated his free self-offering on our behalf that obtained forgiveness. Thanksgiving (*Eucharistia*) and expiatory sacrifice are inseparable.

(b) The risen Christ bears his glorious wounds forever. This shows forth the eternal validity and the inexhaustible power of his self-offering on the cross. Our many acts of eucharistic offerings participate in Christ's one act of self-offering, the self-offering that has become eternalized in the resurrection and ascension.[40]

For this reason, in the eucharistic celebration we are not simply passive recipients of his atonement. Being united with him means being conformed to his state of sacrificial gift that is inseparably praise and atonement, thanksgiving for God's gifts and propitiation for our sins. Thus, union with the eucharistic Christ calls for both sacramental and existential participation in his sacrifice. Although it requires our utmost personal efforts to live, act, and suffer as he did, our participation adds nothing to the universal efficacy of Christ's once-and-for-all self-offering. It rather enables us to share, according to the measure of our faith and love, in its power of atonement and sanctification.

NOTES

1. According to Catholic tradition, all other forms of Christ's presence in the church lead to or derive from the Eucharist. Cf. *Sacrosanctum Concilium* 7, 10.

2. This "more integral" or theological method does not belittle the method of historiography. In fact, it starts with the critique of the critical method by bringing to light tacit or explicit philosophical presuppositions without which no one can investigate history. Precisely the consistent application of the historical-critical method leads us to transcend it. For, if we attempt to understand "the world of a text" through which we hope to grasp its intended meaning, we must appropriate (at least conditionally) the faith suppositions of its author(s). Therefore, in interpreting Christian texts (those of the New Testament, the magisterium, and individual theologians) we will assume that their authors write about different aspects of one and the same divine *reality*, the crucified and risen Christ present in the Eucharist, rather than simply formulate abstract beliefs and theories.

3. *One Loaf, One Cup: Ecumenical Studies of 1 Cor 11 and Other Eucharistic Texts*, The Cambridge Conference on the Eucharist, August 1988, ed. B. F. Meyer (Macon: Mercer University Press, 1988).

4. *Jesus and the Suffering Servant: Isaiah and Christian Origins*, ed. W. H. Bellinger and W. R. Farmer (Harrisburg: Trinity Press, 1998).

5. Collegeville: Liturgical Press, 1998, pp. 215–220.

6. *Eucharistie in der Schrift und Patristik: Handbuch der Dogmengeschichte*, vol. IV/4a (Freiburg: Herder, 1979).

7. *The Eucharist in the West: History and Theology*, ed. R. J. Daly (Collegeville: Liturgical Press, 1998).

8. See, in particular, *The Meaning of Christian Worship and Other Writings*, ed. B. Neunheuser (Westminster: Newman, 1962).

9. Perhaps his most important work on the Eucharist is *das Sakramentale Wesen des Messopfers* (Essen:Wibbelt, 1946). For other authors and works, see the ample bibliography in Kilmartin, *The Eucharist in the West*.

10. The "*Sitz im Leben*" for the institution narratives is most likely the liturgy of the nascent church. What Jesus did and said were first recited as part of the Lord's Supper and only later fixed in writing. The Lord's Supper, according to Paul's testimony, derives from Jesus and has been already firmly established in Corinth as the Lord's institution about twenty years after Jesus' death and resurrection; thus, it can hardly have come from anywhere else but Jesus himself. This evidence is confirmed by the occurrence of the same tradition with secondary variations in the Synoptic gospels and in the eucharistic discourse prepared by prophetic sign-actions in John 6. (See more detail on the convergence of 1 Cor 11, the Synoptic tradition, and John in W. F. Farmer, "Peter and Paul, and the Tradition concerning 'the Lord's Supper' in 1 Cor 11:23–26," in *One Loaf, One Cup*, 35–55; O. Hofius, "The Lord's Supper and the Lord's Supper Tradition: Reflections on 1 Corinthians 11:23b–25," in *One Loaf, One Cup*, 75–115.) Another surprising fact that is usually overlooked: Paul's epistles are a literary genre very different from that of the gospels. He does not intend to present narratives about Jesus, yet he makes one exception, that of the Lord's Supper. Even though Paul is interested in Jesus' origins, teachings, death, and resurrection as well as in the appearances of the risen Lord, he only refers to them. The terse cultic narrative on the Lord's Supper shows its unique importance for Paul and for the Corinthian community.

11. Atonement sacrifice in this context does not suggest any "vicarious payment" for our sins, but rather expresses the fact that the free self-offering of Jesus to God in thanksgiving obtains the forgiveness of sins.

12. In Matt 26:26–29 the giving over of both his body and his blood (the latter explicitly linked to the forgiveness of sins) is embedded in prayers of praise and thanksgiving expressed by two aorist participles (*eulogesas* and *eucharistesas*). The atonement linked to thanksgiving is further enriched by the perspective of John. In the Last Supper of the Fourth Gospel, Jesus' passover from this world to the Father shows the ultimate depth of his love for the Father and for us (cf. especially 13:1; 14:31). The *hyper hymon* of 1 Cor 11:24 should be understood in the perspective of general Pauline soteriology: Jesus gave himself over for us out of love (Gal 2:20; Rom 8:32; Eph 5:2).

13. See on this issue primarily O. Betz, "Jesus and Isaiah 53," and W. R. Farmer, "Reflections on Isaiah 53 and Christian Origins" in *Jesus and the Suffering Servant*, 70–87, 260–280.

14. Cf. 2 Sam 23:16–17; 1 Chr 11:18–19.

15. What Matthew and Mark express by describing the gesture of Jesus (namely that he handed over the cup of his blood to the disciples to drink), in John, Jesus himself makes clear by his words: "Amen, amen I say to you, unless you eat the flesh of the Son of Man and drink his blood, you will not have life in yourselves" (6:53).

16. As Jacques Dupont aptly observes: " At the time of the covenant of Sinai Moses sprinkled the people with the blood of the victims offered to God; we can hardly imagine he could have been content to use a symbol of that blood" ("This Is My Body...This Is My Blood," in Raymond A. Tartre, ed., *The Eucharist Today* [New York: Kenedy, 1967], p. 24). That Christ understood his words over the bread and wine in a realistic (but not cannibalistic) sense is confirmed by the convergent witness of Paul and John (1 Cor 10:16; 11:27–29; John 6:51–65). See more on this in my article, "Eucharist," *International Bible Commentary* (Collegeville: Liturgical Press, 1998), 215–238.

17. See more about this theme in Roch Kereszty, "The Eucharist in the Letter to the Hebrews," *Communio* 26 (Spring 1999): 154–167.

18. Cf. H. Gese, "Die Herkunft des Herrenmahls," in *Zur biblischen Theologie* (Munich: Chr. Kaiser, 1977), 107–127; C. Giraudo, *La struttura letteraria della preghiera eucaristica: Saggio sulla genesi letteraria di una forma: toda veterotestamentaria, beraka giudaica, anafora cristiana*, An. Biblica 92 (Rome: Pontifical Biblical Institute, 1981).

19. "The Eucharistic Provenance of New Testament Texts," 40.

20. *Homilies on the Letter to the Hebrews* XIII, 9.

21. *De Civitate Dei*, 10, 6.

22. Cf. *Summa Theologiae* (*S.T.*) III, q. 83, art. 2.

23. See the theories of Scotus and Biel in E. Kilmartin, *The Eucharist in the West*, 161–163; 172–178. According to Scotus and Biel, the fruits of any individual Mass are limited because the offerer of the sacrifice of the Mass is the church militant here on earth and the merits of this church are always limited. Yet, while not representing a majority of theologians, Cardinal Cajetan keeps alive even at the time of the Reformation the Thomistic understanding of the Mass: it is a sacramental participation in the sacrifice of Christ which is fruitful *ex opere operato*, i.e., "by the work performed," in other words, from what Christ does through the ritual act. Thus, every Mass is of infinite value, but it becomes fruitful only to the extent of the participants' disposition.

24. For instance, one opinion held that Christ had two kinds of priesthood and, correspondingly, two sacrifices: as a priest according to Aaron, Christ offered a bloody sacrifice on the cross; as priest according to the order of Melchizedek, he offers the bread and wine of the Eucharist. An even more extreme view held that the Masses were offered for the sins of Christians that were committed after baptism, while the sacrifice of the cross was offered for the sins of the pagans.

25. Denzinger-Schönmetzer 1743, 1751, 1753–1754.

26. For more detail, see D. N. Power, *The Sacrifice We Offer: The Tridentine Dogma and Its Reinterpretation* (New York: Crossroad, 1987).

27. This statement does not exclude the value of so-called "private Masses" in case a congregation cannot be present, since even a "private Mass" is always offered for the church.

28. See D. Bentley Hart, "Thine Own of Thine Own," in this volume.

29. See A. Dulles, "The Eucharist as Sacrifice," in this volume. St. Thomas describes how the *acta et passa Christi* ("his acts and sufferings") are both efficient and formal causes of our transformation through the sacraments *per spiritualem contactum* ("through spiritual contact": *S.T.* III, q. 48, art. 6). In the light of the Eastern liturgical tradition we should refer the term *"spiritualis"* to the relational activity of the Holy Spirit in whose power the historical mysteries of the incarnate Son transcend time and operate throughout the course of human history.

30. Cf. Roch Kereszty, "A Theological Meditation on the Liturgy of the Eucharist," *Communio* 23 (Fall 1996): 529–530. Of course, the historical events of Jesus' life, death, and resurrection reach us also through our subjective faculties (our memories and imagination); this would explain the great differences in the way authentic visions of Christ and the saints are experienced in different cultures and by different individuals.

31. The fundamental weakness of transignification theories is that they usually do not emphasize this infinite qualitative difference between the human gift of self through signs and the theandric gift of the self by Jesus. The merely human symbol of the gift of self (for instance, a wedding ring) does not ontologically become the self, while the bread and wine, the symbols of the gift of self of the God-man, are transformed in their very being into the sacrificed and risen humanity of Jesus. The proponents of the transignification theories do not need to emphasize this difference, since they suppose that human meaning-giving activity determines the very being of material things. According to them, the wedding ring's deepest reality is that it is the sign of the spouse's fidelity. See in more detail, E. Schillebeeckx, *The Eucharist* (New York: Sheed & Ward, 1968), 107–160.

32. The term "transubstantiation" is misleading in our cultural context. In ordinary speech, "substance" is an empirical reality, while in the Aristotelian scholastic tradition it is either the essence of a thing or a thing as it exists in itself.

33. The early Luther still accepts transubstantiation and articulates our transformation into the "form of Christ" most eloquently: "Christ with all saints, by his love, takes upon himself our form (Phil 2:7), fights with us against sin, death, and all evil. This enkindles in us such love that we take on his form, rely upon his righteousness, life and blessedness. And through the interchange of his blessings and our misfortunes, we become one loaf, one bread, one body, one drink, and have all things in common. O this is a great sacrament, says St. Paul, that Christ and the church are one flesh and bone. Again through this same love, we are to be changed and to make the infirmities of all other Christians our own" ("The Blessed Sacrament of the Holy and True Body of Christ, and the Brotherhoods," *Basic Theological Writings*, ed. T. F. Lull [Minneapolis: Fortress Press, 1989], 243; on how the early Luther maintains transubstantiation and chastises only those who try to explain it, see p. 253).

34. Of course, our transformation into Christ through the Eucharist is different from that of the material elements of eucharistic bread and wine. We do not lose but rather perfect our personal selves (our substance) by being transformed into Christ.

35. On how according to the fathers the Eucharist transforms our souls and bodies, see D. Jeffrey Bingham, "Eucharist and Incarnation: The Second Century and Luther," in this volume.

36. This part of my essay has been taken over with some changes from the corresponding part of my article "Eucharist" in the *International Bible Commentary*, 237–238.

37. Cf. the Constitution on Divine Revelation, *Dei Verbum* 21, 23, 24.

38. The document was approved at the meeting of the commission by more than one hundred theologians coming from among the most important Christian traditions, Catholic, Orthodox, and Protestant. The meeting took place in Lima, Peru, in 1982. See text in *Search for Visible Unity: Baptism, Eucharist and Ministry*, ed. J. Gros, 1984. Cf. the official Vatican response to the document, "Baptism, Eucharist and Ministry: An Appraisal," *Origins* 17 (1987), 403–416. On the reactions by other churches, see *Baptism, Eucharist & Ministry 1982–1990: Report on the Process and Responses* (Geneva: World Council of Churches Publications, 1990).

39. By "substantial" I mean the reality of bread and wine insofar as they exist in themselves, in their own right. After the consecration, their whole reality is exhausted in their becoming effective signs of Christ's real presence. Thus, since they no longer exist in themselves as bread and wine, "their essence" has also changed.

40. In the Letter to the Hebrews Christ interceding for us and his sprinkled blood speaking on our behalf in the heavenly Jerusalem express the unity between Jesus' historical sacrifice and its heavenly consummation (7:25; 12:24).

CONTRIBUTORS

Dr. William J. Abraham, Albert Cook Outler Professor of Wesley Studies, Perkins School of Theology, Southern Methodist University

Dr. D. Jeffrey Bingham, Assistant Dean for Theological Studies and Professor of Historical Theology, Southwest Baptist Seminary

Dr. Peter Casarella, Associate Professor of Systematic Theology, Catholic University of America

Fr. Brian Daley, S.J., Catherine F. Huisking Professor of Theology, Notre Dame University

Dr. Robin Darling Young, Associate Professor of Historical Theology, Catholic University of America

Avery Cardinal Dulles, S.J., Laurence J. McGinley Professor of Religion and Society, Fordham University

Abbot Denis Farkasfalvy, O. Cist., Adjunct Professor of Theology and Research Scholar, University of Dallas

Dr. Everett Ferguson, Professor Emeritus of Biblical Studies, Abilene Christian University

Dr. Durwood Foster, Professor Emeritus, Pacific School of Religion

Dr. D. Bentley Hart, Orthodox Theologian

Fr. Roch Kereszty, O. Cist., Adjunct Professor of Theology, University of Dallas

Fr. Francis Martin, Professor of Sacred Scripture, John Paul II Institute for Studies on Marriage and Family

Rabbi David E. Stern, Senior Rabbi, Temple Emmanu-El, Dallas, Texas

Dr. Richard Taylor, Professor of Old Testament Studies, Dallas Theological Seminary

INDEX